Cattle Colonialism

FLOWS, MIGRATIONS, AND EXCHANGES
Mart A. Stewart and Harriet Ritvo, editors

The Flows, Migrations, and Exchanges series publishes new works of environmental history that explore the cross-border movements of organisms and materials that have shaped the modern world, as well as the varied human attempts to understand, regulate, and manage these movements.

CATTLE COLONIALISM

An Environmental History of the Conquest

of California and Hawai'i

John Ryan Fischer

The University of North Carolina Press / Chapel Hill

*This book was published with the assistance of the
Wells Fargo Fund for Excellence of the
University of North Carolina Press.*

© 2015 The University of North Carolina Press
All rights reserved
Set in Miller by Westchester Publishing Services
Manufactured in the United States of America

The paper in this book meets the guidelines for permanence and durability
of the Committee on Production Guidelines for Book Longevity of the Council on
Library Resources. The University of North Carolina Press has been a member
of the Green Press Initiative since 2003.

Portions of the text were previously published in John Ryan Fischer,
"Cattle in Hawai'i: Biological and Cultural Exchange," *Pacific Historical Review*
76 (August 2007): 347–72.

Jacket illustration: *Port of Honolulu* (1816), watercolor and
graphite on paper by Louis Choris, Honolulu Museum of Art

Complete cataloging information for this title is available from the
Library of Congress.

ISBN 978-1-4696-2512-6 (pbk: alk. paper)
ISBN 978-1-4696-2513-3 (ebook)

To Vanessa, Iris, and Caroline

Contents

Illustrations and Table

Acknowledgments

Many people and institutions have been instrumental in helping me conduct the research and writing of this book over the years. Some of the early research for this book, as well as the intellectual foundation for my exploration of invasive species in history, came from the National Science Foundation's generous Integrative Graduate Education and Research Traineeship (IGERT) on Biological Invasions, which I received while at the University of California, Davis. I would especially like to thank Kevin Rice, Carole Hom, and my fellow IGERT trainees. Research support from the UC Davis Agricultural Resource Center allowed me to conduct archival work in Hawaiʻi, and the Huntington Library's Wilbur R. Jacobs fellowship made possible a valuable stay at that excellent institution. Further funding from UC Davis, including the UC Davis history department, was also instrumental in funding archival research. The archivists and staff at the Huntington Library, the Bancroft Library, the California State Library, the UC Davis Library, the Hawaiʻi State Archives, the Hawaiian Mission Children's Society, and the Bishop Museum Library all played integral roles in my research as well.

Louis Warren helped me through every stage of this project and provided numerous excellent ideas. Alan Taylor and Andrés Reséndez also provided valuable insights, comments, and edits. Conevery Bolton Valencius, Peter Kastor, Clarence Walker, Karen Halttunen, and Eric Rauchway influenced my thinking and development as a historian in seminars and other venues. David Igler, Carolyn Merchant, Virginia DeJohn Anderson, and Matt Chew have provided helpful comments as chairs and/or commenters of conference panels during which I presented some of this work. A particular panel of young historians of Hawaiʻi at the Pacific Coast Branch meeting of the American Historical Association in San Diego was very helpful in my thinking, and I would also like to thank my co-panelists, Seth Archer, Larry Kessler, and Gregory Rosenthal. Robert Chester, Lisbeth Haas, Peter Mills, Joshua Reid, and Kurt Leichtle are among the other colleagues who have offered valuable professional advice, shown me their own work, or provided helpful comments on my work. Editors Susan Wladaver-Morgan and Carl Abbott at the *Pacific Historical Review* provided useful comments on some of the earliest material I wrote for this project. I'd also like to thank the team at the University of North Carolina Press, including my editor, Chuck Grench, who helped to shepherd this book into publication. Andrew Isenberg and an anonymous reviewer gave me essential advice that helped me refine my arguments and improve the manuscript overall.

Last, but far from least, this book would not exist without the love and support of my family. Thanks to my sister, Maggie, for sense of humor and support, and my profoundest thanks to my parents, my mother, Vicki, and my late father, Pete, who gave everything they could to help me achieve my dreams. Thank you to Frank and Carolyn Van Orden, who have been the best in-laws anyone could hope for. Finally, and most importantly, thank you to Vanessa Van Orden, who has been my foundation and inspiration through the long process of working on this book. My two wonderful daughters, Iris and Caroline, were worth every moment of distraction.

Cattle Colonialism

Introduction

In August of 1908, a man named Ikua Purdy roped, threw, and tied a steer in fifty-six seconds at the annual Frontier Days World's Steer Roping Championship in Cheyenne, Wyoming, one of the top rodeo events in the United States. This result shocked most of the 12,000 spectators as Purdy beat out local hero Angus MacPhee, a top broncobuster in Buffalo Bill's traveling Wild West show.[1] Performances like MacPhee's and Purdy's in both the Wild West show and the rodeo competition were a driving force in the turn-of-the-century mythologizing of the American frontier. What made this contest unusual was that Ikua Purdy hailed from the Parker Ranch on the Waimea Plains of the island of Hawai'i and that he was part Native Hawaiian himself. In fact, Purdy's Hawaiian companions, Archie Ka'au'a and Jack Low, placed third and sixth, respectively, to round out an impressive showing by the distant travelers, who all were paniolo, or Hawaiian cowboys.

The local papers were certainly impressed. The *Cheyenne Daily Leader* reported that these "brown Kanakas from Hawaii provided the big sensation at Frontier Park yesterday, Iku [*sic*] Purdy and Archie Tiini [*sic*], lithe youngsters from the far Pacific, invaded the heart of the American cow country and taught the white ropers a lesson in how to handle steers." Nevertheless, the same article expressed reservations about the Hawaiian ropers, who had not yet won their final impressive victory in the competition. It noted that "here was something new, the idea of a Hawaiian cowboy defeating a real cowboy at the cowboy's own particular game, and the crowd made the most of the novelty. Their performance took the breath from the American cowboys, and [they] are demanding that the whites who are to rope today let slip no opportunity to beat the time of the Honolulu experts."[2] The racialization of the paniolo is evident in both of

Ikua Purdy statue commissioned by the Paniolo Preservation Society and sculpted by Fred Fellows (photograph by Shawn G. Fackler, 2014)

these excerpts; the "brown Kanakas" were not "real cowboys," according to the paper, despite their prowess. This telling distinction persists, and neither Hawai'i nor Native Hawaiians are commonly associated with the American West as it has been performed in mythmaking rodeos and shows.[3]

The paniolo could trace their cattle traditions to the vaqueros of California's early nineteenth-century missions and ranchos. At the turn of the twentieth century, California's vaqueros also challenged racial notions of what made "real cowboys." As immigrants flooded westward into California at the turn of the century, the state's past as a Spanish colony became a point of interest. Writers like Charles Fletcher Lummis and Helen Hunt Jackson romanticized Spanish California's ranchos and missions, which had thrived on a cattle economy based mainly on Indian labor.[4] In 1890, when *Century* magazine asked the son of General Mariano Guadalupe Vallejo to write his reminiscences of the "Ranch and Mission Days in Alta California," he took time to recall "the Indian vaqueros, who lived much of the time on the more distant cattle ranges," and who "were a wild set of men."[5]

Around the same time that Ikua Purdy won in Cheyenne, an illustrator named Joseph Jacinto Mora first visited California. Shortly after his

Neophyte Mission Vaqueros (from Mora, *Californios*, 49; used with permission of the jomoratrust.com)

birth in Uruguay in 1876, Mora's family moved to New York, where Mora eventually attended art school and began his career. Mora began to travel around the American West in 1903, and, after spending a few years living with and producing art based on the Hopi in Arizona, Mora settled permanently in California in 1907. He spent most of the rest of his life producing sketches, sculptures, and books based on the missions of California, with a special emphasis on the region's vaquero culture and careful attention to their California Indian heritage. Mora was not alone in his early twentieth-century celebration of California's Indian vaqueros. Arnold Rojas worked as a vaquero in California from the 1910s and later in his life published several works on California vaquero life and folklore. He noted that "when some vaquero had performed his work with great skill, the other men would look at each other, smile approvingly, and say, '*Se crio entre los Indios pues*'—'Well, he was brought up among Indians.'"[6] These writers did not shy away from the multiethnic nature of California's cowhands, and they readily depicted the crucial role that Indians played in the cattle economy of California from the late eighteenth century to the early twentieth.[7]

Rodeo shows and western art, meanwhile, presented a narrative of American progress predicated on the idea of white conquest of an uncivilized frontier; Anglo-American civilization subdued racial others at the same time whites tamed and improved frontier landscapes.[8] As a result, Wild West shows generally presented cowboys as white, effacing the racial diversity of those who labored on the pastoral frontier. To this end, Buffalo Bill's Wild West show maintained a clear distinction between "cowboys," presented as white, and nonwhite "vaqueros," defined as Mexicans or "half-breeds."[9] As Ikua Purdy's victory demonstrates, this narrow construction of the cowboy past not only distorted the history of the West, but it also rewrote the geography of expansion. Unlike what the civilizing westward narrative usually presented, the advance of ranching frontiers did not proceed ever westward from one frontier to the next adjacent, but rather crossed oceans by sail and settled islands, or drove north from arid Mexican valleys, recruiting native peoples as laborers as they moved. It was not a simple story of linear Anglo-American progress, but rather one of overlapping imperial conquerors and indigenous people who alternately accommodated, adapted, and resisted.

More recently, historians have begun to challenge the simplistic frontier narrative, but western history remains overwhelmingly preoccupied with terrestrial stories and questions. This shortcoming has deprived the field of crucial context and insights as the histories of the island and coastal spaces of the eastern Pacific Ocean are essential to the history of the American West. Just a few generations before the West became a subject of performance and memory, cattle were unknown in most of what would become the American West. A few herds clustered around the mission outposts of New Mexico and Texas, the far northern frontiers of New Spain, where they also became commodities in the raiding and trading complexes of groups like the Comanche, Apache, and Navajo. The advent of Western ranching as a part of global economic enterprise, and thus an instigating force in the colonizing efforts that made the West American, came later and even farther west, in Pacific sites like the California coast and the Hawaiian Islands. Spanish padres and soldiers, accompanied by Indian vaqueros from Baja California, herded cattle northward to provide beef and milk in an unfamiliar landscape. A generation later, the British explorer Captain George Vancouver purchased a few breeding cattle from the descendants of these pioneering herds and sailed with them more than 2,400 miles across the Pacific Ocean to land them in Hawai'i. This was only the first time that cattle would link these two Pacific regions.

Once herds of these unfamiliar animals established themselves in these two locales, they became tokens in the games of imperial rivalry that dominated the region for centuries. The Pacific Ocean is vast and encompasses a long history of human habitation with shifting networks of trade and migration that stretch back for millennia. As historian Matt Matsuda reminds us, "the Pacific as a named, comprehensive entity is historically European."[10] European explorers and cartographers, on behalf of their empires, mapped a vast body of water, and, as they sought to understand, conquer, and profit from it, they created the concept of the Pacific Ocean, its boundaries amorphous and many of its constituent parts still unknown. While it is important to remain cognizant of the socially constructed nature of the Pacific Ocean, especially the complexity and deep history that it elides, the concept is still useful, especially when we seek to understand the European conquests that created it.

The search for merchantable commodities, especially for Chinese markets, had driven colonialism since before Columbus. Until the upsurge in overland immigration, and perhaps even until the completion of the transcontinental railroad in 1869, California was a maritime settlement, linked to European and American markets primarily by sea. Trade in furs, otter pelts, and hides and tallow was the basis of California's economy until the gold rush began in 1848, and even then, many of the forty-niners rushed to the gold fields under sail. Whaling, the China trade, and the hide and tallow trade were also vital to Hawai'i's incorporation into a growing world economy after Cook's discovery, and these endeavors helped link the islands to California. Never as valuable as cash crops like sugar, and certainly not as sought after as gold and silver, products from cattle like hides and tallow nonetheless provided enough of an incentive to begin to effect a capitalist transition, engaging European and American military and economic interests and changing forms of labor and land tenure in ways that suited the emerging imperial world order of the nineteenth century. In the constructed imperial space of the Pacific, cattle were the tangible asset that first anchored permanent and growing European presences in its eastern portion.

As Jared Diamond's *Guns, Germs, and Steel* reminds us, and as historians Alfred Crosby and Elinor Melville have established, domestic animals have been a powerful force in world history. The Old World contained many more domesticable large animal species than did the New World. Pre-Columbian North Americans had only domestic dogs, while many Polynesian cultures, like that of Hawai'i, also had pigs that early settlers from Asia had carried to the islands in boats. Cows, sheep, and horses were unknown to most of the indigenous peoples of the eastern Pacific.[11] These animals, with their many uses in agriculture, labor, warfare, as food sources, and even as the ultimate sources of certain diseases, became a vanguard of colonialism.[12] Cattle multiplied even when colonists did not.

However, the story is more complex than the one presented by Crosby and Diamond. Introduced animals did not merely compete with native peoples for resources as a tool of European conquest. That conquest itself was multifaceted and contingent. Recently, historians have focused on the complexity and possibilities created within areas contested by colonial powers. These "borderlands" operate differently than modern nation-states of clearly defined and controlled political borders.[13] European colonial rivalries often created a borderland in territories they sought to conquer by preventing such clear definition and control. Borderlands historians have brought to the fore the fluidity of colonial contestation and the ways that concepts like ethnicity, gender, labor, capital, land tenure, and trade can shift in borderlands and across borders.[14] These insights apply well to the Pacific in the eighteenth and nineteenth centuries, a region in which the English, French, Americans, Russians, and others all sought to dominate. Introduced animals provided a tool for Europeans to impose their authority on new areas of the world, but the greater borderland context shows that domination was not an inevitable result of such introductions. Rather, the colonial powers would use the animals in different ways to varying purposes, and it is not merely the animals themselves but the legal, economic, and social frameworks that each European power brought with the animals that determined their value as implements of colonization. The transition from "borderlands" to "bordered lands" in the eastern Pacific would be shaped, in part, by which European powers could most effectively impose these frameworks through cattle. Native peoples of the Pacific entered into the global workforce as dependent laborers, managing and processing herds for local or colonial elites. Through trade, native elites fell into severe debt to purchase European goods and became ever more tied to the maritime economy, including the hide and tallow trade, to service these debts. And cattle established European concepts of private property that eventually led to the transference of land from the indigenous population to colonizing ranching interests. Thus, systems of trade, labor, and land tenure associated with ranching frontiers resolved the borderlands of the eastern Pacific and, eventually, left the United States as the dominant force in the region in the latter half of the nineteenth century.

At the same time, historians have come to see borderlands, though shaped by European imperial rivalries, as locations of indigenous autonomy. The inhabitants of borderlands regions, like the contested Pacific, could carve out some level of sovereignty until a more monolithic authority asserted itself. As borderlands historians have shown, this autonomy allowed local peoples to negotiate the course of the major transformations wrought by the colonial experience and the accompanying "flow of people, capital, and goods."[15] This book adds "species" to this list and demonstrates that the cultural responses of native people to new species displayed the same innovative responses to colonial introductions. Though biotic, economic, and cultural exchange through trade, settlement, disease, and attempted acculturation transformed the lives of the native peoples of Hawai'i and California, they were not passive observers in this process.[16] Unlike European capital and goods, domestic animals, as a reproducing biological resource, offered more opportunities for indigenous control and did not necessarily lead inexorably to dependence. In fact, such animals could increase the autonomy and mobility of indigenous peoples in borderlands by creating a new source of food and labor that also provided goods marketable to Europeans. For instance, several environmental histories have explored Native American adaptations to European animals, especially the horse, which became central to the cultures of Plains Indians.[17]

In the Pacific, livestock created native cattlemen and ranchers and offered a resource with the potential to create an economic base to protect autonomy from the imperial agenda of competing European powers. California Indians created their own horse cultures and profited from the massive herds of cattle that took hold in California. Indians within Spanish colonial institutions, of which the Franciscan missions were the most important, gained status and wealth from managing cattle as vaqueros. At the same time, Indians that avoided or escaped from the missions used horses to increase mobility and as a food source. By the U.S.-Mexican War, these Indians subsisted on raids against Spanish herds.

Hawaiians already had their own domestic mammals. As Polynesians expanded through the Pacific over several millennia, they brought pigs with them. The ownership and use of a domestic animal allowed the Polynesians in Hawai'i to incorporate the introduced cattle into preexisting categories, but cattle also helped to transform those categories. Cattle were contested within native Hawaiian society. Hawaiian chiefs attempted to use commodities made from the cattle to protect their sovereignty, and they acted to take advantage of the new animals by hiring California vaqueros to train Hawaiian cowboys. At the same time, many Hawaiian farmers suffered from the intrusion of the animals and protested their presence. Both groups, however, sought to manage the animals in different ways, not to reject their presence. Native Hawaiians recognized cattle as a useful resource.

As one of the largest and most commercially exploitable of old-world species, cattle were central to the interconnections and transformations of the late eighteenth-century and early nineteenth-century Pacific. They did agricultural work and provided beef and milk. They transformed landscapes through grazing, trampling, and water consumption, and they spread seeds and pathogens through their waste. Because they were owned in European culture, they brought with them property connections and a complicated package of related meanings. Their hides and the tallow rendered from their fat became the region's most marketable products. Prior to their arrival in the Pacific, there was nothing else quite like them in the lives of native people. After they arrived, those native lives would never be the same.

The surprising victory of Ikua Purdy and the romanticization of Indian cowboys in California in the early twentieth century are hints of a flourishing trans-Pacific cattle culture that thrived in the decades after cattle first entered the region. Together they confront standard notions of the geographic and racial limits of the American West and reveal the contingencies of biological introductions in the interconnected world of the eastern Pacific, and the role those changes played in paving the way for colonialism. Cattle created opportunities for survival and adjustment, but they also caused environmental and economic changes that served the imperial designs of the United States and ended the eastern Pacific's fluid borderlands. The biological and cultural consequences of invasions played a key role in imperial power struggles, but they did not inexorably lead to the subjugation and destruction of native peoples. By examining environmental change and cultural responses to that change across traditional boundaries, we gain important insights into processes of globalization that began centuries ago and continue today.

The history of the American West did not stop at the shoreline but was instead bound to developments in the Pacific Ocean. Hawai'i and California anchored the European and American presences in the eastern Pacific, and ties of trade and diplomacy bound them together. Eventually, they provided the most important bridges between the United States and the Pacific Ocean.[18] Examining these two regions together provides important insights. This is not a strictly comparative work; these two regions share interlinked histories before the gold rush. The juxtaposition of their experiences reveals parallel environmental changes, European incursions, economic developments, and reforms in land tenure occurring almost simultaneously and often influencing each other.

THE FIRST CHAPTER discusses the initial establishment of cattle in California and in Hawai'i. The centrality of livestock to European economies, and European beliefs that domestic animals served as a civilizing force, prompted colonists to transport cattle to these new territories. A herd of cattle accompanied the settlers from New Spain who founded the first Franciscan missions in Alta California in 1769. These settlers believed that their effort to turn California's Indians into "gente de razón" or Christian "rational people" depended in large part on cattle. In 1793, the English explorer Captain George Vancouver transported cattle from the herds established in California to Hawai'i. Vancouver hoped to establish the animals on the centrally located archipelago near shipping lanes for growing trade with the Far East and in an attempt to transform Native Hawaiian culture by adding a pastoral element.

After the introduction of cattle in these Pacific regions, the establishment of the species depended on ecological resources and native responses. The second chapter examines the ecological changes prompted by cattle and the effects of these changes on indigenous subsistence strategies. California Indians intensely managed the California environment in order to attain significant yields and sustain a large population through hunting and gathering. Hawaiians utilized plants and animals brought through Polynesian migration and trade, and they developed their own agricultural regimes to support a large organized population. Cattle grazed on Hawaiian crops and items gathered by California Indians, and they also facilitated the introduction of new species that competed with more familiar resources. Thus, cattle presented a clear challenge to native lifeways. At the same time, introduced diseases and military conflicts destabilized indigenous societies, exacerbating the effects of livestock introductions.

Chapters 3 through 5 trace three major shifts in indigenous labor in the eastern Pacific. Chapter 3 covers the European efforts to ensure the survival of cattle populations in these new lands by eliciting native cooperation and labor in California and Hawai'i. Different colonial systems in the Pacific borderlands led to varying approaches to guiding the management of the new resources that livestock represented. The Franciscan missionaries taught natives European methods of agriculture as part of the conversion process. These agricultural methods included traditional practices of cattle management adapted to the North American context of abundant rangeland. Many Indians in the mission system became vaqueros who utilized the equipment and techniques developed to manage and transport vast herds of cattle in New Spain. In Hawai'i, as cattle from California rapidly multiplied and threatened native fields, native Hawaiians attempted to herd animals that had gone feral and become dangerous. Thus, the initial native response to the introduced animals occurred within the context of sudden environmental change but nevertheless demonstrated rapid adaptations.

The fourth chapter explores the emerging markets in the Pacific that allowed Californians and Hawaiians in the early nineteenth century to profit from the recently established herds and increased the connections that linked the two contested regions in the Pacific borderlands. These markets spurred an intensification in the use of native labor and a strengthening of the ties across the Pacific. The California missions utilized their cattle herds to supply international markets with profitable hides and tallow, often through illicit trade until Mexico's political independence decreased trade restrictions. In the first two decades of the early nineteenth century, European and American traders marketed Hawaiian sandalwood in the Canton trade. When the supply of sandalwood began to diminish on the islands and Kamehameha's kapu on cattle came to an end, Hawai'i became another supplier in the hide and tallow trade. As California and Hawai'i became important depots for whaling ships, beef also became a marketable product to crews in port or to whaling ships seeking to replenish their stores. The trade linkages created by hides and tallow and whaling served to create an interconnected Pacific World served by native laborers.

In turn, these linkages increased the opportunities presented by cattle and allowed for a trans-Pacific exchange of cattle culture. The fifth chapter analyzes these developments in native cattle cultures at the height of the hide and tallow trade. Early management of the feral herds depended on European and American bullock hunters. Around 1832, Hawaiian elites hired vaqueros from California to employ and teach a ranch style of herd management to better control and harvest goods from cattle on the island. California vaqueros and the newly trained Hawaiian paniolo labored with cattle within the European-controlled trade networks of the eastern Pacific. Meanwhile, California Indians outside this system still exploited the predominance of cattle on California's rangelands through banditry.

After these three chapters on the transformation of labor regimes in the Pacific borderland, the sixth and final chapter examines how this changing political context and enhanced economic value of livestock in the Pacific translated into new systems of land tenure. Rancheros in California called for an end to the mission system, as the missionaries' herds competed with their own. In 1834, the Mexican government secularized the mission lands with the claimed intention of their redistribution among the Indian converts. A few Indian ranches thrived for a brief time; however, most of the mission lands found their way into the hands of Mexican rancheros and the increasingly numerous Anglo-American immigrants. Until 1849, the Hawaiian royal family and nobility controlled Hawaiian land. In 1849, under foreign pressure, Hawai'i instituted a land reform called the Great Māhele. The Māhele allowed Hawaiian commoners access to land ownership, but after 1850 it also allowed foreigners to purchase Hawaiian lands. Europeans and Americans with herds of cattle soon established large ranches on several of the islands. These parallel land reforms served as an important turning point in Euro-American imperial projects in the Pacific, as the expression of Euro-American power during land reforms concentrated land in the hands of colonial powers and closed off many avenues of native profit from cattle.

WHILE IKUA PURDY and the California Indian vaqueros celebrated by Jo Mora and Arnold Rojas in the early twentieth century serve as reminders of the fluid trans-Pacific World that briefly flourished in the late eighteenth and early nineteenth centuries, they were workers within a capitalist system dominated by Anglo-Americans. Paniolo and vaqueros remain celebrated aspects of native culture in Hawai'i and California, but they also represent a lost world of native opportunity, brought about by inventive adaptations to a new and exotic species, but closed off by the assertion of Euro-American control over the land. Cattle in the early nineteenth century paved the way for the colonial expansion of Europeans and, finally, the United States in the region. At the same time, they offered some of the most powerful opportunities for indigenous people there to protect their sovereignty. This may seem like a paradox, but it highlights that domesticated animals are tools whose use is contingent on the social, cultural, and economic systems in which they are employed.

CHAPTER ONE

Arrivals

In 1776, two explorers in different hemispheres undertook expeditions on behalf of rival European empires in the Pacific. Their journeys triggered major cultural, economic, and ecological transformations throughout the region. In London, Captain James Cook prepared a fleet for a third mission of exploration into the Pacific Ocean for Britain. Meanwhile, Captain Juan Bautista de Anza marched overland from northern New Spain to settle a mission and fort on the San Francisco Bay. Cook and Anza introduced new ideas and trade items to the eastern Pacific, as well as alien diseases, plants, and animals. Anza brought human settlers with him, while Cook did not; however, both explorers attempted to establish a non-human European presence, domestic animals, in the lands that they explored. These introductions forever altered local lifeways and created new connections across the vast distances of the eastern Pacific.

Anza set out from Tubac, on the northern frontier of New Spain, in October of 1775, with a group of soldiers and settlers to supplement the fledgling military and religious settlements of Alta California. Navigating through the uncharted deserts and mountains and among the mostly unknown peoples of the region, Anza was to establish a new overland route to resupply the faltering missions and presidios and to expand their reach. His party included twenty-nine soldiers and their families (29 wives and 136 "persons of both sexes") to reinforce Monterey, which would soon become the region's capital, and to further establish the Spanish presence on this important Pacific bay.[1] After a 600-mile desert crossing, the expedition reached San Gabriel, one of the missions recently established in southern Alta California, on January 3, 1776. From there, they turned north and traveled up the coast. Anza, the fathers, the soldiers, and the settlers arrived in Monterey on March 10. However, on March 22, a smaller party, still led by Anza, and including his chief chronicler, the expedition's religious leader, Father Pedro Font, set out to reconnoiter a recently discovered large bay about 100 miles north of Monterey Bay. On March 28, Anza and Font chose the site for a presidio and the Mission San Francisco de Asís on the southern peninsula of San Francisco Bay, and thus furthered the extension of Spanish control of North America's Pacific Coast that had begun a mere seven years earlier.

While Anza's settlers were arriving in Monterey on March 10, 1776, workers thousands of miles away in London hauled the HMS *Resolution* from its dock into the Thames River.[2] The government of Great Britain had commissioned James Cook to captain the vessel on a mission to extend its influence in the Pacific, just as Spain had commissioned Captain Juan Bautista de Anza to do much the same. This was to be the *Resolution*'s second voyage of exploration into the Pacific and Cook's third. Cook's first voyage, from 1768 to 1771, on the *Endeavor*, had been to observe the transit of Venus from the southern hemisphere, but it had also provided the first maps of New Zealand and the first European exploration of Australia's east coast. His second voyage, from 1772 to 1775, as captain of the *Resolution*, had consisted of a search for the fabled continent of *terra australis* in the seas north of Antarctica.

Cook's third voyage was planned as a diplomatic mission to Tahiti to return Omai, a native of the Society Islands, who had become a celebrated curiosity in London since Cook had returned from his second voyage with him.[3] This ostensible reason for the voyage alone did not justify the heavy British expense of such an expedition, but Cook's sponsors also hoped for further potential discoveries, new charts, and increasing British influence in the Pacific. The third expedition began on June 24, 1776, and reached Tahiti more than a year later, in July of 1777. After Omai's return, Cook explored the west coast of North America. Cook also established the first recorded European contact with the Hawaiian Islands, which he dubbed the Sandwich Islands in honor of his patron, in January 1778. The contact was ill fated, and on one of the first forays of Cook's crew to the islands, they shot and killed a Hawaiian. These violent beginnings foreshadowed a violent end for Captain Cook on Hawai'i; Cook died on February 14, 1779, in an altercation with the Hawaiians while attempting to recover a stolen boat.[4]

Historian David Igler has noted that "prior to the 1770s, the eastern Pacific encompassed a disconnected set of indigenous homelands and contending European imperial adventures."[5] The projects of Anza and Cook heralded a shift in the region as they brought Hawai'i and California into greater European awareness, beginning processes that saw them move from important but far-flung frontier regions, to key centers of European trade and influence in the eastern Pacific, and finally to Pacific outposts of the American West. The contact made by Anza and Cook, and their forebears and followers, led to drastic alterations in landscapes and cultures across an eastern Pacific maritime borderland. These transformations occurred as a result of adaptation, co-optation, and syncretism, as well as through violence, disease, ecological devastation, and missionization. They also helped unite the region through the movement of people, goods, and organisms, and thus prepared it for eventual incorporation into the westward-expanding United States.[6]

The introduction of old-world plants and animals to newly discovered areas was essential to European exploration and to colonization. Early European visitors to the New World often carried pigs on their ships and deposited them onshore to propagate as a future source of provisions. In the Caribbean, some of these animals became so numerous that maritime marauders could survive off the feral populations on local islands. Buccaneers got their name from the boucan, an apparatus used to smoke the meat of these wild cattle and pigs.[7] Historian Patricia Seed, in her exploration of the different methodologies used by the various colonial powers, has noted that animals played a specific role in establishing colonial control. The English established their colonial authority through "improvement" of the land. In other words, the English believed that they legitimized their conquest of new territory by employing English agricultural practices, from fence building to the utilization of animal manure for fertilizer. The raising of domestic animals like cattle and sheep was a fundamental part of these practices.[8] Pastoral practices also served a purpose in Spanish "ceremonies of possession," though in a different manner. The Spanish did not seek to displace indigenous agricultural practices but rather to subjugate them. The Spanish allowed the sedentary societies that they conquered, like the Nahua in Mexico, to keep many of their traditional practices and even societal structures while exacting allegiance and tribute from them.[9] Less sedentary societies necessitated more significant transformations; making these peoples into farmers became a crucial step in achieving subjugation. To achieve these goals, the Spanish "reduced" or gathered nonsedentary Indians into pueblos and missions where they performed agricultural labor, including the care of domestic animals.[10] For the Spanish, livestock established colonial control by transforming Indians into Spanish subjects. For the English, livestock established colonial control by transforming Indian lands into English lands.

Plants, animals, and even humans escaped many of the predators and germs that controlled their populations in home regions. Free of these limiting factors, populations of the invading species could explode, often beyond the carrying capacity of the local environment. Considering the European conquests that followed rapidly on the heels of Columbus's discovery, Alfred Crosby notes "the successful exploitation of the New World by these people depended on their ability to 'Europeanize' the flora and the fauna of the New World."[11] The British navy developed new technologies and methods specifically for the long-distance maritime transport of plants, both to collect newly encountered species and to introduce European species to new regions. They justified their exertions in the service of introducing plants by citing efforts to increase local productivity or to stave off scurvy with local supplies of citrus, though historians have also attributed them to "the psychology of imperialism."[12]

To the English, the hierarchy of civilization reflected the perceived hierarchy of the natural world. Historian Harriet Ritvo has explained that, "the animal kingdom, with humanity in a divinely ordained position at its apex, represented, explained, and justified the hierarchical human social order."[13] The primacy of human beings in this structure dictated that domestic animals, the most explicitly subordinate to their divinely ordained human masters, held a prime position, with wild animals beneath them. Ritvo has also noted that "the dichotomy between domestic animals and wild animals was frequently compared to that between civilized and savage human societies," a comparison that took on special significance in the context of introducing European animals to non-Western landscapes.[14] These dynamics manifested in the English settlement of North America.[15] English settlers saw livestock as an "important hallmark of civilized society," and the English encouraged native peoples to assume the responsibilities of husbandry in order to advance themselves. Meanwhile Indians had to adapt a cosmology built around the hunting of wild animals to these new, more docile creatures.[16]

Both land *and* people would be "civilized" through the care of livestock. European settlers' attitudes toward their livestock motivated introductions as much as the animals' material functions within European economies did. English settlers in North America "declared that livestock would improve the land and its native inhabitants."[17] Eighteenth-century thinkers believed that all human societies followed the same evolutionary trajectory. This path can generally be broken down into four major sequential stages: nomadic hunter-gatherers were followed by pastoral societies that kept domestic animals. They then became settled agriculturists before finally developing commercial societies like Europe's. Pastoralism was a crucial step-up from nomadism and toward settled agriculture in this inexorable pattern of social development.[18] Thus, animals were the key to the evolution of human society from its crudest stages. In the late nineteenth century, Colonel Richard Irving Dodge wrote, "The possession of domestic animals may be regarded as an exponent of civilization, the number and variety possessed by a people usually in direct proportion to its advancement. Domestic animals indicate stability, and he who possesses them in variety must have a home."[19] By herding animals, native peoples could advance from the lowest state of human society on their way to the modern civilized state of commerce that the Europeans saw themselves as occupying. Richard White notes that, in the American West, Europeans "on the basis of utility" considered their own coevolved animals "as superior to the native wild fauna."[20] The mountain man Jedediah Smith put it most simply when he first journeyed to California in 1827 and remarked that "some fine herds of Cattle in many directions" that he sighted were "sure evidences of Civilization."[21]

European Rivalries in the Pacific

The Cook and Anza expeditions belonged to the broader extension of European power into the Pacific. Since the sixteenth century, the Pacific had served as a route for imperialistic European powers whose true destinations were in East Asia. The value of Pacific trade drove much of European imperial expansion in the Western Hemisphere, and European explorers sought journey-shortening passages and lost continents full of riches.[22] In 1542, the viceroy of New Spain commissioned Juan Cabrillo to sail up the Pacific coast of North America and on to China to establish a trade route linking Spain's American colonies to the highly valued goods of East Asia. When they went ashore at San Diego Bay on September 28, 1542, Cabrillo and his crew became the first Europeans to set foot in the future Alta California. The impact of this landing on the local Indians is unknown because the next European visit would not be for decades. Cabrillo did not mention trading with the natives, and he did not intentionally bring European domestic animals or plants, but he may have brought disease, and a virgin soil epidemic could have had long-lasting effects in the region. Although Cabrillo did not make it to China, later explorers eventually established a trans-Pacific route. Beginning in 1565, with the establishment of Spanish colonial power in the Philippines under Miguel López de Legazpi, Spain shipped specie mined or pillaged in the New World across the Pacific in the Manila galleons. The galleons traded American gold and silver for spices from the Indian Ocean and Chinese silks and porcelain, and then returned to Acapulco. The Spanish then carried the Asian goods overland to Vera Cruz and shipped them back to Spain via the famed treasure fleet. This trade led to increased interest in the Pacific among Spain's principal rivals.[23] Spanish colonial efforts typically focused on conversion through missionization; the fact that they eschewed these efforts in their earliest explorations of the California coast speaks to their priorities at the time. East Asian markets trumped the standard operating procedure.

The privateer Sir Francis Drake led the first English foray into the Pacific. In 1578, Drake explored the western coast of North America, raiding key Spanish seaports along the way.[24] The English knew of Spain's use of the Pacific to link their American and East Asian colonies, and had similar hopes. Drake probably landed in California.[25] Claiming the coast for England, he dubbed it Nova Albion and proceeded westward along the same pathways used by the Manila galleons en route to circumnavigating the globe. This early English voyage into the Pacific succeeded more as piracy than as colonization, but it did foreshadow a growing Spanish-English rivalry in the region.

Joined by the Portuguese, the Dutch, the French, and finally the Russians, this rivalry continued for centuries. Advances in naval technology and new markets for American products (especially fur) in China increased the perceived value of the Pacific among these imperial rivals. Russia's pursuit of valuable furs had led to the settlement of Siberia during the seventeenth and early eighteenth centuries, bringing Russian explorers across the North Pacific into Alaska. A series of wars between France, Spain, and Britain throughout the eighteenth century often moved into Pacific theaters. In 1743, British Commodore George Anson took a galleon near the Philippines during the War of Jenkins' Ear. In 1762, the British would go on to seize Manila itself during the Seven Years' War, though the British returned Manila in 1764, shortly after the war. That war also consolidated British control in India and North America east of the Mississippi at the expense of the French. The French, however, did not abandon their ambitions in the Pacific. Both France and Britain began to send scientific expeditions into the Pacific in the latter half of the eighteenth century.

Most of the region remained relatively unexplored by Europeans until the middle of the eighteenth century. While the rivalries were fierce, even the ascendant British lacked the power to project their influence around the Pacific Rim. To Europeans, that ocean was little more than a vast wilderness of water, crisscrossed by a few uncertain shipping lanes. They possessed limited knowledge of the Pacific's ocean currents and trade winds, and it would require large-scale expeditions by Cook and others to chart many of the region's landmasses. Explorers had yet to disprove the existence of the long-sought-after Northwest Passage and *terra australis*. These gaps in European power and knowledge spurred further missions like those of Anza and Cook in the 1770s.

Cook's Introductions

On June 10, 1776, Cook had a veritable Noah's ark of old-world animals loaded onto the *Resolution* for the coming expedition. In his journal, he stated that they "took on board a Bull, 2 Cows with their Calves & some sheep to carry to Otaheite [Tahiti] with a quantity of Hay and Corn for their subsistence. These cattle were put on board at His Majestys Command and expence with a view of stocking Otahaite and the Neighboring Islands with these usefull animals."[26] Cook and the British government made explicit plans to seed European species on the islands. While familiar with the advantages of creating a stocking station in the Pacific with known supplies, Cook emphasized the animals' usefulness to the natives. This emphasis on utility underscores the European belief in the superiority of their own flora and fauna and points to the animals' perceived power to change native societies. The animals could fulfill the Western civilizing mission by transforming Tahiti into a pastoral society that would make good use of them for material, and subsequently cultural, benefit.

The ostensible reason behind Cook's third voyage, Omai, was a Ra'iatean man who had been living in Tahiti and was probably in his twenties when he joined Cook's second voyage as an interpreter. He was not of the chiefly caste, but in London he was a celebrated curiosity, especially among natural philosophers and Christian missionaries. He also had an audience with the king and queen.[27] Omai's own apparent interest in domestic animals further drove home the point that they could be used to civilize the "noble savages" of the Pacific. In a letter to his patron, the Earl of Sandwich, Cook explained that "the takeing [*sic*] on board some horses has made Omai completely happy, he consented with raptures to give up his Cabin to make room for them, his only concern now is that we shall not have food for all the stock we have got on board.”[28] Omai's excitement about the animals provided proof of their excellence, as well as of a Polynesian desire to use them. Cook observed that “the greatest benefit these islands will receive from Omais [sic] travels will be in the Animals that have been left upon them, which probably they would have never got had he not come to England; when these multiplies [sic] of which I think there is little doubt, they will equal, if not exceed any place in the known World for provisions.”[29] Cook explicitly linked European domestic animals, and the trade they would help provide, with the improvement of the Polynesians he encountered in the Pacific. Animals were to provide the connecting link between Europeans expanding into the Pacific and the native peoples who would benefit from their civilizing influence.[30]

Transporting domestic animals thousands of miles by sail was not an easy proposition. Cook stocked the *Resolution* with “Hay and Corn” to feed the animals, sacrificing scarce space and putting them in competition with the expedition's human crew for provisions. The animals often fell ill or starved over the long voyages. While sailing toward Antarctica in late November 1776, Cook remarked that “a very strong gale . . . made the ship tumble exceedingly and gave us a great deal of trouble to preserve the Cattle we had on board, and notwithstanding all our care several goats . . . died.”[31] Cook added to his menagerie while stopped in South Africa, where he lost two sheep while grazing them onshore. He wrote that he “added two young Bulls, two Heifers, two young stone Horses, two Mares, two Rams, several Ewes and Goats and some Rabbits and Poultry, all of them intended for New Zealand, Otaheite, and the neighbouring islands, or any other place we might meet, where there was a prospect that the leaving of them might prove usefull to posterity.”[32] Once again, Cook emphasized that the animals would be “usefull.”

His journals also indicate, however, that not all peoples and places that he encountered could benefit. In January of 1777, Cook landed in Tasmania (or Van Diemen's Land), where he once again landed a breeding pair of pigs to populate the island with the animals and create future resources for European sailors, regardless of the local ecological cost. After chasing off a group of Tasmanians with a demonstration of European firearms, he related that

> after they were gone I tooke the two Pigs a boar and a Sow, and carried them about a mile within the woods at the head of the bay and there left them by the side of a fresh Water brook. I did intend to have left also a young Bull & Cow, some sheep and Goats, and should have done

it had I not been fully satisfied that the Natives would destroy them, as I am persuaded they will do the Pigs if ever they meet with them; but as this is an animal that soon becomes wild and is fond of the thickest part of the woods, there is a great probability of their escaping, whereas the other Cattle must have been left in an open place where it would have been impossible for them to remain concealed many days.[33]

This passage reveals not only the distinctions between cows and pigs as feral animals and ecological invaders but also the logic of such introductions. Cook utilized the same reasoning as Spanish explorers in the Caribbean who introduced self-sufficient pigs on islands to propagate away from human populations. Pigs and cows inhabited different positions in the late eighteenth-century view of domestic animals. Europeans saw pigs as independent and gluttonous, while they saw cows as stolid and obedient.[34] Cook took these perceived characteristics into account in his introductions, leaving the pigs to fend for themselves as an increasing feral population instead of attempting to subordinate them to local peoples in an attempt to create a pastoral, developing civilization. These differing views of the two species may have colored Cook's views of pig-raising Polynesians, though he did seem to place them above people like the Tasmanians, who had no agriculture or domestic animals.

While Cook often claimed to focus on animals that would be "usefull" to both native peoples and European settlers, he had no inhibitions against overriding native wishes to establish European animals in locales with unwelcoming inhabitants. Cook often spoke of "soft primitives" and "hard primitives," who were less amenable to English civilization. Cook's grouping of the Tasmanians in the latter category and his dismissal of them foreshadowed the brutal genocide that occurred with the British settlement of Tasmania in the nineteenth century.[35] Considering the disruptions to ecosystems that pigs can cause, Cook's introduction may also have played some small role in the collapse of the aboriginal Tasmanian population, though there is little evidence to compare with the clear and disturbing record of white violence there. Cook's account demonstrates that native peoples often took an active role in the establishment of alien species, as Europeans recognized that newly established populations (especially cattle) remained vulnerable to human predation.

In September of 1777, Cook finally brought Omai back to Tahiti; Cook then delivered his bovine cargo to the island's King Tu. Cook found the Tahitians far more accepting of the "civilizing influence" of European domestic animals than the Tasmanians were. In fact, he had a difficult time negotiating the distribution of the animals among various chiefs eager for a share. The Tahitians already saw the domestic animals as a source of wealth and an addition to their gift economy. After describing the conflicts that developed among the cattle's recipients, Cook related, "I thought it best to leave them all with Otoo [Tu] with a strict injunction never to suffer them to go from Oparre not even the Spanish bull, nor none of the Sheep, till he should get a stock of young one[s], which only he was to dispose of to his friends and to send to the Neighboring islands."[36] Cook helped to establish cattle in Tahiti by integrating them into the local social networks of hierarchical gift giving. He found this society more amenable, and usable, than the hunter-gatherers of Tasmania.

Cook's instructions also demonstrate the desire to educate the Tahitians in the proper care of the animals, and a paternalistic attempt to ensure their establishment through coaching. Omai again acted as the mediator in these processes. Cook noted that, before he explained the "several uses" of the cattle, sheep, and horses to the islanders, "Omai was desired to till [sic] them that there were no such animals within many Months of sail of them, that they had been brought them at a vast trouble and expence, and therefore they were not to kill any till they became very numerous, and lastly, they and their Children were to remember that they had been from the men of Britane."[37] Cook hoped to buy future credit for his nation once the Tahitians realized how useful and important the animals were, as he seemed to assume they invariably would, but he also asked for their protection in the meantime. Cook also left Omai several European animals and a garden of European plants. In 1789, when HMS *Bounty*, commanded by one of Cook's former mates, Bligh, landed at Tahiti, the crew learned that Omai had perished of disease four years after Cook left him. He had apparently killed one of his goats after it had gored his stallion, and his garden had been destroyed by hogs and goats after Omai's demise. Only a mare survived near his house.[38] Introductions did not always succeed.

Cook also left domestic animals at the site of his last great "discovery." Shortly after sighting the Hawaiian Islands in January of 1778, Cook sent his men ashore at the island of Niʻihau for supplies. Although Cook described serious problems with thievery on the islands, he was able to gather the necessary supplies, including much-needed drinking water. On February 1, upon deciding that the location was potentially advantageous, Cook planted more of his European flora and fauna on the island.

He left "a Ram goat and two Ewes, a Boar and Sow pig of the English Breed, the seeds of Millons [sic], Pumpkins, and onions."[39] Surprisingly, Cook included the breeding pair of pigs despite knowing that the Polynesians of Hawai'i already possessed significant stock of the animals. On January 23, some of Cook's men had come from Kaua'i with "a few hogs," and Cook had gone on to relate that Hawaiians "had come from all parts of the island, and had brought with them a great many very fine fat hogs to barter, but my people had nothing that would purchas [sic] them, nor indeed did we want them, having already as many on board as, for want of salt, we could dispence with."[40] While willing to take on a few Polynesian pigs, Cook felt that "the English Breed" was superior enough to stock Pacific islands, even those already inhabited by species of the animal. A subspecies of *sus scrofa* descended from Asian pigs, Polynesian pigs were smaller and more docile than the European pigs.[41] These differences seem less likely to disqualify the animals for marine transportation (Polynesians had carried them thousands of miles in smaller watercraft for centuries) than Cook's cultural preference for the more familiar subspecies. Despite the rhetoric of advancement to civilization, Europeans like Cook often dismissed indigenous domestic animals, and indigenous agriculture in general, which served the English ideology that they could "improve" these areas and take possession of them in the process.

Cook also brought germs to the islands despite his attempts to shield local people from diseases borne on his expeditions. In his journal, he wrote on January 20, "As there were several venereal complaints on board both the Ships, in order to prevent it being communicated to these people, I gave orders that no Women, on any account whatever were to be admitted on board the Ships, I also forbid all manner of connection with them, and ordered that none who had the venereal upon them should go out of the ships."[42] Many historians have noted that Cook tried harder than most European explorers to prevent the spread of sexually transmitted diseases like syphilis to the peoples he encountered. But he failed. When the *Resolution* and *Discovery* returned to Hawai'i in late 1778, Cook and his men discovered that diseases unfamiliar to the natives preceded the expedition to the more eastern islands of the group. While charting Maui in November, Cook noted that word of their earlier visit to Kaua'i and Ni'ihau had traveled to the Hawaiians there, as well as diseases: "as these people had got amongst them the Venereal distemper, and I as yet know of no other way they could come by it."[43] Cook acknowledged with sadness that his prohibitions on contact had failed. Lieutenant King noted on November 28 "three of the Natives have apply'd to us, for help in their great distress: they had a Clap, their Penis was much swell'd, & inflamed. The manner in which these innocent People complained to us, seem'd to me to shew that they consider'd us as the Original authors."[44] King also noted that some of Cook's crew thought the rapidity with which the diseases had spread from west to east indicated that the conditions were preexisting, but King explained that it was unknown in the surrounding islands they had visited before their arrival and that in "a people ignorant of its contagious effects . . . its rapidity may be astonishing."[45] Thus, at the same time Cook was planting seeds and distributing animals on Ni'ihau, his crewmen also introduced invasive pathogens that would have a dramatic effect on the islands' native populations and presaged a demographic collapse.[46] These "virgin soil epidemics" were especially destructive because native peoples had no previous exposure, and thus no acquired immunities, to diseases familiar to European bodies.

While Captain Cook's visits to the Hawaiian Islands were brief, he initiated changes that would have long-lasting effects. As we shall see, the next few decades would be a time of immense upheaval in the archipelago. Hawaiians built a radically new political structure by the end of the eighteenth century, followed by fundamental transformations in economic and religious institutions. Introduced European animals helped change basic Hawaiian notions of property and class. Biological and ecological revolutions accompanied these shifts, and Cook's implantations of plants, animals, and disease were only the beginning. More large domestic animals would soon bring still larger alterations on physical and cultural landscapes. Their presence would give Hawai'i a key position in the Pacific whaling circuit and tie the islands into a hide and tallow trade bridging the Pacific. As a result, people and goods began to move back and forth between California and Hawai'i. However, ironically, the initial animals introduced by Cook struggled. A broken foremast forced Cook to return to the islands shortly after his departure. When he returned, he faced increased Hawaiian hostility, and on February 14, 1779, Hawaiians killed Cook during combat over a small boat that a Hawaiian had stolen from the expedition. On February 28, 1779, mate Charles Clerke noted that on Ni'ihau the "2 Ewes and one Ram Goat . . . had now increased to 7 and were in fine order till they unluckily fell a sacrifice to the ill fortunes of their benefactor."[47] The Hawaiians had killed the alien animals after Cook's death, perhaps because of the religious implications of Cook's killing.[48]

Spanish Introductions to California

By the time of Cook's death, Juan Bautista de Anza's party had founded a new settlement on the San Francisco Bay that expanded the reach of the Spanish Empire in the Pacific Rim. Anza's expedition both depended on and stimulated the expansion of old-world organisms to this newly discovered region. A large herd of cattle accompanied Anza's party, and these animals were crucial to the success of the expedition's goals. Before they left Tubac, Pedro Font enumerated the various people and baggage that would make the treacherous journey north, including "three hundred and twenty-five beeves to provision the expedition on the way, those left being designed for stock cattle for the new settlement and missions of the port of San Francisco" and "thirty beeves belonging to individuals."[49] Cattle served an important purpose in supplying the large expedition with sustenance during their months-long overland journey. The expedition could drive its food supplies as a herd without expending the energy of its human component or pack animals. Instead, they would harvest the grasses of the intervening territory. As Font noted, the cattle would serve as foodstuffs and also as the backbone of the economy of the soon-to-be-founded San Francisco settlement.

While Cook's goats were the first of their kind to set foot on Hawai'i's shores, Anza's cattle joined a burgeoning population of the alien animals in the region. Anza augmented Spanish settlements and extended Spanish power on the Pacific coast of North America. His settlers and his cattle expanded a line of missions and forts along the Pacific coast in Alta California that were less than a decade old. His expedition served as a capstone on Spanish plans to push north along the Pacific Rim.

To increase the efficiency of New Spain's colonial government during the Bourbon Reforms, King Carlos III had sent José de Gálvez as visitador general to oversee the viceroyalty in 1765. Gálvez focused much of his attention on expansion to the north; he knew of British explorations in the Pacific, as well as the presence of Russian fur hunters exploiting sea otter populations on the Pacific Coast of North America. Well publicized in Spain, Vitus Bering's 1741 exploration of Alaska prompted fears that either the English or the Russians would soon encroach on Spain's North American possessions, if they had not already. Spain's influence on the Pacific, once called the "Spanish Lake" because of Spain's early dominance from the Philippines to Mexico, would subsequently suffer. To verify Spanish claims, and to create a buffer between the profitable mines of northern New Spain and other European powers' fur frontiers and ambitions, Gálvez enacted a plan to settle the region that became known as Alta California. The settlement expanded from the successful mission settlements of Baja California; from 1697 to 1768, a series of Jesuit missions on the peninsula had worked to convert local Indians into gente de razón, or civilized Christians. Although the Indian population collapsed during those seventy years, the missions allowed the Spanish to establish the first permanent settlements in a region that Europeans had barely touched since Cortés's first attempt at conquest in 1533.[50]

In 1767, the Spanish had expelled the Jesuits from all Crown lands, and the Franciscans had inherited the missions in Baja California. Now Gálvez recruited Franciscans to help settle California alongside military commanders. Gálvez appointed Captain Gaspar de Portolá as the military leader and Fray Junípero Serra as the religious leader of the expedition to found settlements in Alta California. Earlier expeditions had uncovered two favorable bays in the region, San Diego and Monterey, which were to be the sites of the first European settlements. Two ships set out from the port of La Paz in early 1769 to land the first soldiers to prepare for the arrival of an overland expedition containing Serra and Portolá.

On March 24, 1769, the first overland expedition, led by Captain Fernando de Rivera y Moncada, left from a camp at Velicatá in Baja California. Portolá and Serra followed on May 13. As in the later Anza expedition, a large herd of domestic animals traveled with them. The manifest for Portolá's party mentioned "306 Cows and heifers, 6 ewes and 2 sheep, 153 Chickens and Cocks," as well as "262 Horses and Mules, 2 female Burros" accompanying the "Seven Missionary Priests" and 243 officers and soldiers for the soon-to-be-built presidios.[51] An overland expedition could move many more domestic animals than a naval expedition could, and settlement necessitated domestic animals to support the colony. Whereas climate and season, unfamiliar soils, and scarce labor constrained early crop yields from a new settlement, cattle could transform California pasturage to an immediate food resource for the colonists that could withstand aridity and even store calories to be taken in the winter. They also provided power to move wagons and farm implements, leather goods to make tools and clothe settlers, and oil from rendered fat for nighttime light. These latter two resources gave cattle a commercial use that would become important to Alta California's economy in the coming decades. Furthermore, the entire project of the settlement of California hung on the use of domestic animals to civilize California Indians, to turn them from gentiles to "people of reason" (gente de razón).[52]

Because much of Mexico was too arid for traditional European crops like wheat, and because of acute labor shortages and land newly "opened" by demographic collapse of native populations, ranching prevailed in much of New Spain. While Europeans readily adopted New World crops like maize, squash, beans, and potatoes, they still focused on familiar European grains for much of their production, and they remained committed to the pastoral lifestyle dominant in Spain and so central to their vision of civilization. Before the colonization of the New World, the Iberian regions of Extremadura and Andalusia had developed a unique system of animal husbandry to raise large herds of cattle.[53] Cattle abounded throughout the Old World, but most European pastoralists on feudal landholdings possessed or raised only a few of the animals. However, in these arid regions of the Iberian Peninsula, cattle ran in large herds on open estates with brands marking their ownership. In a practice called transhumance, the vaqueros who managed the herds for the cattle barons moved the cattle seasonally to mitigate their impact on rangeland.[54] Because they ran in large herds on relatively open range, Spanish cattle retained more of their defenses than other European breeds did. Hardy animals, the Spanish longhorns possessed feral instincts and the long defensive weapons on their skulls that gave them their name.[55] The conquest of the Americas required the transfer of these distinctive animals, and the unique cattle culture that produced them, to the New World.

The animals succeeded in New Spain, and ranches proliferated as the cattle population expanded rapidly. One biological invasion necessitated another; as virgin soil epidemics depopulated the region, the widespread availability of land and the scarcity of labor favored cattle ranching in Mexico, as large herds required relatively few drovers.[56] Land use rested on a Spanish tradition emphasizing commonage—more an ideal in Iberia than a reality—as the Crown attempted to retain ultimate control over all of the colonial lands.[57] This open land policy allowed certain barons to establish extremely large herds and then appropriate specific rangelands as ranching estates, or estancias. These barons did not own their estancias outright in the early sixteenth century, but they gained exclusive rights that eventually evolved into ownership.

Cattle flourished from these large economies of scale and a propitious environment. Records indicate that in the late 1530s herds "nearly doubled in fifteen months."[58] The animals and the culture built around their management flourished in the New World, and adapted to the new conditions.[59] In the process, they also promoted Spanish conquest and expansion in the Americas. Mission instruction included learning a trade, which for many Indians meant working with horses, cattle, and sheep, the cornerstones of the ranching industry in New Spain. Thus, the cattle not only supported the expedition; they also supported the new colonies and helped to transform the Indian converts into Hispanic peoples.

Velicatá in Baja California served as an ideal point of disembarkation for Portolá and Serra because of its good pasturage. Moving an entire herd of cattle through the dry, mountainous, and relatively unknown country to San Diego was as difficult and dangerous as the long passages at sea undertaken by Cook. Fortunately, as Junípero Serra explained, Velicatá "has the advantage of a convenient watering place midway, unknown till now, with good pasturage for the animals."[60]

The centrality of the cattle to the entire venture of settling Alta California meant that similar considerations for the animals remained paramount throughout the journey. The expedition set out from Velicatá on May 13, 1769, and spent much of its time looking for feed and water for the animals. The journals of early expeditions in Alta California are littered with dozens of examples of the words "pasto" and "zacate," synonyms for pasture that specifically implied grasslands suitable for the grazing of domestic animals.[61] When they discovered a patch of cottonwoods on May 25, they dug for water to "quench the thirst of man and beasts."[62] These concerns dominated the journey through the desert to San Diego. Restless animals could also be a disturbance. In his journal of the expedition, Portolá noted on May 29 that the party "spent a bad night, the animals repeatedly being stampeded all night long, and so lay by on the following day."[63] When they passed over their final hillcrest above the bay, Serra exulted that "we found the country was not only nice pasture land, but that it had also a pleasant river of good water. . . . There the animals traveled splendidly, and we went without further anxiety."[64] The expedition made excellent time and arrived at the bay July 1. The two ships that had preceded them in January and February, the *San Carlos* and the *San Antonio*, respectively, had not fared as well, and Serra noted that they had arrived "with nearly all the people ill, many having died every day and every other day continuing to die from the sickness of Loanda, or scurvy."[65]

Despite the dire straits of the naval expedition's crewmen, the foundation of San Diego went ahead as planned. Further considerations for the well-being of the livestock dominated the founding of the first mission. Upon arriving in San Diego, Serra was pleased to find plenty of souls for him to save. In listing the site's virtues, he noted "above all a large population of gentiles, both in this locality and in the surrounding country.

They visit us frequently, but first they put aside their bows and arrows."[66] Serra carefully observed the natural environment to be certain that the land would also support the pastoral economy of a Franciscan mission. A mission needed fresh and abundant water to prevent the cattle from bunching near it and overgrazing the local range.[67] In the dry warmth of San Diego, the average adult cow would require more than ten gallons of water a day.[68] At San Diego, Serra observed that "land here is plentiful and good, and a river goes with it. Although not long ago it had flowing water, at present, this being the driest part of the year—there is no water running it. But there are still large and good pools."[69] Water to "quench the thirst of both man and beast" remained essential to the settlement.

By the next year, Serra hoped to expand the cattle culture at the missions. In a letter to the president of the missions, Antonio María de Bucareli y Ursúa, Serra enumerated a series of measures that would improve the new California missions. He asked for the recruitment in San Blas of "day laborers, cowboys, and mule drivers" to manage the growing herds.[70] He added, "It is of no less importance that, when the livestock arrives . . . some Indian families from the said [Baja] California should come, of their own free will, with the expedition."[71] Thus, Serra would acquire more laborers to tend his herds and gardens and serve as examples of newly converted gente de razón through their work in a European system of pastoral agriculture.

By 1775, the missions and presidios at San Diego and Monterey had grown, and the Spanish had founded three more missions. As the settlements in Alta California expanded, the Fathers selected Juan Bautista de Anza to lead an expedition to found a mission at a large bay sighted by Portolá as he had searched for Monterey Bay. As in all the settlements in California, cattle underwrote Spanish control of this strategically vital region. Anza's expedition followed previous expeditions in including a herd of more than 350 cattle to feed the settlement to be founded at San Francisco Bay. Fray Pedro Font described Anza's party as it departed on October 22, 1775, noting that "ahead went four soldiers, as scouts to show the road. Leading the vanguard went the commander, and then came I. Behind me followed the people, men, women, and children, and the soldiers who went escorting and caring for their families. The lieutenant with the rear guard concluded the train. Behind him the pack mules usually followed; after them came the loose riding animals; and finally all the cattle, so that altogether they made a very long procession."[72] The sheer size of the expedition attested to the importance of buttressing New Spain's

California holdings and supporting the mission there with the European animals necessary for its viability.

This "very long procession" followed the trail blazed by Anza himself in 1774 from Tubac in New Mexico to the San Gabriel mission north of mission San Diego. On November 18, Font noted that "the camp site is very short of pasturage, as there is only some bad Carrizo [reeds or beach grass] in a flat formed by the river."[73] The problems persisted. On December 10, 1775, Font complained that "all this land is difficult to cross because of the great scarcity of pasturage and water and because nearly all of it is very sandy."[74] Death also stalked the animals in these long overland crossings, just as it did at sea. On Christmas Eve, after the party had crossed through some cold mountain passes, Font noted that "the cattle were so used up with the snow that yesterday in so short a journey three beeves became tired out and today another one."[75]

Soldiers from San Gabriel had founded the mission of San Juan Capistrano in November of 1775, but when Font visited it in mid-January of 1776, he found the mission site abandoned. While the settlers rode north, a battle had broken out between a group of soldiers and Indians at San Diego, and they had returned to fortify the presidio there. Local gentiles had burned and looted the San Diego mission and murdered and mutilated Father Luís Jayme. Anza, Font, and a small group of soldiers left the expedition to restore order. As Font surveyed the abandoned mission site of San Juan Capistrano, he attributed the rebellion to the dispersion of the missions, soldiers, and cattle. Font explained that "in more than seven years they [the missions] have made little progress, and have suffered extraordinary trials and need. . . . That the provisions . . . for the promotion of the missions were meager is a matter of great certainty. And as proof of it, without attempting to specify all cases, it is sufficient to know that as a beginning of stock only nine cows and one bull were sent to each mission."[76] Font claimed that the small numbers of livestock sent to found the later missions explained their failure and proved that New Spain had not done enough to ensure their success. European animals were the basis of the Franciscans' plans; how were they to expand Christian civilization if they could not feed the soldiers or show the virtues of European animal husbandry to the Indians?

On March 11, 1776, the party reached the mission of San Carlos del Carmelo, near Monterey, where Fray Serra greeted them. Then Anza and Font led a smaller party north to choose the site of the settlement on the San Francisco Bay. Among their highest concerns was choosing good ranching land. On March 27, Font evaluated one possible site for the new settlement and observed that "the place and its vicinity has abundant pasturage, plenty of firewood, and fine water."[77] He also noted that "here and near the lake there are *yerba buena* and so many lilies that I had them almost inside my tent."[78] The next day, they founded the presidio nearby, and a party of settlers ventured north to occupy it that summer. The eventual pueblo that began to grow around the San Francisco mission in the 1830s came to be known as Yerba Buena for the medicinal herb that Font had observed in abundance there. Yerba buena (*Micromeria douglasii*) is a forb on which the cattle grazed.

Over the next two decades, cattle did quite well in the settlements on the San Francisco Bay and throughout California as a whole. On November 15, 1792, when Captain George Vancouver and some of his men first went ashore at San Francisco, he remarked that "the herds of cattle and flocks of sheep grazing on the surrounding hills were a sight we had long been strangers to, and brought to our minds many pleasing reflections."[79] Later, when Vancouver observed the slaughter of twenty-two of these cattle at Santa Clara, he remarked that "hence it is evident, as the whole of their stock has sprung from fifteen head of breeding cattle . . . that these animals must be very prolific to allow of such an abundant supply."[80] By the 1790s, the gambit to escort the herds thousands of miles over dry and difficult land had paid off for the Spanish settlements in California, which could now feed the populations of its frontier settlements from the burgeoning herds on its hills. Vancouver also noted that those in charge of the settlements had carefully nurtured the expansion of the herd. He explained that "their great increase in so short a time is to be ascribed to the rigid œconomy of the fathers, who would not allow any to be killed, until they had so multiplied as to render their extirpation not easy to be effected."[81]

Vancouver's Hawaiian Introductions

Vancouver wanted to establish domestic animals on the Hawaiian Islands, where he had been as a member of Captain James Cook's third (and final) voyage. Vancouver's own voyage followed a series of British explorations in the Pacific Ocean of which Cook's shone as the brightest exemplars. Just as the late eighteenth-century Spanish missions into California existed to counter Russian advances in the Pacific from the north, this round of British exploration served as a response to perceived challenges from imperial rivals in the Pacific. The northern extent of Spain's North American possessions along the Pacific coast remained unclear, and the Pacific Northwest with its riches in sea otter pelts for fur traders had become the center of conflict in the late 1780s. Cook had reported the existence of Nootka Sound in March 1776, and a British fur trader named John Meares had stopped there to build a permanent trading post in 1788. In 1789, Estéban José Martínez seized Nootka Sound for the Spanish. War threatened as the British and the Spanish prepared expeditions to assert their authority over the sound. Alejandro Malaspina sailed for Spain in the summer of 1789, but George Vancouver's expedition for Britain overshadowed his discoveries. Vancouver's voyage lasted from 1791 to 1795, and he sailed on the HMS *Discovery*, named for one of Cook's ships. Vancouver returned with detailed charts of Nootka Sound that allowed the British to strengthen their claims. The Spanish had already relented and abandoned their first settlement, and they never regained a toehold in the area.[82]

Vancouver also revisited regions "discovered" by his predecessors. Although Hawai'i had remained in constant contact with Europeans after Cook's voyage, Vancouver's visit had a profound effect on the archipelago. He managed to gain provisions for the three ships of his expedition, and he even received a confused (and never enforced) cession of the islands' territory to the British king. He also established a variety of plants and animals on the island, including orange trees and domestic animals that would aid later British mariners in the Pacific. These domestic animals included cattle, which Vancouver, like other European explorers, hoped to introduce as a convenient source of beef provisions for ships in the mid-Pacific, as well as a civilizing tool to transform the Hawaiian people.

Vancouver visited California to secure supplies to feed his crew and animals to stock the Hawaiian Islands.[83] In January 1792, Vancouver purchased from the Spanish authorities in Monterey "some black cattle and sheep, for the purpose of establishing a breed of those valuable animals in the Sandwich Islands."[84] Once again, carrying these animals on a maritime voyage was uncertain and dangerous work. When they arrived in Hawai'i in February of 1793, Vancouver refilled the ship's water casks, because, as he explained, "the vast consumption of water by the cattle on our passage hither, made the quantity we now required very considerable."[85] As in Cook's voyages, cattle competed with crew for stores, utilized a great deal of resources from the scarce shipboard space, and required great care and supervision. Vancouver noted "the unfortunate losses we had suffered in our passage amounting to three rams, two ewes, a bull and a cow."[86] In fact, the first cattle to ever set hoof upon the Hawaiian

Islands were the most ill of the remaining stock. Vancouver described that "the only bull that remained, and a cow that had brought forth a dead calf, were no longer able to stand on their legs, and it was evident, that if a speedy opportunity did not offer itself for relieving them by sending them ashore, their lives could not possibly be preserved. . . . The loss, particularly of the bull, would have been a cruel disappointment to my wishes."[87] The introduction of cattle to Hawai'i was of great importance to Vancouver, despite the inherent risks, so he rushed through diplomatic protocols with the Hawaiian chiefs to get the sick bull and cow ashore.

In correspondence with Phillip Stephens, the Secretary of the Admiralty, Vancouver claimed that he and his crew were "highly indebted to the civil, honest and friendly behavior of the whole of the inhabitants of the Island, whose study seems to emulate the behavior of Tamaah Maah [Kamehameha I], their King." As a result, he noted, Hawaiians had supplied "all our wants of wood, water, and various refreshments of hogs, fish, vegetables, &c. which the country affords, and in such abundance as we have from time to time demanded for the use of our three Vessels, without the trouble of bartering for those things." Vancouver revealed to Stephens his plans to stock the island with livestock "as some return for the honorable and hospitable behavior we have in every instance experienced from the islanders, I have at length effected the establishment of a breed of black cattle in Owhyhee [Hawaii] . . . ; there is little doubt under the promise of Tamaah Maah of the inhabitants taking the greatest care of them, that they will soon propagate, to the advantage of the whole of these worth [sic] people, and their future visitors."[88] Vancouver hoped that his introduction would result in a mutually beneficial future trade in the animals. In Vancouver's vision, native Hawaiians, while eating a beef-filled diet themselves, would happily share some of the beef from the cattle they raised with British ships stationed in their fair harbors, as they had so generously shared with him.

To ensure that the introduced domestic animals would establish a reproducing population, Vancouver called upon the king to place a strict religious ban on killing them. He "demanded that they [livestock] should be *tabooed* for ten years, with a discretionary powering [sic] the king alone to appropriate a certain number of the males of each species, in case that sex became predominant, to the use of his own table."[89] However, Vancouver would violate Hawaiian religious norms to complete his plan. After demanding the taboo, he elaborated that "in so doing the women should not be precluded of partaking of them, as the intention of their being brought to the island was for the general use and benefit of every inhabitant of both sexes, as soon as their numbers should be sufficiently increased to allow of a general distribution amongst the people."[90] This gender equality in beef consumption contradicted native traditions that barred women from eating any foods defined as delicacies. Vancouver's demands, while possessing an air of class and gender equality, also spoke to the cultural dimensions of his biological introductions. Vancouver insisted that the production and consumption of European beef and mutton would follow the European patterns, including their social and gender dimensions. In granting some of Europe's animal assets to Hawai'i, Vancouver felt an obligation to ensure that the Hawaiians used them according to European standards.[91]

Further introductions followed, as Europeans continued to reshape the Hawaiian landscape, including its people, into a pastoral mold. In 1803, American merchant Richard Cleveland traveled from California to Hawai'i. Cleveland hoped to please King Kamehameha with a gift of horses, and, as a result, he introduced another biological element essential to European cattle culture. Cleveland and his partner, Captain William Shaler, sailed on the *Lelia Byrd*, a commercial vessel engaged in the Canton trade. Cleveland's account of his efforts to stock Hawai'i with horses focused more on the animals' ability (or failure) to astonish the natives. Both Cleveland and Shaler saw great benefits to the Hawaiians of these old-world animals while denigrating the local fauna. As Shaler put it, "These islands were very poor in animals."[92]

Cleveland diligently worked with the friars of California's missions to acquire his animal gifts for Kamehameha while there in the spring of 1803. Cleveland and his crew had difficulties with mission leaders farther up the coast, but they finally encountered a padre with whom they could deal in Mariano Apolonario at Mission San Miguel. He provided them with two horses, a male and a female, and they later added another mare with foal. Cleveland remarked that "in return for those, and a flagon of wine and dried fruits, we gave him such manufactures as he desired, to more than their value."[93] Attaining the horses was a matter of importance to Cleveland, who desperately wanted to make a good impression on Kamehameha.

But Cleveland's investment in horses failed to please Hawai'i's king. Cleveland noted that "desirous of conciliating the good opinion of a person whose power was so great, we omitted no attention which we supposed to be agreeable to him. But whether he had left some duty unperformed on shore, or whether he had met with something to disturb his serenity of mind, we know not; certain it was, that he did not reciprocate our civilities."[94] This disappointing reception continued with the presentation of the horses, as "after walking around the deck of the vessel and taking only a careless look at the horses, he got into his canoe, and went on shore."[95] Hawai'i's other inhabitants did not share the king's disinterest. At Kealakekua Bay, Cleveland encountered John Young, an Englishman who had unwillingly become one of the island's first European residents after Kamehameha detained him in 1789.[96] Cleveland noted that on June 24, 1803, the *Lelia Byrd* "anchored in Tooayah [Kawaihae] Bay, for the purpose of landing the mare with foal, for which Young was very urgent."[97] Young shared his fellow Europeans' esteem and concern for the horses. As a permanent resident, he was deeply invested in the future of the islands, and he probably desired the power inherent in European animals to transform his new home into something more akin to a European civilization.[98]

The horses also intrigued many of the natives. After the landing of the mare with foal, Cleveland explained that "this was the first horse that ever trod the soil of Owhyhee, and caused, amongst the natives, incessant exclamations of astonishment."[99] He added that "the people showed none of the indifference on seeing them, which had been manifested by the King, and which I believe to have been affectation, but on the contrary, expressed such wonder and admiration, as were very natural on beholding, for the first time, the noble animal."[100] Cleveland delighted in the Hawaiians' excitement over the animals and refused to believe that the horses did not similarly amaze Kamehameha. Cleveland also recorded that

> while the crowd were apparently wondering what use they could be put to, a sailor from our ship jumped upon the back of one and galloped off amid the shouts of the natives, who, with alacrity, opened a way to let him pass. . . . The King was among the number, who witnessed the temerity of the sailor; but with all the sagacity for which he has been justly praised, remarked, that he could not perceive that the ability to transport a person from one place to another, in less time than he could run, would be adequate compensation for the food he would consume and the care he would require. As a dray or a dragoon's horse there was no prospect of his being wanted, and hence our present was not highly appreciated. In this we were much disappointed, but hoped, nevertheless, that the king would be influenced by our advice to have them well taken care of; that they would increase, and eventually that their value would be justified.[101]

Cleveland argued that Kamehameha's reluctance to accept the horses showed keen but misguided insight. While the captain admitted that the colt would not be of great use on the islands, he still saw potential future uses. Like the other European maritime voyagers traveling within the Pacific Rim at the turn of the eighteenth century, Cleveland perceived the European domesticated animals as indispensable. He thought that Hawaiians would certainly be awed at the sight of the supposedly superior European animals, and he was disappointed when the king failed to meet his expectations.[102]

In fact, Kamehameha showed foresight in his doubts about the animals. On the American plains, horses increased mobility and speed, but they also had considerable impacts on the Native American groups that adopted them. The Pawnees quickly incorporated the animals into the buffalo hunt, which had great dietary and cultural significance. The horse also became an important part of the Pawnees' economy and served as a status symbol. However, the animals also had major drawbacks. Horses threatened plants that had served as important food staples, and the animals required close monitoring to protect them from raids and prevent them from breaking into the fields from which the Pawnees gathered plants. Even on the vast grasslands of the plains, feeding the horses year-round required constant effort.[103] Thus, the king's doubts that the benefits of the horse "would be adequate compensation for the food he would consume and the care he would require" demonstrate his acumen for assessing the opportunities and costs that new animals presented. Nevertheless, Hawaiians would eventually require Cleveland's horses to deal with the rapidly expanding and destructive cattle population. The Hawaiians' mixed reactions to horses demonstrate the often complex interactions that native peoples had with newly introduced animals, which heralded a series of dramatic post-contact cultural and ecological transformations.

Conclusions

After centuries of fitful exploration and risky crossings of the Pacific Ocean, Europeans began to establish a permanent presence beyond the fringes of this vast region in the second half of the eighteenth century. Explorers like Portolá, Anza, Cook, Vancouver, and Cleveland knew that expanding imperial frontiers into the Pacific would require the establishment of familiar old-world elements, especially livestock, which could provide reliable supplies while transforming newly encountered peoples and places. As a result, Europeans fought and suffered to establish old-world domestic animals in the western coast of North America and in the eastern Pacific. They recognized that livestock underlay their agriculture, trade, and culture, and thus their colonial and commercial efforts in newly encountered places. Consequently, they expended energy to transport animals and to ensure their success in unfamiliar pastures.

Cook charted Pacific coasts and evaluated the indigenous people he met to decide what animals he would introduce. Though he would meet his end in Hawai'i, Cook's voyage established British influence in the island chain, and Vancouver worked to complete his agenda when he brought cattle to Hawai'i. Vancouver had a convenient source for the animals because the Spanish had fought so hard to bring herds to extend the northern frontier of New Spain. These soldiers and missionaries had carefully evaluated the landscapes of Alta California to find a safe home for herds of cattle that could feed priests and settlers and transform indigenous people. Cook and Vancouver made great strides in establishing British power in the "Spanish Lake" of the Pacific Ocean, while José de Galvez countered by extending the Spanish presence north along the North American coast. All of these Europeans saw the animals as a tool of survival, a commodity, and a marker of civilization; they believed that indigenous people would come to see the animals in these ways too. The English saw domestic animals specifically as carriers of ideas of property, while the Spanish saw the animals as crucial in the transformation of native cultures to their conception of Christian civilization.

In the process of these introductions, they often disregarded or encouraged the ecological and cultural ramifications of their actions, which fundamentally and irreversibly changed the lives of native peoples. As Richard Cleveland learned, indigenous people did not always cheer the gift of domestic animals. The fragile breeding pairs of cattle in Hawai'i would require careful husbandry by natives to survive, and even the invading herds of Spanish cattle in Alta California were vulnerable to the dense Indian populations there. Native reactions would determine the course of livestock populations in these regions. European explorers created a new world in the Pacific with their cultural encounters and biological introductions, and this Pacific World served as the backdrop to the continuing adaptations and conflicts between European settlers, indigenous peoples, and domestic animals.

CHAPTER TWO

Landscapes

In 1840, almost fifty years after Vancouver's initial introduction of cattle, American naval explorer Charles Wilkes visited Hawai'i as part of the high-profile United States Exploring Expedition in the Pacific. Wilkes spent some time on the Big Island and made an ascent up the slopes of the volcanic Mauna Loa. Along the way, he took note of the Waimea Plains, where so many of Vancouver's cattle grazed. He was disappointed by what he saw. He stated that "the district is famous, according to report, for the number of wild cattle found on it, and from that circumstance would be supposed to produce fine pasturage." However, he said, "this is far from being the case, for there is nothing but a few scattered tufts of grass, and a species of ranunculus, which is of so acrid a nature that the cattle will not eat it."[1] The predominance of a plant species unpalatable to cattle suggests that grazing pressure may have severely impacted other plants more favorable to consumption by cows. Probably, the barren field had been swept by cattle, who had left behind only the acrid ranunculus.

A few months later in the summer of 1841, Charles Wilkes's expedition had taken him to California. Again, he complained, stating that "instead of a lively green hue, it had generally a tint of a light straw-colour, showing an extreme want of moisture . . . owing, as I afterwards observed, to the withered vegetation and the ripened wild oats of the country."[2] The "want of moisture" in the summer months had been a consistent trait in California, but the "ripened wild oats" were a more recent addition, a plant that the Spanish had probably introduced unintentionally, but that was well adapted to the grazing of their cattle.

Wilkes's expedition's journey in 1841 from Hawai'i to North America's Pacific coast followed a route that was becoming heavily trafficked by that time. Along the way, he was able to witness some of the effects wrought by a half century of cattle, the animal that would come to drive a significant portion of that traffic, in the eastern Pacific. Borderlands are places of transformation, and this was certainly true of the Pacific borderlands. European introductions of old-world animals caused dramatic and rapid changes in the local environments of both California and Hawai'i, and the native peoples in both regions had to reckon with these new arrivals. Both groups lived in complex societies with long histories of habitation in the region. Over time, they had developed traditions and practices suited to these landscapes, and they had survived through periods of disruption and conflict in the past. The newest changes were likely the most dramatic and rapid that they had ever faced, and they presented dangers and forced adaptations. This chapter briefly discusses the unique geographies of California and Hawai'i, examines some of the lifeways of the native peoples in each region, and then analyzes the ecological transformations wrought by the introduction of cattle and other livestock. The altered landscapes of California and Hawai'i would serve as the backdrops for the indigenous responses, new labor regimes, and changes in land tenure that would reshape the Pacific borderlands in the decades to come, creating the pastures that disappointed Charles Wilkes. At the same time, cattle also provided many of the eastern Pacific's inhabitants with their livelihoods and served as a tool for the colonizing powers, including (and especially) the United States, which Wilkes represented.

Island Biogeographies

The Hawaiian archipelago is the product of a single volcanic "hotspot" in the middle of the Pacific Ocean. Over the past 80 million years, as magma emerged from beneath the earth's surface through this hotspot, it formed mountainous underwater shield volcanoes that eventually broke through the surface of the Pacific Ocean. The volcano would emerge as an island, then eventually go dormant, and slow processes of erosion began to wear it down, leaving fertile volcanic soils as it crumbled back into the sea over several million years. As the tectonic plates shifted, the location of this hotspot relative to the earth's surface changed; the plate moved west and north, leaving a chain of dormant volcano-formed islands with the youngest, and still active, Big Island of Hawai'i, in the southeast.[3]

The nearest large landmass is the West Coast of North America, more than 2,000 miles away; because of this isolation, each emerging volcanic island would have been all but barren of life. Slowly, however, flying animals, seeds, and insects hitchhiking on driftwood colonized each island.

Separation from parent populations and new ecological niches prompted these residents to evolve rapidly into new and unique species in a process known as adaptive radiation.[4] Ninety-six percent of Hawai'i's native flowering plants occur naturally nowhere else.[5] This property of island biology made the Galápagos Islands the background for the development of Charles Darwin's theory of evolution. Evolutionary distinctiveness also makes specialized island biota especially vulnerable to exotic generalists that evolve in larger populations with broader and more varied habitat ranges and niches. The difficulty of the oceanic barrier dictates what types of creatures colonize islands. Marine animals arrived first, followed by birds. Plants arrived by floating across the vast oceans or as seeds carried by birds. Before humans arrived, only two mammal species, a bat and a seal, inhabited Hawai'i. Purely terrestrial land mammals would have to wait for humans to transport them to the islands.

The trade winds that blow east to west in the Pacific have a dramatic effect on the climates of the Hawaiian Islands. The eastern, or windward, sides experience significant regular precipitation and consequently have lush tropical rain forests. The western, or leeward, sides lay in the arid rain shadows of the eroding volcanic peaks of the islands. Dry forests flourished on the leeward side of the islands and on the slopes of their volcanoes at higher elevations.

Because of its unique geography, California shares some characteristics with Hawai'i. California encompasses a large and amazingly flat central valley surrounded by the imposing and ever-rising Sierra Nevada to the east and the smaller coastal mountains and eventually the Pacific Ocean to the west. Though mostly circumscribed by political boundaries rather than the ocean, scholars have nonetheless described California as having many of the attributes of an island, including adaptive radiation, owing to the diversity of its topography and climate and the difficulty many organisms have crossing the imposing deserts, mountains, and ocean that surround it.[6] California has notable biodiversity and many unique endemic species; out of the 6,300 plant species native to California, a third of them grow nowhere else.[7]

California features rich aquatic communities along its long seashore, wetlands along the coast, fertile grasslands in the central valley, arid deserts, coastal hills, foothills, volcanoes, and one of the world's tallest mountain ranges. Throughout the state, and even in the wettest areas along the northern coast, most precipitation falls in the winter months, while the summer is almost completely dry. The Sierra Nevada holds much of the winter precipitation in snowpacks that melt in the spring and feed rivers that flow to the sea. Many of these rivers flow through the central valley and eventually join together in a system that drains into the immense San Francisco Bay. Redwoods, the world's tallest trees, grow along the coast. Large stands of pine cover the mountains, and oaks flourish in the central valley, coastal hills, and foothills.

In the late eighteenth and early nineteenth centuries, most visitors emphasized the area's diversity in their descriptions of California. Charles Wilkes claimed that "there is perhaps no other country where there is such a diversity of features, soil, and climate as California."[8] The flora of the Sacramento Valley impressed John C. Frémont during his 1846 overland exploration. He described the area as "being gay with flowers, and some of the banks being absolutely golden with the California poppy (*eschscholzia crocea*). Here the grass was smooth and green and the groves very open, the large oaks throwing a broad shade among sunny spots."[9]

This natural abundance extended to California's fauna as well. At one point in his exploration, Frémont noted that "from the fresh trails which occurred regularly during the morning, deer appeared to be remarkably numerous."[10] Charles Wilkes claimed, "The variety of game in this country almost exceeds belief. The elk may be said to predominate, but there are also many bears, black-tailed deer, wolves, foxes, minxes, hares, muskrats, badgers, antelopes, and ovis Montana [a species of wild mountain sheep]."[11] Alfred Robinson, a New Englander who traveled to California in 1828 and settled there, noted that "game is plentiful" and that "the rivers and creeks are supplied with an abundance of salmon and other fish."[12] Twice a year, millions of salmon swam against the currents up California's rivers to spawn, and California's lakes and rivers were also rich in trout. These fish helped sustain populations of bear and otter, but the abundance and diversity of the coastal fisheries dwarfed these massive runs.

California Indians and the Environment

Of course, the sheer size of California plays a clear role in this abundance. Today, the state of California covers over 155,000 square miles, and the Spanish claimed even more territory within Alta California, including most of the modern state of Nevada (though they never effectively controlled more than the territory north to Sonoma and less than a hundred miles inland).[13] Peoples in California confronted myriad landscapes: mountains, deserts, wetlands, grasslands, and forests. This diversity of ecotypes and the natural abundance and size of California combined to help produce a plethora of different Indian societies. Estimates generally count 300,000 people living in California before European settlement in 1769, which represented the densest native population north of Mexico. California contained more than a hundred different native languages from seven different language families, a quarter of the native languages and two-thirds of the language families spoken in all of North America north of the Rio Grande. Tribal designations refer to groups linguists and anthropologists categorize by language. California Indians actually lived in smaller autonomous groups anthropologists have called "tribelets." Tribelets usually consisted of a single village, or ranchería to the Spanish settlers, of 300 to 500 individuals.[14]

Only the Yuma in the South, bordering today's Arizona, practiced agriculture. The Yuma utilized the milpa complex of corn, beans, and squash, which originated in Central Mexico and spread to the Southwest and then eastward. Throughout the rest of California, most Indians were semisedentary hunter-gatherers who survived by exploiting a variety of niches provided by the region's natural diversity. The Chumash of Santa Barbara and the Channel Islands grew rich enough from exploiting sea creatures that they developed a hierarchical society, much like the coastal Indians of the Pacific Northwest.[15] The Ohlone made use of the estuaries of the San Francisco delta, as well as coastal fisheries and the terrestrial resources of the coastal mountains. Farther north, the Karuk, Yurok, and Hupa survived off annual salmon runs. Inland, Pomo, Miwok, and others harvested acorns from the numerous oaks growing throughout California.

In all of these groups, the men hunted game, while the women gathered fruits, nuts, and vegetables to round out their diet. Acorns, the seeds of California's oak trees, were among the most crucial foodstuffs eaten by the native Californians. In the fall, the acorns would ripen on the branches of various species of oaks, and Indians would gather them. The nuts were easy to store and thus could be consumed throughout the year; however, they were not easy to eat. The Indians had to process the hard and tannic acorns to leach out the toxic acids and to render them edible. To this end, native women ground them into dust with a mortar and pestle and then mixed them with water to make a paste that could be eaten or baked into a bread. Pine nuts in the coastal mountains and foothills also provided a rich source of calories.[16]

The French explorer Jean François de Galaup, comte de La Pérouse remarked that "prior to Spanish colonization, the Indians of northern California grew only a little maize and lived almost exclusively on the product of their fishing and hunting; no country has more fish and game of every kind; rabbits, hares and deer were as common as in the royal hunting grounds; otters and seals are as plentiful as in the N., and in winter they kill a very large quantity of bears, foxes, wolves and wild cats."[17] The Indians were not mere passive recipients of California's bounty, however. Archaeological evidence shows that humans have lived in California for at least 12,000 years. The evidence also suggests periods of resource scarcity and overexploitation. In response to these challenges over the centuries, California Indians developed a set of strategies to utilize the region's productivity. For instance, acorn harvesting probably began around A.D. 1000 during a period when game populations were at a nadir, perhaps due to overhunting.[18] Long habitation in the area provided Indians with detailed knowledge of the various species in the region. More intensive management of California's resources helped to create the abundance that awed European visitors.

Local knowledge allowed the Indians to develop strategies to change their environment in dramatic ways in order to promote the plants and animals that most interested each particular tribal cultural group. The practice with the most impact was the use of controlled or prescribed burning. As in other regions of North America, Indians in California occasionally lit grasslands and allowed them to burn. Fire provided one of the Indians' most powerful tools in shaping their environment. The French explorer Camille de Roquefeuil noted one such fire near Mendocino, which he first took to be an erupting volcano. He later learned from the Franciscans in San Francisco that "the natives, at this season, set fire to the grass, to dry the pods of a grain which they use for food, to render it more easy to gather."[19] This helped create and sustain grassland areas out of forests or shrublands, and thus made the area more easily navigable and lessened the number of insect pests. It also prompted production of foods, like acorns, and caused some species of plants to sprout, which in turn could encourage the population of game.[20]

Indians used their knowledge of animal behavior as a tool in their hunting. They dug pits in carefully chosen locales to trap large animals. While visiting Monterey in 1786, La Pérouse, admiring the Indians' skills as hunters, noted that "we all of us saw an Indian with a deer's head tied over his own, crawling on all fours, pretending to eat grass, and carrying out this pantomime in such a way that our hunters would have shot him from 30 paces if they had not been forewarned. In this way they go up to deer herd within very close range and kill them with arrows."[21] Intimate knowledge of game animals allowed for a skilled mimicry and subsequent close approach on a hunt.

In the earliest years of the missions, Junípero Serra became aware of the Indians' ability to procure game meat. In a 1774 letter he related, "The gentiles [unconverted Indians] in all directions are drawing nearer. Yesterday, some from the mountains sent word for us to bring mules to get some meat. They sent us four big pieces of bear meat, and a whole deer. Today, and tomorrow, our people are going to feast off it sumptuously."[22] While the missionaries worked to establish cattle, the Indians were able to supply supplementary gifts to the colonizers. Before the arrival of European cows, horses, pigs, and sheep, the Indians' main experience with large mammals involved the elk, deer, and bear. The Indians believed that they had a special relationship with these mammals, and they incorporated them into their kinship groups, so that certain clans claimed a familial relationship with certain animals. A set of cultural practices, such as elaborate rituals of reciprocity, population control, and territorial rights, existed to deter overexploitation of these valuable resources.[23] These rituals served both the supernatural function of protecting food supplies by keeping their metaphysical source pleased and perhaps the practical function, developed over long periods of trial and error, of preventing degradation of food supplies.[24]

While the Indians did not utilize the same concepts of private property and landownership as Europeans did, they did have a sense of individual or clan usufruct rights that families could transfer to their descendants; for instance, the same family might have exclusive access to the acorn harvest of a specific oak tree for generations.[25] Furthermore, clans and villages could be territorial, and incursions into a group's traditional hunting and gathering grounds often caused conflict between California's diverse and decentralized Indian groups.[26] The Indians also paid careful attention to seasonal cues, assuring a variety of caloric sources throughout the year, and they carefully observed the favored environmental conditions of preferred plants and animals and sought to promote these conditions when possible.[27] New plants and animals soon strained these carefully developed relationships with the land, and new ways of looking at the land would prompt conflict, change, and adaptation.

Environmental Change in Spanish California

The history of California's missions is especially contentious. On one side, advocates of American Indian rights point to brutal Spanish depredations against California's earlier inhabitants. On the other, a proud Catholic tradition portrays the missionaries, who put their lives at risk to bring the word of God to the heathen of the frontier, as heroes or even saints. The central question underlying this contested scholarship is "Why did the Indians come to the missions?" Did the Christian messages of the Franciscan monks draw them into the missions? Did they willingly seek conversion? Or did Spanish soldiers recruit them to the missions though force of arms? Or did the destruction of their traditional lifeways force them into the shelter of the missions?[28] The environmental changes that the Spanish wrought through their introductions of livestock have come to play a central role in this debate. In her influential study of the role of sheep in the dispossession and destruction of Indians in central Mexico's Valle de Mezquital, Elinor Melville stated that "sheep did not simply replace men, however, although that was the final outcome; rather, they displaced them—ate them, as the saying goes."[29] By overrunning native lands, and destroying native resources in the process, this "ungulate irruption" of woolen grazers literally ate the Indians of Valle de Mezquital out of house and home. Historians of California's missions have begun to claim that this process repeated itself as Mexico's conquerors moved to the northern frontier. Did cattle so transform California that they ate the Indians out of the countryside and into the missions?

While Spanish livestock almost certainly added to the disruptions that California's Indians faced in the late eighteenth and early nineteenth centuries, they were not the Indians' chief antagonists or the prime movers of the Indians to the missions. The animals wrought ecological change and exacted a toll on resources, but recent scholars may be exaggerating these costs and underplaying the opportunities that the animals provided. Most importantly, the legal and cultural frameworks of colonialism in which the animals were introduced exacted a higher toll while also channeling the destructive potential of introduced species against the subjects of colonization.

The cattle populations of the missions did increase rapidly after the original arrivals of 1769. While Vancouver and Kamehameha conspired to leave the Hawaiians with a religious kapu to protect the animals, in California their populations expanded under the careful oversight of mission padres desirous of their increase. With a minimum breeding age of one year, the rare birth of twin calves, and predominantly female herds, a cattle herd could, theoretically, almost double its size in the first year. This number is all but unattainable, but biannual doubling is an outside possibility under the most ideal conditions.[30] The Franciscan settlers of California nearly managed to reach these numbers in some years. The fathers of San Antonio de Padua claimed a near doubling of their stock between their first annual report of 1773 and their second in 1774. They started with thirty-eight cattle; twenty-nine were born, and "four were eliminated, that is to say, one bull slaughtered to feed the guards, one cow slaughtered to provide for the troops of J. B. Anza; an ox died and another lost."[31] While Junípero Serra's letters demonstrate that agents of the missions continued to drive cattle to Alta California during the 1770s, as in Anza's drive from New Mexico in 1776, most of the dramatic increase can be attributed to the fecundity of the cattle, the escape from disease and predators provided by the new environment (despite the bears and wolves that could prey on the unfamiliar herds), and the stewardship of the missionaries.[32] Walter Colton, an American who lived in Monterey in the mid-nineteenth century, claimed that the California environment had a distinctive effect on livestock. He noted that "the fecundity of nature here is not confined to the vegetable kingdom . . . a sheep has two lambs a year; and if twins, four; and one litter of pigs follows another so fast that the squeelers and grunters are often confounded."[33]

The natural increase that followed through the second and third decades of the mission presence in Alta California is just as dramatic. Fermín Francisco de Lasuén, the second presidente of the missions following the death of Junípero Serra in 1784, compiled the annual livestock censuses of the missions. His numbers show the dramatic increase in the mission herds within the first few decades of their introduction to Alta California (table 1).

The rapidly expanding herds soon overwhelmed the lands near the missions. The fathers established ranchos affiliated with the missions near each establishment (which numbered eighteen by the end of the eighteenth century), and set the cattle loose in the countryside to graze. Steven Hackel has noted a "rough correlation" between the baptisms of specific Indian villages at San Carlos Borromeo and when livestock arrived in their environs. That is, as cattle moved into new territory, their ecological impacts forced the local Indians into the missions.[34] Furthermore, a severe drought in the mid-1790s (the effects of which on cattle can be seen between 1793 and 1796 in table 1) hastened this process.[35]

There is no question that cattle caused massive disruptions to the ecosystems of the California coast. Cattle travel in larger herds and graze on a wider array of species than native ungulates do, and they tended to move about the countryside less, which could concentrate the damage. However, these changes played out over decades rather than years. The most direct competition between Indians and the cows from New Spain would have been for the seeds and acorns that they gathered, and by the

Table 1. Censuses of Mission Cattle in Alta California, 1785–1802

YEAR	NUMBER OF COWS	PERCENT INCREASE (DECREASE)
1785	6,813	
1786	8,266	21.3
1787	10,269	24.2
1788	11,747	14.4
1790	19,398	65.1*
1791	25,180	29.8
1792	30,081	19.5
1793	31,070	3.3
1794	32,117	3.0
1795	31,167	(−2.9)
1796	32,460	4.1
1797	34,674	6.8
1798	40,012	15.4
1799	45,739	14.3
1800	54,321	18.8
1801	57,973	6.7
1802	67,782	16.9

Information from Lasuén, *Writings*, 2:394–426.
*Note that there was no census for 1789, so this increase is over two
   years; the average increase is 28.4 percent per year.

mid-nineteenth century some Europeans observed that such competition had become a problem at specific sites.[36]

The most revealing evidence of such depredations in the eighteenth century comes from a land dispute between the Mission Santa Clara and the pueblo of San José. The fathers of Santa Clara complained to Junípero Serra that "the animals, both large and small, belonging to the townsfolk have caused unceasing damage to the crops put in by the Indians."[37] The padres complained, as they often did, that the secular settlers impeded their efforts to turn the heathen Indians into gente de razón, this time by foiling the successful efforts to teach the Indians civilized cultivation of crops. Similarly, the pueblo's livestock was "getting mixed up with the livestock belonging to the Indians of the mission," that is to say, the mission livestock.[38] They explained that "the consequences will be, perhaps, that the Indians will have to stop their field work, so as not to labor in vain; and they will have to rely for their food on the herbs and acorns they pick in the woods—just as they used to do before we came. This source of food supply, we might add, is now scarcer than it used to be, owing to the cattle; and many a time the gentiles living in the direction of the pueblo have complained to us about it."[39] While the missionaries of Santa Clara ignored any deleterious effects of their own larger herds, their complaints nevertheless demonstrate that Indians noted the impact of domestic animals of their own food production, both traditional and in the mission.

It is important to remember that the missionaries employed this evidence to guard their property against secular rivals, and it is difficult to assess the eighteenth-century damage from a single, localized complaint. Cattle did eat seeds from grasses like chia that served as a staple in some coastal regions, but generally there is little overlap in bovine and human diets (which is one of the main benefits of the animals: they convert energy stores that are difficult for humans to digest into a more palatable form). Most California Indians traditionally harvested acorns before they fell, a point at which cattle would not have access to most of them.[40] Grazing cattle may have eaten oak saplings and thus encouraged long-term deforestation and an eventual decline in acorn production, but the short-term effect on acorn production would have been more limited.[41] The Indians would also certainly have cause for concern as the cattle chewed favored herbs and medicinal plants, though these were not key caloric elements. However, coastal fishing, which underlay the economies of the numerous Chumash Indians who would have made up most of the converts at Santa Barbara and several other southern missions, would have remained mostly unaffected. Intensive cattle grazing can poison some waters with bacteria and nitrogen from waste, but this is more a phenomenon of the modern factory farm than the extensive ranchos of the missions, and there is no documentary evidence to support cattle-generated pollutants damaging California's fisheries in the late eighteenth or early nineteenth centuries.

Cattle also had indirect impacts on Indian subsistence. They brought other invasive species with them, as ecological relationships that they had formed with other species in the Old World carried over to their new home. Wild oats (*Avena fatua*) came to dominate the California landscape by the mid-nineteenth century, and the source oats almost certainly traveled via hay along with the cattle.[42] The Spanish cattle and horses had co-evolved with oats in Mesopotamia, and these animals helped spread the plants. Cows not only spread seeds, but their close grazing of grasses not evolved for their presence created a disturbance in native ecosystems that allowed invasive or weedy species to move in. Before cattle, many historical ecologists believe that California's grassland pasturages probably consisted mainly of perennial bunchgrasses, especially two species of needlegrass (*Nassella cernua* and *Nassella pulchra*), that could conserve water in their dense root systems.[43] These root systems did not extend as deeply as those of annuals, and they were easily uprooted by grazing domestic animals.[44]

The disturbance of cattle grazing and the animals' ability to spread seeds led to the rapid spread of exotic annual grasses like bluegrass (*Poa annua*), filaree (*Erodium cicutarium*), brome (*Bromus spp.*), and ryegrass (*Lolium spp.*) that had evolved in concert with old-world grazers. Cattle and their associated disturbances also promoted the invasion of weeds (so defined because they were less palatable to livestock) like black mustard (*Brassica negra*), amaranthus, Saint-John's-wort (*Hypericum perfora-tum*), and Russian knapweed (*Centaurea repens*).[45] Analyses of the composition of adobe bricks have shown that many of these invasive grasses and weeds (like ryegrass and wild oats) had established themselves by the mid-1770s, and others, like the pernicious brome and bluegrass, by the end of the eighteenth century.[46] The similarity of California's seasons to Mediterranean Spain's facilitated both intentional and unintentional introductions. One Spanish naturalist observed that "the four seasons of the year are very like those of Spain. Thus it has been seen that all the trees and seeds that have been introduced from the country multiply with the same abundance and quality as in that climate."[47]

The seeds of displaced native plants like chia (*Salvia columbariae*) and purple needlegrass (*Nassella pulchra*) had served as an important food source for California Indians.[48] Furthermore, the disturbance caused by grazing, as well as the loss of biodiversity promoted by the invasive species, also likely promoted erosion, as cattle removed the tangled roots of bunchgrasses that held soil fast.[49] Protection of pasturage for Spanish livestock was also one of the motivations for suppressing Indian burning, which also would have indirectly diminished the yields of traditional subsistence methods.

The effects of introduced cattle on California's large endemic ungulates, the deer and elk that served as key elements of California Indians' diets, were complicated and are difficult to fully assess. Cattle are less discerning in the calories they consume than deer or elk are, and competition for food may have forced out these animals. Research has demonstrated that there is significant overlap in the animals' diets, which suggests they may compete for food when they share a range.[50] Furthermore, large mammals in California moved to higher altitudes in the dry summers, while Spanish livestock exerted their grazing pressure in riparian areas year-round.[51] Midcentury land management researchers considered competition between livestock and game animals to be a serious concern.[52] More recent research suggests that despite the overlap in diets, the animals generally avoid each other for much of the year. Furthermore, cattle-grazing regimes can be a net positive for game animals, as their destruction of some brush plants can expand accessible range and palatable pasturage.[53]

Other new old-world grazers, like horses and sheep, could also displace game. The Spanish herded thousands of sheep at the missions; the population continued to expand into the hundreds of thousands before collapsing with the secularization of the missions in the 1830s. Sheep do graze closer than cattle do, but they require less forage, about one-fifth that of cattle or horses, because they are smaller. The overall population of sheep in California fluctuated, but it never reached as high as double the cattle population, and because sheep were more vulnerable to predation than the Spanish longhorns were, missionaries and rancheros kept their herds smaller, closer, and under constant oversight, whereas cattle were allowed to graze on an open range. Therefore, sheep probably did not have a significant impact on Indians beyond the range of the missions, especially compared with cattle.[54]

The missions and ranchos owned large herds of tame horses, while vast numbers of wild horses roamed the interior by the early nineteenth century. At times, the Californios had to slaughter massive numbers of horses to protect pasturage for cattle. In the 1840s, British explorer George Simpson related that "horses had at one time become so numerous as to encroach on the pasturage of the cattle; and accordingly they were partly thinned by slaughter, and partly driven eastward into the valley of the San Joachin [sic]."[55] Horses also quickly began to spread beyond the Spanish sphere of influence into the interior. A Spanish expedition sighted wild horses in 1806, and many noted the existence of large wild herds in the San Joaquin Valley in the following decades.[56] Again, this population expansion probably did not happen quickly enough to explain the initial eighteenth-century mission baptisms, nor is there evidence that horses impacted the mule deer and tule elk populations. Perhaps the greatest threat to native ungulates were new diseases brought by the introduced livestock; for instance, many old-world domestic animals carried brucellosis, a disease that affects reproduction and could infect species like elk. The impact of these diseases and competition has to be balanced, however, with the impact of epidemic diseases on humans, which would have reduced overall predation on game animals. Observers frequently comment on the easy availability of game alongside horses and cattle through the mid-nineteenth century. In the 1820s, William Beechey said that San Mateo, one of the ranchos for Mission San Francisco, "strongly resembled a nobleman's park: herds of cattle and horses were grazing upon rich pasture, and numerous fallow deer, startled at the approach of strangers, bounded off to seek protection among the hills."[57] This anecdote suggests a significant deer population living alongside livestock. One final factor in these new animals' interactions is the population of other animal predators; although the Spanish actively hunted bears to protect their herds, the grizzly bear may have actually increased away from Spanish settlements, with the new food source that the herds provided.[58] Thus, the impact of introduced animals on endemic animals is unclear. However, even if exotic animal species did impact deer and elk populations, it is still likely that the overall availability of calories from large mammals increased during these decades, owing to the growth of wild horse and cow herds and human depopulation.

During the mission period, evidence indicates that the Indians actually ventured out of the missions to supplement their caloric intake from traditional food sources, rather than the other way around. Some historians have argued, somewhat controversially but with evidence from travelers' accounts, that the lack of significant provisions contributed to the missions' high mortality rates among neophyte, or recently converted, Indians.[59] There is clear evidence that lack of food in the missions was a problem at times. Mission superintendent Francisco Fermín de Lasuén revealed in an 1801 letter that it was standard practice for "hungry" Indians "to go to the mountains for a week" to tap traditional food sources.[60]

As dramatic as the transformations wrought by cattle might have been, the loss of a significant population of the region's keystone species, humans, probably would have been even more transformative. From the first arrival of the missionaries, and probably earlier through trade networks and from early European explorations, the populations of California's Indians faced severe epidemics caused by introduced diseases. The English explorer William Beechey noted that a third to two-thirds of the neophyte population gained every year at the missions through baptism was subsequently lost through deaths. Looking at censuses, he observed that in 1786, 7,701 baptisms compared with 2,388 deaths; in 1813, there were 57,328 baptisms and 37,437 deaths.[61] The mission padres recorded an influenza epidemic in 1801, and measles in 1806 and again in 1827–28.[62] Fray Lasuén reported that he had to allow the neophyte Indians of Santa Clara to scatter away during a "plague" that struck the mission in 1802.[63] The padres also recorded that syphilis, the same disease that Cook had introduced to Hawai'i, was endemic in the mission populations; first transmitted by visiting sailors or Spanish soldiers, it contributed to declining birthrates in California's native population. In 1813, Fray Ramón Olbés of Mission Santa Barbara explained that "the most pernicious [sickness] and the one that has afflicted them for some years is syphilis. All are infected with it for they see no objection to marrying another infected with it. As a result births are few and deaths so many that the number of deaths exceed births by three to one."[64] While the concentration of populations at the missions would have made those institutions particularly deadly, the movement of runaways and furloughs would have also served as vectors to devastate the gentile populations of California in a similar manner.

Alta California avoided one of the most devastating old-world diseases, smallpox, until the 1830s, despite epidemics throughout Mexico, including one that ravaged Baja California in 1781. Though mission fathers' policies of quarantine and even vaccination played some role in protecting the Indians from at least this one virus, the colony's relative isolation probably played an even bigger role.[65] Smallpox did arrive in the 1830s and ravaged Indian communities throughout the region. Malaria probably came with a fur-hunting expedition from Fort Vancouver into the Central Valley in 1833.[66] Livestock may also have become a new vector for diseases as their waste polluted Indian water sources and spread the bacteria and protozoa that cause dysentery and other ailments.[67]

The demographic disaster that befell the Indians of California would have had an effect on the local environment tantamount to that of the exotic species introduced at the same time. The falling population would have had less of an impact on the local environment, allowing certain species like elk to proliferate as their chief predators diminished. Even as fewer Indians consumed the natural resources they had carefully husbanded, societal disruptions also interrupted food production. For instance, fewer able bodies gathered and processed acorns, however abundant or scarce in the era of European livestock. Thus, while the details are impossible to assess, it seems unlikely that introduced animals were the main factor pushing Indians into the missions. Certainly, they would have effected significant changes in the landscape, but the results would have been too slow and too mixed to lead to the immediate destruction of all traditional caloric sources. However, that still leaves the central question of Indian missionization unanswered.

Pre-European rivalries and resultant warfare are perhaps the least examined factor in the Indians' movement to the missions. Descriptions of conflicts between Indian groups within California suggest that security may have pushed Indians to the missions more than disruptions of traditional subsistence patterns did. The French explorer La Pérouse suggested this explanation in 1786, and he noted that "independent Indians [on rancherías] are very frequently at war, but fear of the Spanish makes them respect the missions, and this may well be one of the reasons for the increase in Christian villages"[68] Could the missions have served as a sanctuary from warfare?

While some California Indians scholars have characterized their subjects as generally peaceful, contemporary accounts suggest warfare as a consistent factor in California Indian life.[69] The influential early twentieth-century ethnographer Alfred Kroeber recorded stories of warfare from Indians throughout California. Kroeber was always quick to describe these conflicts as "only feuds that involved large numbers of kinsmen," revealing preconceptions about the simplicity of hunter-gatherer societies.[70] While modern anthropologists see more complex motives behind warfare, the presence of conflict in Kroeber's accounts cannot be ignored.

Archaeologist Steven LeBlanc has cited evidence of millennia of conflict in California. In his arguments about the role of ecological competition in violence, LeBlanc claimed that California Indian exploitation of acorns and marine resources was intense enough to create population densities on par with agricultural societies, which likely also led in some areas to numerous conflicts over land and resources in the region.[71] In 1792, Spanish naturalist José Longinos Martinéz observed near Santa Barbara that "their wars are frequent and always originate over rights to seed-gathering grounds."[72] Archaeological evidence of such conflicts includes evidence of injuries from clubs, arrows, and spears, as high as 22 percent of the remains in one site.[73] La Pérouse thought warfare so dominant that it constrained Indian movement, stating of one ranchería "as their people are at war with their neighbors, they can never travel further than twenty or thirty leagues."[74]

In 1814, Fray Juan Martín and Fray Juan Cabot, missionaries at San Miguel, explained that "the sum total of the prowess of these miserable people consisted in taking their bows and arrows and taking each others' lives. They realize and acknowledge the fact that they would have exterminated themselves if the missionary had not come and induced them to live in peace."[75] We don't have to agree with the fathers' harsh judgments of the Indians' "miserable lives," but we cannot completely disregard their testimony of serious conflicts that raged between different groups in California. The fathers of San Carlos stated that the Ohlone and Esselen Indians that came to their mission were at first so contentious that they could not assemble together for church services.[76] During William Beechey's visit in 1826, he witnessed a battle between mission Indians and a nearby ranchería. He noted that "the tribes are frequently at war with each other, often in consequence of trespasses upon their territory & property; and weak tribes are sometimes wholly annihilated or obliged to associate themselves with those of their conquerors."[77] He went on to explain that such conflicts often led to raids in which mission Indians captured gentiles as labor for the missions, and that "these misunderstandings & captivities keep up a perpetual enmity amongst the tribes, whose thirst for vengeance is almost insatiable."[78] This last statement raises the possibility that the Spanish colonial presence intensified these conflicts.[79]

Examples from the Central Coast, long dominated by the Chumash cultural group and missionized fairly early with Mission Santa Barbara, demonstrate this point. Anthropologist John Johnson has argued that an alliance of rancherías in the Santa Ynez Valley raided the coastal Chumash from the 1770s into the 1800s. Ambushes and scalpings between Indians from Goleta and Dos Pueblos even led to the abandonment of a village site that the Spanish dubbed La Quemada ("the burned site," present-day Arroyo Quemado).[80] In 1787, Lasuén recorded a battle between the ranchería of Kalawashaq' and a group of recent neophytes led by a high-status Indian named "José María," who had to take shelter in the nearby village of Teqepsh.[81] These examples demonstrate that Indians from within and around the missions became involved in intergroup rivalries. Indians even managed to involve Spanish troops in a series of Chumash counterraids in the area of Mission Santa Barbara in 1790, and this conflict led to the deaths of two Spanish soldiers. Johnson also noted a gender imbalance in the Chumash mission population in 1782; the higher proportion of women in the mission could be explained by mortality from warfare.[82]

There are reports that some groups, like the Juaneños and the Mojave, took women and children as captives after a successful battle.[83] It is possible that, as in other regions of North America, disease may also have increased captive raiding as groups attempted to replace lost population. By the Mexican period, the Shastas were raiding for slaves in the borderlands between Alta California and the Oregon Territory.[84] On a fur-trapping expedition for the Hudson's Bay Company, John Work noted a raided village, relating that "all had the appearance of devastation, the most of the huts were burnt, large caches of provisions principally acorns, remained but much broken down. We found the places where four individuals were burnt . . . their schulls [*sic*] remained, the hard parts of which were broken so that there is little doubt they died by violence. . . . The

Indians who came to camp yesterday reported their visit and by signs made it understood that a few nights ago a party of savages from across the mountains probably the chastys [Shastas] had fallen upon the camp above alluded to while people were all asleep, killed two of them and carried off several into slavery."[85] Though relatively far from the corridor of coastal missions, these raids may have echoed similar attacks that occurred during the depopulation that followed initial Spanish settlement.

In 1829, a rebellious Yokut neophyte from Mission San José named Estanislao led a two-year rebellion in the interior that repeatedly repulsed Californio expeditions against them. The ranchero Antonio María Osio recalled that the members of the third and most successful expedition sent against Estanislao "were joined by some inhabitants of the pueblo of San José and some allied Indians who were long-standing enemies of Estanislao's ranchería."[86] This alliance further suggests the importance of rivalries between California's Indian communities to the Spanish and Mexican colonial mission there.

Economist Marie Duggan has analyzed mission records and accounts to argue that political alliances formed by these conflicts aided mission recruitment. She discovered that much of the mission budgets went to the purchase of gifts, which the fathers used for negotiations within California's gift economies to build local alliances. Venetian glass beads, followed by cloth, were the most important gifts, and the peak of such purchases correlates with the high baptism rates of the 1790s observed by Hackel.[87] She notes that the Tamien at Santa Clara, the Kumeyaay (Ipai-Tipai) at San Diego, and a Chumash band at Santa Barbara used negotiated alliances to maintain their traditional territory and a modicum of independence within the mission system.[88] Anthropologist Lynn Gamble has proposed that the Chumash fought primarily to manage and expand networks of exchange; Spanish trade goods would likely have heightened the stakes of such battles.[89] Anthropologists have also argued that the missions contributed to the dissolution of political alliances within cultural groups like the Chumash and destabilized traditional systems for conflict resolution like reciprocal gift exchanges.[90] As historian Lisbeth Haas has noted, "Indigenous political life rested on this production of wealth through acknowledged possessions of land, oak groves, hunting sites, and other resource areas."[91] While the overall damage to traditional productivity may have been more limited than it is sometimes portrayed, even a highly localized impact could heighten competition for resources and destabilize existing power structures, and thus increase conflict. In other contexts, such as colonial Peru, Indians used missions as a refuge from both warfare and economic exploitation within the colonial system.[92] Virgin soil epidemics, and perhaps some local ecological change from introduced old-world species, probably accelerated these rivalries by disrupting villages, opening new territory for exploitation, and prompting kidnapping raids to replace lost members of society.[93]

Thus, disease and ecological change destabilized native communities and the interrelationships between different groups while the arrival of missionaries and settlers further complicated the situation. The padres exploited the resulting chaos to draw Indians into the missions and thus to Christianity. While destructive introduced animal and plant species may have played a role in this narrative, plagues and wars probably served as stronger, more immediate motivators. At the same time, introduced species presented new opportunities for California Indians following the seismic shifts that accompanied Spanish colonization.[94]

Hawaiians and the Environment

Unlike most native Californians, the Hawaiians before contact with Europeans practiced agriculture. Polynesians first settled the islands between A.D. 300 and A.D. 600 after a 2,500-mile journey in canoes from the Marquesas.[95] They brought their own Polynesian portmanteau biota, which included taro, sweet potatoes, bananas, breadfruit, coconuts, chickens, dogs, and pigs, and they effected their own dramatic changes on the Hawaiian landscape.[96] Their staple crop was taro (or kalo in Hawaiian), a root vegetable that could be grown and harvested year-round in Hawai'i's tropical climate. They harvested this vegetable and mashed it into a paste called poi that served as the foundation of the Hawaiian diet.

Hawaiians farmed in a feudal-like system in which chiefs, or ali'i, controlled tracts of land that radiated from the islands' mountains to the beach in slices and followed watersheds. Each of these ahupua'a thus contained a variety of the resources that Hawaiians would need for the taro plantations, including water for irrigation. The common farmers, or maka'āinana (which means "eyes of the land"), grew the taro for their own subsistence, but paid a portion of their crop in tribute to the konohiki, resource managers and tax collectors, who in turn supported the ali'i. Highest of all were ali'i nui, chiefs who often controlled entire islands or even multiple islands.[97] Birth and inheritance determined the individual's status within this system.

Taro is a labor-intensive crop that requires wet conditions. Planters had to clear fields and dig irrigation ditches to water the plant.[98] Around

A.D. 1100, the Hawaiian population began to expand rapidly, and the Hawaiians constructed large stone irrigation projects to increase agricultural production.[99] On the geologically younger islands of Maui and the Big Island, dryland, or kula, agriculture was even more important than irrigated wetlands, and these agricultural areas required even more labor in weeding and harvesting. Important kula crops included breadfruit and sweet potato and a dryland variety of taro. Dryland agriculture overlapped more with potential rangeland and was thus a key area of conflict with cattle. Kula lands also became vulnerable to cattle because ali'i and konohiki often allowed the commoners to use them as common lands on the ahupua'a. Maka'āinana could grow supplementary foodstuffs there without paying tribute, but, increasingly after Vancouver's introduction, cattle owners used them as open range.[100]

Hawaiians grew a wide range of crops in different regions and thus showed a detailed awareness, developed over centuries, of the variations in climate and soil conditions and the suitability for agricultural production of each.[101] Hawaiians slashed and burned vegetation to clear and enrich fields; they also fertilized the soil with seaweed or manure, and periodically fallowed the fields.[102] Hawaiians enclosed shallow coral reefs near the shore to create saltwater fishponds. At low tide they could collect fish trapped in the pond. They used the fishponds to practice aquaculture by keeping and breeding select species of fish.[103] The same canoes that allowed the Polynesians to carry their culture over great oceanic distances allowed them to harvest significant resources from oceanic fisheries.

Hawaiians, unlike the California Indians, had brought their own livestock across the Indian and Pacific Oceans. As mentioned in chapter 1, the Hawaiians raised a Polynesian breed of pig. This crucial element of the Polynesian portmanteau biota gave the inhabitants of Hawai'i a different context than California's Indians for their confrontation with the Europeans' cattle when Vancouver introduced them in 1793. Pigs were far more than a food source to the Hawaiians. Just as California's Indians considered game animals as sacred and ritualized interactions with them, Hawaiian culture ritualized and sacralized the raising and consumption of pigs. In Hawaiian cosmology pigs were a manifestation of the trickster and shape-shifter god Kamapua'a, who was in turn a manifestation of the important fertility god Lono.[104] In Hawai'i, as in California, kinship networks identified with certain animals, and some clans aligned with pigs.[105] The Hawaiians raised pigs more like household pets than livestock. Consequently, though pigs are famously invasive, Hawaiians generally confined the animals to the household, although some evidence exists of pre-European wild pig populations.[106] Pigs' high value in Hawaiian society and the danger that they posed to taro crops also probably motivated the Hawaiians to watch their animals carefully. One English explorer explained that "hogs are kept in pens, and fed on taro leaves, sugar canes, and garbage."[107] The omnivorous pigs often consumed the same food as their human owners.

Because of their value and their connection to the divine, pigs played an important role in Hawaiian sacrifices to the gods. By killing and consuming part of a pig, and leaving other portions for a deity to consume, the Hawaiians could gain some of the gods' power, or mana, which they could parlay into influence, draw on for sorcery, or use to mark special occasions. The sacrifice of pigs acted as a token in the relationship between the human and the divine.[108] Scholars have interpreted the elaborate rituals that regulated human relationships with pigs as functional adaptations to previous environmental crises, as with the Native American relationship with game animals. Rituals for the raising and slaughter of pigs in New Guinea protected the local environment by keeping the animals contained and tame. By controlling the ownership and consumption of pigs, these rituals discouraged conflict in New Guinean societies.[109]

As in all Polynesian cultures, the Hawaiians held strong ideas about purity and divinity, and certain spaces, people, or items could be marked as sacred, or kapu (taboo).[110] Different classes of people could corrupt something kapu by touching it, and the penalty for breaking a kapu was usually death. The king was kapu to a commoner, as were temples. The Hawaiians saw women as spiritually impure, and as a result, divine foodstuffs, like pig, but also sharks, sea mammals, and certain breeds of dog, were kapu, and women faced severe penalties, including death, for eating them.[111] Women did apparently consume the non-kapu breeds of Polynesian dog.[112] By the same token, because taro was always sacred (hiwa kalo, or black taro, for instance, represented another manifestation of Kamapua'a, the pig god, and thus shared the animal's sacred character), women could not work in the production of poi at any level, though they could consume it. Men cleared and irrigated the fields, sowed the taro cuttings, harvested the roots, baked the taro, and made the poi paste. The Hawaiian men prepared the women's portion of poi separately first, so that it would not pollute their own portions.[113] Women were more active in food production (both farming and cooking) in dryland areas on Maui and the Big Island, perhaps because of the additional labor required in those agricultural regimes.[114]

Though these strong prohibitions against women's activities in the realm of food production and consumption suggest that native Hawaiian culture treated women as inferiors, anthropologists like Jocelyn Linnekin argue that the situation is more complex. Spiritual segregation did not necessarily translate into secular denigration. Women in precontact Hawai'i, in fact, had a great deal of temporal power and often took key political positions.[115] Rank also played a role, as chiefly women were much less likely to face punishment, or faced lesser punishment, for breaking kapu compared with common women.[116] Hawaiian genealogical traditions, key to tracking a family's rank and power, often followed the female line of descent, and women could inherit property, which they did more and more often as colonial disruptions of Hawaiian life made men more mobile.[117]

Environmental Change in Hawai'i

The lack of a Western presence on the islands until the establishment of the Protestant mission in 1820 creates a paucity of sources that makes it difficult to track the establishment of the cattle in Hawai'i and their immediate effects on the native population. Without the head counts of animals as in some of the Spanish missions, the writings of Western visitors alone offer sporadic insights into the state of the archipelago's newest animal inhabitants over the course of the next few decades. For instance, accounts of a growing cattle population on the islands and indications of large herds by the 1830s show that Hawaiians did abide by the kapu, and the cattle population, freed from hunters by edict, did expand rapidly. Amasa Delano, a merchant who plied the China trade out of Massachusetts, visited the islands several times at the beginning of the nineteenth century. While at the islands in 1806, he noted that the locals explained that "they had not killed any of the black cattle that Capt. Vancouver brought there; and that they had multiplied very much."[118] Although distance made further importations more difficult, the islands' isolation may have prevented the spread of disease among the Hawaiian cattle population. Furthermore, and unlike California, no predators like bears or wolves lived in Hawai'i. The first reliable census of the animals counted 40,700 cattle in 1852, 12,000 of them wild.[119]

While Vancouver's seeds of a new bovine population expanded into herds, contact with Europeans had already set in motion a series of transformations to Hawaiian society every bit as dramatic as those prompted by the Franciscan missions in California. In 1792, Vancouver noted that "the village of Whymea [Waimea on Oahu] is reduced at least two-thirds of its size, since the years 1778 and 1779. In those places where, on my former visits, the houses were most numerous, was now a clear space, occupied by weeds and grass."[120] Vancouver blamed this precipitous decline in the population on warfare. He explained that since Cook's European discovery of the islands, there had been "incessant war, instigated both at home and abroad by ambitious and enterprising chieftans [sic]; which the commerce for European arms and ammunitions cannot fail of encouraging to the most deplorable extent."[121]

In a parallel to the battles waged around California's missions, warfare had raged throughout the islands since Cook's visit, and Vancouver's three voyages to Hawai'i from 1792 to 1795 took place against the backdrop of the climax of a fierce internal contest for control of the islands. Before Cook's arrival, an independent ali'i nui controlled each island. These different chiefs may have come into conflict, and some larger island ali'i received tribute from some smaller islands (for instance, Molokai and Lanai were subordinate to Maui), but none could control the entire chain of islands. The Big Island chief who had been in power at Cook's death, Kalaniopuu, died in 1782, and his son Kiwalao and his nephew Kamehameha fought a war of succession to control the island. The ali'i nui of Maui, Kahekili, meanwhile had gained enough strength to take over Oahu.[122] Warfare had always been a part of Hawaiian life, and distinct traditions and rituals governed its conduct. As in most other regions, including California, contact with Europeans accelerated conflicts and heightened the stakes, as disease destabilized political infrastructure and iron and guns made warfare more deadly. Cook's discovery opened Hawai'i to fur traders from the American northwest, who shipped their wares to the Chinese city of Canton in exchange for Eastern luxuries. Needing supplies and more trade goods for China, like Hawai'i's rich sandalwood forests, these European and American traders of the Pacific Ocean were selling guns to the warring Hawaiian chiefs throughout the 1780s.[123]

In 1790, Hawaiians on the Big Island and Maui harried the American merchantman *Eleanora* under Simon Metcalfe, and at one point captured a dinghy, which they burned to extract the iron nails. When the *Eleanora*'s companion ship, the schooner *Fair American*, under Metcalfe's son Thomas, arrived at the Big Island some months later, an ali'i under Kamehameha ambushed the ship and threw its six crew members into the sea.[124] Only a Welsh sailor named Isaac Davis survived. Kamehameha managed to keep the seizure of the *Fair American* from the elder Metcalfe, and he held one of Metcalfe's crew, an Englishman named John Young, when it seemed that he might be able to convey the information to the *Eleanora*. Kamehameha now had an American schooner with its own guns and two British advisers. He put these resources to good use against Maui's Kahekili, who had allied with the ali'i of Kaua'i, Kaeokulani.[125]

When Kahekili died in 1794, his heir Kalanikupule, who controlled Oahu, began to fight with his father's ally Kaeokulani, who now controlled Maui and Kaua'i. Kalanikupule allied with an English trader, William Brown. Brown and Kalanikupule routed Kaeokulani in a battle on Oahu in late 1794. On January 1, 1795, Kalanikupule killed Brown and attempted to take his two ships, the *Prince Lee Boo* and the *Jackall*, for himself. The crews escaped and sailed on for Canton, leaving Kalanikupule vulnerable. Meanwhile, Kamehameha had consolidated power on Hawai'i. Kamehameha, with the aid of John Young and Isaac Davis on the *Fair American*, quickly swept through Maui and Molokai, and finally took Oahu in 1795 by defeating Kalanikupule at the battle of Nu'uanu Valley. He now controlled all the islands except for Kaua'i. Kaua'i alone remained independent during Kamehameha's reign, and a typhus epidemic foiled his last attempt to take the island in 1804.[126]

Despite this series of bloody conflicts, disease caused most of the depopulation that Vancouver observed. As we have already seen, an epidemic of virulent venereal disease had broken out across the islands in the single year between Cook's two stops there.[127] As in California, and as the conflicts for succession narrated above help illustrate, disease destabilized political structures and helped breed chaos and warfare. It is also worth noting that Hawaiian land tenure shifted dramatically during this time period as a result of the twin ravages of conquest and disease. Kamehameha often promoted loyal followers to landlord, or konohiki, status, and he granted ahupua'a to loyal ali'i, especially on the conquered island of Oahu.[128] Some Hawaiian sources suggest that these new chiefs made more dramatic demands for tribute, making the tributary system even more onerous than it had been, and making commoners more vulnerable to ecological shifts.[129] As in California, microscopic invaders and political conflicts helped create social and cultural disturbances that paved the way for the invasion by larger exotic species like Vancouver's cattle.

In seeding the Hawaiian Islands with domestic animals, Vancouver had made no provisions for the containment or control of the cattle population, and they became feral as they reproduced and spread out across the islands. Unfortunately, islands like those of the Hawaiian archipelago are especially sensitive to the negative effects of a biological invasion. As mentioned above, the spatial isolation of islands leads to the process of adaptive radiation as organisms that colonize islands quickly evolve into a variety of specialist species. Thus, islands tend to have a high degree of biodiversity but are highly vulnerable to invaders.[130] Hawai'i also provided an escape for the organisms, since the islands had no predators to control the cattle population. Native plant species had not adapted to the pressures of domestic cattle grazing and trampling. Ecologist Christopher Lever notes that on the Hawaiian Islands "feral cattle have had a serious negative impact on the vegetation of dry, mesic, and wet forests at both high and low altitudes. Indeed, it has been claimed that they have been the single most destructive animal in the islands."[131] Lever goes on to note that cattle have been instrumental in the transformation of many Hawaiian forests into open pasture, as well as having an adverse effect on native Koa trees and rare plant species *Vicia menziesii* and *Cyanea superba*. Lever concludes, "The impact of overgrazing pressure on plant gene pools, nutrient cycling and plant evolution through natural selection is undoubtedly significant."[132] Naturalist Albert Koebele reported that "some four or five species of trees are destroyed by the cattle that eat off the bark, like 'wiliwili,' the 'papalo,' and other soft-wooded species."[133] Clive Roots, a zoologist, explained that "the Hawaiian forests are particularly susceptible to damage by heavy artiodactyls—even-toed species—whose trampling and overgrazing of the undergrowth dries out the soil and denies the shallow-rooted trees sufficient water."[134]

The environmental impacts of the introduction affected more than plant life. Soon, cattle became a nuisance to native Hawaiians. As the feral cattle population expanded, the animals threatened and destroyed native crops like taro.[135] On Maui in 1806, Amasa Delano noted that a newly arrived bull "made very great destruction amongst their cane patches, and tearing them to pieces with his horns and digging them up with his feet."[136] The bull's behavior on Maui typified cattle behavior throughout the islands. The completely unsupervised lives of the feral cattle of the islands also seemed to prompt behavioral changes. Often aggressive Spanish longhorns used their horns as weapons wherever they went, but the animals proved especially deadly in Hawai'i. This served to further the cattle's ecological "escape" as they became harder for native populations to control. As one British visitor noted in 1813, the cattle were "so wild the natives scarcely ever catch them."[137] In the 1860s, a Hawaiian named Levi Ha'alelea testified that during his youth in the 1820s and 1830s "the cattle were very wild and would run after a man."[138] As a result, many Hawaiians, unable to kill harassing cattle because of the kapu, built stone fences and walls to protect their crops.[139] However, in 1822, Archibald Campbell noted that "the fences" were "not . . . sufficient enough to contain them."[140]

The largest populations of cattle inhabited the Waimea Plains on the island of Hawai'i ("the Big Island"). In the shadow of the 13,000-foot Mauna Kea volcano, the plains offered one of the largest relatively flat areas on the islands on which the cattle could graze. The plains also served as the home to a major American mission after 1830. The Reverend Lorenzo Lyons resided at the mission from 1832 until his death in 1886, and he observed the changes wrought by the cattle on the plains and their effect on natives. He stated that "people are compelled to leave their cultivated spots and seek distant corners of the woods beyond the reach of the roaming cattle . . . but the cattle follow, and soon destroy the fruit of their labor. There is a despairing spirit among my people, and great suffering among them."[141] Cattle interrupted traditional agricultural relationships with the land and pushed people out of their established croplands, which would have already been severely disrupted by the rampant disease and resulting rapid demographic change resulting from contact with Europeans. The agricultural Hawaiians were probably more vulnerable to cattle than California Indians, who hunted and gathered from a wider variety of sources, were.

The animals also contributed to deforestation and other associated problems. The cattle's hooves damaged roots, and the browsing animals ate new shoots and prevented the regrowth of forests decimated by trade and agriculture. An anonymous article (probably written by the missionary Lorenzo Lyons) in the February 1856 issue of the *Sandwich Island Monthly Magazine* described the dramatic changes wrought by cattle on the Big Island. The article noted that "it is the memory of many foreigners now living here, when the whole of these plains were covered in a thick wood . . . where hardly a tree stands for miles."[142] The article painted a vivid portrait of just how this deforestation occurred. "Thousands of old dead trees both standing upright and lying prostrate, from the present boundary of these woods, exhibit a mode in which the destruction is effected; for whilst the old trees die of age, no young ones are seen taking their places, as during the last thirty or forty years, the cattle have eaten or trodden them down."[143] Ha'alelea gave a similar report, and he related that "in former times when I was a boy . . . Waimea was a thickly wooded region all about there . . . but of late years round about where I lived, it is as cleared of trees as the Esplanade is."[144] He explained that white settlers had felled the trees for fuel and fences for cattle pens, and that "a good many of the young trees were destroyed by the cattle."[145]

Lorenzo Lyons also noted that "Waimea of an evening is a perfect cloud of dust. The soil is remarkably dry, and so extremely fine that water does not seem to wet it."[146] Deforestation and trampling led to erosion in this relatively arid, leeward part of the island, and topsoil loss would have further impacted native lifeways. According to Waimea's residents, cattle even affected the weather. The aforementioned *Sandwich Island Monthly Magazine* article traced the changes in a wind pattern known to the natives as mumuku, and explained that "it was formerly so strong that natives always lashed canoes to the rocks, stakes, or trees."[147] Even the patterns of winds that natives had grown used to seemed to shift under the environmental strain of grazing at Waimea. The article discussed how the climate differed from before the arrival of cattle, and claimed that "at that time there was far more rain at Waimea than there is now, which indeed might be readily inferred, as clearing the land of trees invariably lessens the quantity of rain. This clearing of the land has been almost entirely effected by cattle."[148] This is an interesting inversion of the concept of "rain following the plow," but it fits in with popular nineteenth-century Euro-American beliefs that proper use of the land would have beneficial climactic effects and vice versa. Deforestation may have actually led to local climactic change or these changes may have been imagined or coincidental, but either way, the account suggests the extent to which cattle transformed Waimea.

During his expedition's visit, American explorer Charles Wilkes, who complained of the invasive ranunculus in the famed pastures of Waimea in this chapter's introduction, faced other environmental problems caused by the five decade presence of cattle in Hawai'i. His first meeting with the king (Kamehameha III) revolved around one such issue. Wilkes noted that the king "spoke of the decrease of the depth of the water in the harbour, imagining the quarrying of the coral had been in part the cause of it, and asked me to direct my attention to it."[149] Honolulu harbor was crucial to the economic well-being of the maritime-trade-dependent islands, and the king showed foresight in his concern. Wilkes's staff of scientists investigated, and Wilkes reported that it was not coral mining but silt deposits that caused the problem. He explained that "within these last fifteen years much alteration has taken place, by the deposit of mud, which will in time close it entirely up, if not removed or prevented. The stream coming down the Nuuanu valley, though small, makes a considerable deposit."[150] Though neither the king nor Wilkes seemed to realize it, increased erosion would have caused this acceleration in deposits. This erosion, in turn, was likely the result of deforestation caused by the sandalwood trade and cattle grazing on the site of Kamehameha's great and final victory.

Other invasive species often accompanied cattle, including weed species that spread through grazing. In his memoir of life in Hawai'i, Charles de Varigny noted "numerous signs of deterioration and ruin" in 1855, as he explained that "noxious weeds, above all the wild indigo, have invaded the most fertile plains and each year have taken over land where in earlier times hundreds of thousands of beef cattle could wander for forage."[151] It was not coincidence that the weeds that caused this "ruin" followed the cattle, which spread seeds with their digestion and movement, and opened niches for new species with the disturbance of heavy grazing.

Conclusion

Despite European dismissals of the natives of California and Hawai'i who did not possess the civilization of Old World pastoralism (or an inferior version of it, in the case of the pig-raising Hawaiians), both groups had complex relationships with their local environments and dramatic impacts on the landscapes that they inhabited. Both regions were geographically isolated and had high degrees of biodiversity and numerous unique species. Indigenous people in both California and Hawai'i had developed long-standing practices to manage and harvest the resources of these environments. They had developed methods of earning their subsistence and husbanding resources over centuries, and even millennia, of trial and error. The European introduction of their own food items in the forms of old-world domesticated animals disrupted these relationships and forced California Indians and Hawaiians to adapt to a new agricultural order and a new environment.

Rapid changes followed eighteenth-century encounters with Europeans in the Pacific. Native Hawaiians and California Indians dealt with new disease environments, and warfare seems to have increased in both areas. They also encountered new goods and new social and economic relationships with agents of European imperialism. Among these goods were the old-world animals that spread from European introductions, with large cattle having an especially large effect on local landscapes and native subsistence. California Indians and native Hawaiians would have to adapt to the new pastoral order in their landscapes, but they would have to do so under colonial regimes in the eastern Pacific borderlands. The next chapter begins to examine the changing labor regimes of the new pastoral landscapes of the eastern Pacific.

CHAPTER THREE

Reactions

When Portolá's party returned to San Diego from its long and fruitless search for Monterey Bay in January 1770, they found the new settlement under siege by the local Ipai Indians.[1] Miguel Costanso explained that "on the 15th of August, the Indians of the nearest village attacked the camp."[2] The garrison at San Diego, despite serious illness, had fought the Indians off and shot three; however, the Indians had remained close, and Costanso noted that "since that time . . . they [caused] occasional harm, killing a horse or mule now and then and shooting arrows into others, though by night and unseen."[3] Tense, and often violent, relations between the Spanish and the Indians plagued the colony's beginnings, and the Indians quickly realized the importance of the interlopers' domestic animals to their presence. The animals also sometimes attacked the Indians. On May 21, 1806, a neophyte man in his fifties who had taken the Spanish name of Melquiades died "violently, by the fierceness of a bull" at or near the Mission San Luis Obispo.[4] Melquiades had changed his name from Suxuocoyo at his baptism in November 1794, when he had come to the mission from the ranchería of Cheptu, probably a northern Chumash village (though possibly Salinan).[5] The mission father did not record further details, and we do not know if Melquiades was a vaquero, was otherwise employed in caring for cattle, or happened to be in the wrong pasture at the wrong time. However, this is just one of many similar incidents of neophytes killed by bulls recorded by the mission fathers in the early nineteenth century.[6] On June 11, 1828, a neophyte named Camilo died in the corral, "trampled by a bull." The place of death suggests that he was laboring for the colonizers to harvest their animal products for them.[7]

In the same year that Melquiades was killed by a bull, 1806, New England sea captain Amasa Delano stopped at the Hawaiian island of

Maui on his way from South America to China. He noted that the native Hawaiians "had very recently brought to this island one of the bulls that Capt. Vancouver landed at Owhyee [Hawai'i]." He went on to relate that "he would run after and frighten the natives, and appeared to have a disposition to do all the mischief he could, so much so that he was a pretty unwelcome guest among them."[8] In 1805, Russian explorer Urey Lisianski visited Hawai'i and learned that "some time ago a herd came down from the mountains, and committed great ravages in the plantations in the valleys." Spanish longhorns were large aggressive animals with sizable horns that they used to gore any perceived threats. When these dangerous longhorns attacked the Hawaiians' crops, "a body of armed men was sent to drive them away; and in effecting it, four lives were lost."[9] Native Hawaiians, like California Indians, sometimes found themselves at war with European domestic animals in the late eighteenth and early nineteenth centuries. These violent conflicts were just one manifestation of the destabilization brought by contact with Europeans as California and Hawai'i transformed from native lands to borderlands contested by distant imperial powers.

Fatal meetings with animals, very rare compared with the deaths that resulted from other European introductions like guns and diseases, show the negative impact that livestock had on native societies. However, most of their confrontations with cattle were less violent and far more complex. Colonial context played a significant role in shaping these complex interactions; for instance, the pull of trade with the English motivated native Hawaiians to capture cows for sale to passing ships, while the Spanish missions dictated oversight of the labor of California Indians as they managed herds. However, neither California Indians nor native Hawaiians were passive victims of bovine depredations under colonial domination. They actively responded to these four-legged intruders with cultural and economic adaptations that represent attempts to assert some modicum of control over these new arrivals and a level of self-determination in the shifting political landscapes of the new eastern Pacific borderlands that Cook, Vancouver, Serra, and Portolá had helped create.

California Indian Reactions to European Animals

In Alta California, the Spanish settlers forced California Indians to deal with cattle within the structure of the missions. However, Indians often found their own uses for and interpretations of the animals. The first obstacle that California's Indians had to overcome in adjusting to the arrival of European livestock was understanding or conceptualizing the animals. Europeans arrived in the Americas with a variety of unfamiliar technologies and customs, but their domestic animals stood out as the strangest new concepts to which native peoples in the Americas had to adjust.[10] Initially, horses and mules most fascinated Indians; no familiar game animal could or would carry a human being.

In his diary of the initial expedition to found the mission at San Diego in 1769, Fray Juan Crespí noted an astonished reaction upon California Indians' first sighting of domestic animals. He noted that "the mules caused the natives much fear and astonishment, and even when they were in the midst of our people, in perfect confidence, if they saw the mules come near they all trembled, and calling out 'mula, mula,' a term which they quickly learned, they tried to get away."[11] The mules apparently fascinated (and frightened) the Indians more than the Spanish missionaries and soldiers did. The Indians also quickly adopted the Spanish terminology for the animals. In a 1774 memorandum, Junípero Serra told of an exchange he had with some local Indians. Serra asked one of them if he had imagined that there were such people as the Spanish in the world. According to Serra, "He answered no, that they thought all countries were like their own. As regards the soldiers and the Fathers, after carefully looking them over, they had come to the conclusion that they were the sons of the mules on which they rode."[12]

Hugo Reid, a Scotch rancher in Southern California, later recorded similar myths connecting the Spanish to their domestic animals. In his mid-nineteenth-century survey of Indians living around Los Angeles, Reid noted that at the missions "the number of hogs was great and [they] were principally used for making soap."[13] However, he also learned that "the Indians, with some few exceptions, refused to eat hogs, alleging the whole family to be transformed Spaniards!"[14] This belief, though apparently not as common as Reid reported, still suggests efforts to create a series of indigenous cultural values around the new arrivals to California. This particular dietary restriction served the dual purpose of potentially protecting the Indians' health and satirizing their imperial conquerors.

The first full-scale rebellion by California's Indians against the Spanish missionaries occurred in November 1775. A group of Tipai Indians, responding to a rash of conversions and the depredations of some of the Spanish soldiers from the nearby presidio, set fire to the San Diego mission and killed Father Luís Jayme and two other Spanish settlers.[15] A long series of skirmishes preceded this explosion of tensions, including the sporadic attacks against animals that Portolá's party witnessed in 1770 after they returned from their expedition to Monterey. These attacks on animals fit the pattern of Indian warfare to protect resource rights.

In 1780, Serra wrote from San Carlos that "last year's alcalde . . . is in revolt in the mountains with a considerable number of followers, among whom are those we most need, such as the blacksmith, a number of carpenters and day workmen."[16] An Indian named Baltazar from an Ohlone tribelet near Point Lobos had gained the trust of the missionaries and had taken the job of alcalde, or overseer, in 1779. In 1780, he had left the mission with some of the best-trained Indians in a challenge against the fathers' authority. Serra explained that "about three days ago, in full light of day, and inside the mission compound, a number of gentiles shot some cattle with arrows."[17] While it is not entirely clear that this incident connected to the revolt, it seems as though the rebelling neophytes may have incited unconverted Indians to attack the Spanish herds. The Indians understood the centrality of the animals to the Spaniards' colonial mission.[18]

In December 1800, the mission fathers at La Purísima reported to Governor Don Diego the most common crimes for which they had to punish neophytes. They first explained that "the punishments, which we apply to the Indians, of both sexes, are whipping, sometimes shackles, very seldom stocks, and also the lock-up."[19] They listed the most common "misdeeds" as "concubinage, theft, and running away," but then explained that "when the transgressions are against the common good, like killing cattle, sheep, or firing pastures, which has occurred sometimes, the corporal of the guard is notified."[20] Not only did neophyte Indians in the missions still attempt to use fire to manage grasslands; they also killed mission animals. The fathers called on the military to punish these most serious crimes of attempting to maintain native subsistence regimes.

In 1781, the Yuma, the agriculturalist tribe in southern Alta California, revolted against the Spanish. Captain Rivera y Moncada was returning with reinforcements of settlers and cattle for which Serra had sent him to Baja California. The Yuma, perhaps enraged by the thousands of horses and cows with Rivera's expedition that grazed their arid lands and threatened their crops, killed almost all the settlers.[21] Eighteenth-century Franciscan historian Francisco Palóu related that when a surviving cavalry officer "went to look for the soldiers who had remained behind with the cattle . . . he found them already dead. And the cattle also."[22] While the animals that the Spanish often drove through their territory between 1769 and 1781 may have been strange and unfamiliar to the Yuma, they understood the possible dangers the animals posed to their way of life, and they acted on that understanding. The revolt became an insurrection, and an especially crippling one at that, as the most direct overland route from Mexico to Alta California's missions ran through Yuma territory. The Spanish remained unable to pacify the Yuma, and the route did not re-open until 1822.

Most of California's Indians, however, did not attack and kill livestock, as the rapid growth of the herds demonstrates. As Indians, dislocated by disease and environmental change or drawn by gifts and alliance, settled in the missions, accepted baptism, and became neophytes, many developed new relationships with the animals that hint at accommodation and adaptation to the rapid changes taking place. Historian Lisbeth Haas has noted "that despite the physical dislocation and death the missions represented, they became sites of indigenous authority, memory, identity, and historical narration."[23] Indian culture was not overwritten by Spanish power but rather accommodated and interpreted, and sometimes resisted, Spanish imposition on Indian culture, and this certainly holds true for the mission Indians' dealings with old-world animals. For instance, the Luiseño word for introduced domestic animals is "as," which is also their name for a shaman's familiar spirit. Haas has argued that this repurposing of the word "drew the horse and cow into the world of the Luiseño sacred," and appropriated the animals' power, which had so augmented the Spanish invaders.[24]

As chapter 1 has shown, the Spanish missionaries believed that the acceptance of a pastoral lifestyle was a crucial step in the transformation of "salvajes" into "gente de razón." The fathers enforced agricultural discipline, as they enforced all forms of discipline in the missions, with the threat of corporal punishment. When the missionaries believed that neophytes had misbehaved, they imprisoned the offending Indians in isolation or publicly in stocks, or they whipped the Indians in public.[25] In 1779, the viceroy of New Spain mandated that missionaries teach mission Indians pastoral skills.[26] These skills included a distinctive cattle culture that had evolved in arid regions of Spain. Environmental conditions and the shortage of labor and availability of land following a demographic collapse had further transformed Spanish American cattle culture in New Spain. In this system, rancheros allowed cattle to wander on the pastures of an unfenced open range. They drove the cattle to new pastures periodically, and vaqueros would gather cattle for branding with a hot iron, gelding bulls, or for slaughter, often using a lasso to help gather and hold members of the all-but-wild herds.[27] This method may have required less labor than a carefully watched and fenced herd, but it depended on more highly skilled labor. While still in Baja California, Father Lasuén complained that since his mission had "only runaway cattle, going to get meat is like going to catch wild beasts; and in order to get the required amount, it was necessary to keep six or seven skilled cowboys perpetually on wages."[28] The most significant skill required for a vaquero's management of cattle herds was riding a horse. To catch and direct the large four-legged animals, humans required their own similar beast.

The mission fathers not only had to teach the specialized methods of the Mexican vaquero to peoples whom they had just encountered and whose language they did not speak. They also had to overcome a culture carefully calibrated to hunting game animals.[29] Many Indian groups did eventually incorporate horses or sheep into their own myths and gave domestic animals spiritual significance, and the Navajo even believed that raising sheep had always been one of their cultural practices.[30] Anthropologist James Downs has argued that most Indian cosmologies view animals and humans as of the same cloth and that the greatest obstacle to overcome in the Indian adoption of domestic animals is the separation of animal and human into different classes.[31] The Indians had to subsume their reciprocal relationship to animals represented by the ritual of the hunt into a willingness to manage, control, and live with a herd.

Throughout Spanish colonization of the Americas, Indians had made these adaptations within Catholic missions. For instance, Indian vaqueros from Baja California missions drove cattle to the first mission and presidio at San Diego for its initial foundation. The first Indian vaqueros from Alta California appear in records of Juan Bautista de Anza's expedition to the San Francisco Bay in 1776. Palóu noted that the expedition included "three unmarried Indian neophytes, two of them from Old California and the other from the mission of Carmelo, who drove the cattle for the mission, numbering eighty-six head, which were incorporated with those of the presidio."[32] One of the early converted Indians from San Carlos de Borromeo, on the Monterey Bay, had already acquired the skills for the drive through relatively unknown territory. He could have come from one of the Esselen or Ohlone rancherías; unfortunately, the Spanish did not record if or which particular tribes took to the saddle more quickly.

Nor do the records indicate how the fathers chose which neophytes to train as vaqueros. The fathers of Santa Cruz in 1814 explained simply that the baptized Indians "are taught those occupations towards which they have an inclination so that they keep busy and avoid idleness to which they are very prone."[33] Eulalia Pérez, who worked as a llavera, or housekeeper, for Mission San Gabriel as a girl in the early nineteenth century, recounted late in her life that "if the Indians showed a liking for a certain job, then that was the job they were taught. Otherwise, they would work in the field or care for the horses and cattle . . . others had jobs as cart drivers or cowherds."[34] Pérez suggested that herding cattle served as one of the menial jobs given to those who did not show an aptitude for an artisanal job, like blacksmithing or carpentering. However, her account also reveals that not all the Indians who worked with animals at the missions were equal. She explained that one of her duties as llavera was to distribute food to the "vaqueros—those who rode with saddles and those who rode bareback."[35] The herds were numerous enough that they apparently required different skill levels. The more highly trained Indians used saddles and thus received the same clothing as the gente de razón. The mission fathers gave them "a shirt, a vest, pants, a hat, boots, shoes, and spurs. And they were given a saddle, a bridle, and a reata for their horse. Each vaquero would also receive a large kerchief made of silk or cotton, and a sash of Chinese silk or red crepe cloth or whatever other material might be in the storehouse."[36] Meanwhile, Pérez noted that "those who rode bareback received nothing more than their shirt, blanket and loincloth."[37] Some fathers from San Juan Bautista recorded that "the clothing of our neophytes comprises a blanket . . . the cowboys and the more outstanding Indians wear trousers, socks, shoes, and hats which are sometimes those manufactured here while at other times they come from Spain."[38] This association between the vaqueros and the "most outstanding Indians" reveals the high esteem in which the fathers held the Indians who mastered herding cows on horseback. Many neophytes learned how to ride horses, which would have proved a dramatic adjustment to new exotic animals in itself. However, some Indians apparently showed more skill and thus received better accoutrements.

It seems reasonable to speculate that missionaries chose neophytes to train as vaqueros in the same manner that they chose neophytes to train as artisans. The expensive supplies, like saddles, that the missionaries lavished on these vaqueros indicate that missionaries prized their labor more than that of many of the other Indians. Saddles were valuable tools that allowed greater comfort and protection for the rider and took some stress off of the horse. Other tack would have allowed the riders more control over the horse and allow them to better hunt stray cattle in difficult terrain. Overall, about 20 percent of Indian laborers at the missions worked as vaqueros.[39] All of them were men; managing longhorns on the open range was considered a masculine job within Spanish culture, and this dovetailed with the Indian gender division of labor in which men hunted animals.

Rodeo, by E. Wyttenbach (from the California History Room, California State Library, Sacramento, California)

The Indians also would have had a great deal of agency in the choice to become vaqueros. It would be difficult for the Spanish to force an Indian to mount a horse for the first time. Furthermore, a successfully trained vaquero, if unhappy in his job, could always ride away. Beyond having some of the best equipment of any of the neophytes, the very nature of the vaquero's job gave him a great deal of power in the form of mobility. The Spanish did recognize this power. In the 1780s, the new viceroy of New Spain, Bernardo de Gálvez, issued a series of "instructions" that included a prohibition on teaching Indians how to ride horses, and Pedro Fages, the governor of California, singled out the Franciscans in California as the worst violators of this point. The policy change made sense for the Spanish Empire in the late eighteenth century; mounted Indians had caused problems for New Spain throughout their northern frontier, from the Chichimecas to the Comanche. An irate Father Lasuén responded that "no one is more concerned and more interested than the missionaries that the Indian should continue in his native ignorance of horsemanship. But Your Lordship is well aware of the cattle and horses which, with the King's pleasure, every one of the missions possesses, and that horsemen are needed to look after them. And these have to be Indians, for there are no others."[40] Despite the long-standing policy of training Indians to manage domestic animals as part of their agricultural training, Lasuén claimed that the missionaries had no interest in doing so but that conditions forced them into this Promethean role. The father also implicated the soldiers in failing to do their part to herd the cattle. Regardless, the missionaries moved forward training Indians to become expert horsemen, even as they acknowledged the dangers inherent in the act. The Indian vaqueros gained significant power and autonomy within the mission system by performing this function. The alcaldes were the only other Indians allowed to ride horses in Alta California.[41]

Vaqueros' mobility and prestige placed them in an intriguing position within the mission system. On the one hand, their work made it necessary to move far and wide throughout the countryside, and this probably allowed them more communication with Indian settlements beyond the missions' spheres of influence. At the same time, their lofty positions within the neophyte hierarchy may have allied some with the culture of the fathers. There is some evidence that some vaqueros took quite readily to Christianity. Many neophyte vaqueros appear as godparents for the baptisms of converting Indians. Some vaqueros actually appear in mission records as officiants for baptisms. For instance, on August 14, 1801, a neophyte vaquero named Bernardo José from Mission San Buenaventura ("el Baquero Bernardo Jose Neofito de esta Mision") baptized a dying Indian in the Chumash village of Mupu. The padres later recorded this Indian's name as Occóu õ Tatopo, and he took the Spanish name of Antonio Abad.[42] He survived whatever ailment led Bernardo José to take spiritual action, received a "sub conditione" baptism from the mission fathers in case the neophyte vaquero's spiritual authority was lacking, and married another neophyte from Mupu in February of 1802 at Mission San Buenaventura.[43] He lived until April 17, 1804; cause of death was not recorded.[44] Mission records give some additional insight into the life of the vaquero who performed this baptism, Bernardo José. His original name had been Calatu, and he had been baptized by Fray Francisco Dumetz on May 29, 1785, after coming to Mission San Buenaventura from the Chumash settlement of Somis.[45] Dumetz put Bernardo José's age at six or seven (this may have been a mistake since he would get married less than five years later).[46] As in the case of Antonio Abad, Dumetz recorded that the Indian boy was baptized because he was dying ("murio"), though he obviously survived for decades.

On May 29, 1829, a vaquero named Magin served as an officiant for the baptism of a child of neophytes "born in the cornfields" (nacido en las milpas) at Mission San José.[47] The baby was named Dioscoro, a name shared with his father and mother, who married as gentiles from the village of Tammukan before taking similar names (Dioscoro and Dioscora) when

Fray Narciso Duran baptized them when they were twenty-five in 1811.[48] We can again assume emergency measures led to this important ceremony being presided over by a layperson as the child passed away a few days later. Perhaps Dioscora was working when she went into labor, and Magin was riding nearby and attempted to practice the Catholic rites he had seen in order to save the ailing newborn's soul. On August 22, 1800, Fray Magin Catalá had baptized the eleven-year-old Indian Geluas "from the estuary" and given the boy his name in the chapel at Mission San José.[49] Twenty-five years later, the Indian vaquero Magin had done the same for a dying infant in the cornfields near the mission.

We cannot assume that Magin and Bernardo José were fervent Catholics because they administered these rites under special circumstances. Their motives may have ranged from comforting the afflicted to currying favor with the mission fathers who controlled so many aspects of their lives. Furthermore, it is impossible to make assumptions about other vaqueros' faith based on these two data points. Nonetheless, the evidence suggests that the long tenure in the missions, and perhaps the prestigious position as vaqueros, led these two men to embrace aspects of the beliefs of their masters.

Pastoralism also spread rapidly beyond the missions. The Luiseño ranchería of Topome, for instance, began to grow wheat and raise cattle and sheep while remaining ostensibly independent from the nearby mission of San Luis Rey, founded in 1798.[50] The people of Topome clearly saw benefits in producing and trading agricultural items favored by the mission even if they did not choose to enter it. The village was closely associated with the mission, and missionaries provided the initial crops and animals and presumably training; Topome, however, retained some level of autonomy. Similar settlements existed near most missions sites, and in them, "individuals even held a few cattle and an occasional horse in their villages as family property."[51] In the interior, especially in the large San Joaquin Valley, which the Spanish usually referred to as the Tulares, horses were becoming an integral part of Indian societies. The Spanish worried that runaways from the missions spread knowledge about livestock among interior Indians. According to a letter from one of the missionaries, many neophytes that left the mission for the Tulares took animals with them.[52] Spanish words like "caballo" (horse), "ganado" (cattle), "silla" (saddle), and "espuela" (spurs) entered into the Miwok language during this time period. "Vaquero" also became a Miwok word, and it also made its way into the Maidu and Mono languages, all of which were spoken by Indians in the interior.[53]

Visitors to California almost always remarked upon Californians' skill on horseback, and we can be certain that some of the Californios they saw were Indians. American Walter Colton claimed that "a Californian is most at home in his saddle."[54] French visitor August Duhaut-Cilly noted that Californians "excel in everything that has to do with riding."[55] However, he also lamented that they "do not make a good show of their height; their habit of being always on horseback gives them an awkward posture. So little accustomed to the use of their legs are they that they walk with the weight of their body shifting from side to side as if they were crippled."[56] Duhaut-Cilly further explained that "the Indians imitate the Californians in their horseback maneuvers and are equally good riders."[57] In 1820, mission Indians painted the fourteen stations of the cross at Mission San Fernando, and scholars have analyzed these works as a window into cultural adaptation and syncretism in the missions. Eight of the fourteen paintings depict horses, suggesting the impact that animal had on the mission Indians. Lisbeth Haas noted that the horses in the paintings always look out at the viewer, giving them "a human quality consistent with native narrative traditions in which animals share all the attributes of humans."[58]

The particular nature of herding in California also required skill with the lariat, or lasso. When German explorer Georg Heinrich Langsdorff visited California in 1806, he explained that "the cattle, horses, and sheep do not require any particular attention . . . When a supply of cattle is wanted, some of the neófitos [neophytes] and soldiers are sent out to the pastures, on horseback, and with riatas, which they throw very dexterously, catch by the horns the number required"[59] Duhaut-Cilly explained that Californians used lassos "to manage their herds of mules, horses, and cattle. With it they throw them down, whether to kill or brand or geld them. Without the aid of this instrument, it would be impossible to control animals that live in liberty on vast lands and are almost as wild as if they had no masters. It is even imprudent for us Europeans, unskillful horsemen, to ride among the enormous herds without being accompanied by some men of the country, who can at a distance recognize the fiercest bulls and who can, when necessary, save us from their fury by lassoing and harassing them."[60]

The Spanish training of neophytes within the missions further introduced European domestic animals into Indian culture through the consumption of beef. In the 1814 *Respuestas* to the questionnaire on Indian life posed to all the missions, most of the fathers report the regular slaughter of cattle to feed their neophyte populations. Mission San Diego slaughtered twenty-four head every fifteen days for food, while the fathers of San Buenaventura claimed that the Indians received "their share of fresh beef in ample abundance. . . . At this mission every week there are slaughtered sixty, fifty, or at least forty-five head of cattle."[61]

The consumption of these varying amounts of beef represented a distinct change in diet and thus in culture. How and when Indians ate beef seems to have varied. While the fathers at San Gabriel claimed that neophytes "have three meals a day comprising corn, wheat, beans, and meat," Fray Felipe Arroyo de la Cuesta of Mission San Juan Bautista complained that "we can say that the Indians eat only one meal because they are eating all the time unless they are filled up or unless work impedes them."[62] He elaborated that "the mission holds a weekly slaughter. On that day they eat until they can take no more from which they suffer a great deal of indigestion. During the rest of the week they do not care to eat jerked beef and eat it only when they are hungry."[63] Rather than eating three square meals, metered out throughout the day like the gente de razón, the Indians at San Juan Bautista treated the weekly slaughter like a successful hunting expedition. They gorged themselves on fresh meat rather than eating the jerked beef at regular intervals. Archaeological evidence from Mission San Antonio de Padua suggests that the Indians adopted Spanish butchering techniques, despite the Indians' experience preparing large game animals.[64] Beyond the missions, there is evidence that Indians did not make the same changes in their animal-preparation practices. Anthropologist Kent Lightfoot has observed that the Kashaya Pomo Indian laborers at the Russian outpost of Fort Ross "treated beef, sheep, and pigs like any other large ungulates—the meat butchered and cooked as if deer or elk."[65]

Nineteenth-century ethnographer Stephen Powers revealed other limits of Indian adoption of foods from European animals. Powers claimed that "it is a singular fact that the Indians generally have no word for 'milk.' They never see it, for they never extract it from any kind of animal, because that would seem to them a kind of sacrilege or robbery of the young."[66] Indians, like most non-Europeans, had not evolved the ability to metabolize lactose properly, which caused health problems within institutions like the Franciscan missions.[67] To the extent that the Indians utilized them mostly for meat, and not for milk, Indians continued to treat cows more like game animals than like livestock.

Other California Indians besides the neophytes also developed a taste for beef. Whether through deserters who had eaten beef at the missions, through an indigenous dietary experiment, or owing to the starvation caused by a less fecund transformed local environment, Indians outside the missions soon moved from merely killing European livestock to killing and eating it. As early as 1773, Serra complained that Mission San Carlos was running out of mules. He blamed the presidial soldiers for overworking the animals, but he noted that "the deserters assist, with those that they carry off, and the heathen, with those which they have eaten."[68] Unconverted Indians helped diminish the population by consuming them. Similarly, the soldiers who escorted the Franciscans to found Mission Santa Clara in 1777 discovered missing mules roasting in a nearby Indian village.[69] Indian bandits from outside the mission system, either gentiles or runaways, began to find their own uses for Spanish livestock, and this would become an increasing problem for Alta California and its Euro-American inhabitants in the first half of the nineteenth century.

Native Hawaiian Reactions to European Animals

How did the Hawaiians initially respond to Vancouver's "gifts" of cattle in 1793? The journal of one of Vancouver's mates, Thomas Manby, provides us with our most detailed account of the native Hawaiians' reaction to the new species upon their introduction by the British explorers. Manby related that the cattle

> were sent on shore in his Canoes to his Village; a Chief of consequence and a party of men were appointed to attend them, and very particular orders were given with the sick Bull to see him nursed. The four cows were in tolerable condition and had got very tame by being on board. The concourse of people to see them landed was immense; we were a good deal diverted at seeing the terror the whole Village was thrown into by one of the cows galloping along the beach and kicking up her heels. Thousands ran for the Sea and plunged in; every Cocoa Nut Tree was full in a moment; some jumped down precipices, others scrambled up rocks and houses, in short not a man would approach for half an hour.[70]

Manby may have exaggerated the wild scrambling for comedic effect, but it is not surprising that the initial reaction to the unfamiliar animals would be trepidation. Manby extended this description to Kamehameha himself, though he also noted the Hawaiian leader's interest in the animals. Manby claimed that "the cattle greatly delighted him, though it took some time to quiet his fears lest they should bite him. He called them large hogs and after much persuasion we prevailed on him to go close up to them."[71] While Manby again plays up Hawaiian fears, his account also demonstrates that the king readily incorporated them into a familiar taxonomy. Kamehame-ha's terminology stuck, as the Hawaiians named cattle pua'a pipi or "beef pigs" and thus integrated them into a familiar conceptual framework by naming them after the animals the Hawaiians themselves had introduced to the islands when they had first arrived.[72]

Archibald Menzies, the naturalist on Vancouver's cruise, recorded a revealing incident concerning the birth of the first calf in Hawai'i. He explained that one of the cows landed in 1793 was in calf. When it gave birth, he stated that "the natives were so elated at this unexpected circumstance and so anxious that . . . they immediately bundled the young calf upon a man's back, and carried it from this side across the island in a journey of several days."[73] Menzies conveyed a sense of excitement among the Hawaiians to show their gratitude for the introduced livestock. He also used the story, however, to show the native Hawaiians' ignorance of the exotic animals. He explained that on the long trek across the island of Hawai'i, the Hawaiians fed the newborn calf, unhealthily separated from its mother, "fish and water." They continued this diet once the calf arrived in Hilo. Menzies stated that "with this unnatural food the animal had been reared without the least aid from its mother, and they assured us that it was at this time very fat and doing well."[74] Menzies then related the instructions that he gave to the Hawaiians as supplements to Vancouver's earlier mandates: "We endeavored to impress upon their minds the impropriety of separating it from its mother, who was fully capable of rearing it had it been suffered to remain with her. We also pointed out to them the absolute necessity of suffering all cattle to live together at one place in quietness for the purpose of breeding and rearing their young, and not to kill or dispose of any of them at least for some years till they became more numerous . . . to be careful that they properly paired them or at least accompanied them with a bull."[75] As experienced owners of their own domestic animals, the Hawaiians certainly understood such basics as the necessity for breeding pairs, and much of Menzies's lecture illustrates typical European pastoral chauvinism. However, some of his advice probably helped the Hawaiians, who had evidently utilized their experience with pigs as an erroneous guide to the caretaking of cattle. Omnivorous pigs could better survive on a diet of fish, and a young pig would be more likely to survive separation than a calf would. Bovine herding behavior would have been unfamiliar to Hawaiians. Considering the rapid growth and spread of the cow population in Hawai'i over the succeeding decades, the Hawaiians either followed Menzies's advice or made their own adjustments.

Hawaiians weathered the inconveniences of the feral herds and rapidly began to harvest the population for profit in burgeoning Pacific markets once the original ten-year kapu ended. American merchant Ross Cox purchased two cows from the king while stopped at the islands in 1811. His narrative illustrates that, while the Hawaiians were actively engaged in attempting to exploit and control the cattle population, they were ill equipped to do so. Cox bought two cows from the king to supply his ship, but found it difficult to collect his purchases. Cox explained that the king sent

> upwards of one hundred men of his bodyguards, with several chiefs, to proceed to the place where the animals were grazing to assist us in catching those we had bought. . . . They proceeded cautiously in the first instance, until they surrounded the herd, which they succeeded in driving to an inclosure [sic]. One more expert than the rest then advanced under the cover of some trees with a long rope, at the end of which was a running noose. Having quietly waited for some time until a proper opportunity offered, he at length threw the rope, and succeeded in catching a young cow. On feeling the noose round her neck, she became quite furious, and made a desperate plunge at him, which he skillfully avoided by running up a cocoa-nut tree . . . and being apprehensive that the captive might break loose, we fired, and shot her. . . . Finding it impossible to catch another, we were obliged to fire among them, and killed a second.[76]

Native Hawaiians developed ingenious methods for capturing the dangerous longhorns, including a lasso-like rope and coordinated hunting, but it remained extremely difficult to capture a live animal on foot for easy sale as live provisions. The Hawaiians probably had some experience with escaped feral animals, since they did raise pigs. The descendants of Vancouver's cattle were far larger, however, and potentially more dangerous than any porcine fugitives.

The Hawaiians also attempted to domesticate the growing feral herds. After his 1805 visit, Russian explorer Urey Lisianski explained that Kamehameha attempted "to breed some of the animals in a domesticated state; and I saw a very handsome cow and calf, in an enclosure set apart for the purpose."[77] The king actively attempted to control the cattle population and harness it for his people at a very early date, but the feral and unfamiliar cattle proved difficult for the Hawaiians to manage safely. The Hawaiians also seeded other islands in the chain themselves. Had Hawaiians been entirely victimized by the cattle, they could have at least used the oceanic barrier to contain the burgeoning species on the island of Hawai'i, where Vancouver left them. However, as Amasa Delano recorded, the native Hawaiians had moved cows to Maui by 1806.[78] It is likely they had moved the animals to the other islands by that time, as well, and there were herds present on all the major islands by the height of trade in cattle products shortly thereafter.

While the king attempted to utilize the cattle, native Hawaiian planters took an active role in trying to stop the depredations of the cattle on their crops. There was a proper place for cattle within native croplands; the Hawaiians differentiated between kula and kalo lands. The latter were flooded fields used for growing the taro from which they took their name, and the former was a place for dryland agriculture. Hawaiians increasingly kept livestock on kula lands at the expense of dryland crops.[79] Several groups sent petitions to complain about large herds of stray cattle or to ask the government to improve law enforcement practices regarding cattle owners. A group of planters from the village of 'Ewa on Oahu petitioned the island's governor, Keoni Ana, explaining that "there are a hundred and more cattle roaming here, every day, without any keeper. . . . Women and men have tried their best to cultivate; cultivation has not been successful on account of this pest."[80] Stray cattle had a conspicuous and detrimental effect on indigenous planting. As the petitioners noted, "This was a beautiful place before, taro, corn, potato, bananas, and other crops grew nicely."[81] Hawai'i's chiefs and kings encouraged cattle, but at least some of the maka'āinana resented the animals.

It also seems that Hawaiians ate little beef in the first two decades of the animals' presence on the islands. The kapu prevented such consumption for the first ten years, and the dangerous nature of the feral longhorns may have delayed it much further. Though European travelers in the Pacific requisitioned the animals for their own stores, they do not mention sharing it with their Hawaiian hosts at meals. Ross Cox stated that "the king preserved the cattle for the purpose of bartering with ships touching there for provisions; and although he killed none for the royal table, he very condescendingly accepted from us a present of a sirloin."[82] Hawaiians had apparently not developed much taste for beef but instead maintained the troublesome animals solely for trade purposes.

Vancouver had utilized and changed Hawaiian rituals in his introduction of cattle. He had asked for and received the ten-year kapu, which set the cattle apart as sacred and untouchable. However, he had also demanded that women have the same access to beef as men. This would signal that cows were not as pure or sacred as pigs. The alien nature of the animal, and its association with the haole outsiders, may also have set cows apart as ʻumakua or unclean. Either Vancouver's dietary enjoinder or Hawaiians' own perceptions of the animals separated cattle from pigs. Even as Hawaiians often understood cows through their experience raising pigs, they did not grant the same ritual significance to the bovine species. There is no evidence of cattle's use in sacrifices, and while Hawaiians continued to keep pigs carefully in households and tied to Hawaiian kinship groups, cattle remained distant, loose, feral, and unfamiliar.

There is evidence that Hawaiians came to consume cattle products over time. In 1840, when native Hawaiian historian David Malo listed introduced animals in his second *Moolelo Hawaii*, he described "the cow (bipi, from beef)" as "a large animal, with horns on its head; its flesh and its milk are excellent food."[83] When Kamehameha died in 1819, one of his wives, Kaʻahumanu, governed alongside his son Liholiho, and Hawaiʻi's parliament eventually recognized her position as kuhina nui or prime minister. Shortly thereafter, she and the young king's mother Keōpūolani dined with Liholiho and broke the kapu on men and women eating together at the same time. Their example led to the destruction of these gendered prohibitions throughout the islands. Beef played no recorded role in this religious transformation, but the desacralization of eating may have opened the door to a newfound popularity of beef. Or it may simply have been a generational shift in tastes as Western contact increased.

Hawaiian Levi Haʻalelea testified that Hawaiians were attempting to exploit cattle as a food resource by the time of his youth in the 1830s. He recalled that he "and other Natives had gone and killed the cattle. . . . 10 natives would go with axes and hack him all to pieces. They were cattle that had been speared and were lame, we pounded on them with clubs."[84] The island's governor, "John Adams" Kuakini, disagreed with this method of hunting and slaughtering the animals, and he eventually forbade Haʻalelea and his cohorts from further killings. Haʻalelea explained that "the reason he tabooed me and other natives with me from killing the cattle was this, that we had a very bad way of killing the cattle, not shooting them down."[85] It is unclear why the governor so objected to these native slaughters. Haʻalelea believed that Adams preferred a Western method for killing the Western animals, though this may have served as a convenient excuse for protecting the profitable animal resources from wider exploitation. Haʻalelea was from the aliʻi class, though those with him might have been makaʻāinana.

Like California Indians, Hawaiians did take to horse riding. Although horses remained less common than cows and far rarer than they were in

California until the 1830s, horses became a key element in Hawaiian play. In the 1820s, Otto von Kotzebue observed that "the Wahuaners [residents of Oahu] have a great passion for horse-racing . . . and without hesitation venture their whole stock of wealth on a race. The purchase of a horse is, indeed, the great object of their ambition." He also explained that "in these races the horse is not saddled, and a string supplies the place of a bit; the rider is usually quite naked, but very skillful in the management even of the wildest horse."[86] Another visitor noted in 1836 that "though few years have elapsed since the introduction of horses . . . the Hawaiians have become dexterous horsemen."[87]

Charles Wilkes, during his exploring expedition for the United States, also noted the native Hawaiian horseplay in Honolulu in 1840. Wilkes claimed that on Saturday afternoons, everyone gathered to race and practice tricks. Wilkes noted that they wore "every variety of costume," and concluded that "the national taste, if I may so speak, is riding horses; and the more break-neck and furious the animal is, the better."[88] Another member of the expedition, George Colvocorresses, remarked on this new tradition; women's participation particularly interested him. He stated that he "met great numbers of native women, who were riding out on horseback for pleasure" and that "the females ride like the men."[89] He noted how happy they seemed and explained that they "appeared to be very fond of showing off their horsemanship, and the mettle of their steeds. Running and leaping over every wall that could be seen on their path was the order of the day . . . the more break-neck and wild the animal the better."[90] This indigenous skill with horses would be of use when the Hawaiians attempted to learn and adapt European cattle culture to deal with the islands' feral herds.

Conclusion

The unified authority and relative political autonomy of King Kamehameha in Hawai'i served as a principal difference between native reactions to cattle there and in California. Though people in both regions found themselves attractive targets for imperial powers in the late eighteenth century, the Pacific borderlands allowed some freedom, and their cultures remained flexible and adaptive in the face of transformative introduced organisms. Hawaiians as a whole had more indigenous legal control over the animals, though class differences in Hawai'i complicate this story. The maka'āinana, the main victims of cattle depredations on agricultural fields, were subject to the whims of their feudal lords, the ali'i, as far as policy toward the animals was concerned. Kamehameha chose to declare and enforce the kapu on killing cattle, and, as we shall see in coming chapters, the Hawaiian legal system attempted to control the animals and reconcile the conflicts between cow and planter in Hawai'i. California Indians, despite increased struggles for control over territory, remained divided into small local polities. Thousands of them took shelter from a changing world, with varying degrees of agency, in the Franciscan missions, and Spanish soldiers and missionaries mediated California Indian relationships with cattle, especially in the coastal areas settled by the Spanish.

Despite these major differences, there remain many parallels in how indigenous people reacted to cattle. They coped as well as they could as their worlds shifted around them. Playful horse riding, beef consumption, surrounding and trapping cattle, and changing vocabularies are all examples of creative adaptations by native people to unfamiliar and often dangerous old-world animals. Even working as mission herdsmen may have been a way to gain a measure of freedom and mobility within an often oppressive colonial system. Efforts to mitigate the impact of cattle and use them to native ends complicate the narrative of native decline in the face of introduced species. California Indians and Hawaiians remained crucial to the establishment of the animals, and they successfully utilized cattle as key elements of their survival strategies in the face of imperialistic European powers.

Many of these adaptations required changes in labor. Hawaiian leaders began to detail workers to build fences and try to corral animals, and then to capture the animals for sale to passing ships once the kapu ended. The Spanish, meanwhile, trained select Indians as vaqueros to manage herds in order to organize and process the open range cattle for their own economic purposes. Thus, the animals played a role in shifting modes of labor within a system in which most workers existed in a paternalistic labor regime. Vaqueros may have had more freedom and mobility than most mission neophytes, but they were not as free as Indians beyond the reach of the missions, and the average native Hawaiian answered to feudal demands on their labor. The feudal system in Hawai'i predated contact with Europeans, and the Franciscans in California sought to control many aspects of neophytes' lives; neither system of labor was necessarily dependent on the ranching economy in these early years of contact and adaptation. However, as the Pacific borderlands shifted in the early nineteenth century and these regions became more integrated into a global economy, the lack of freedom of laborers working with cattle would become more important.

CHAPTER FOUR

Trade

In the 1830s and 1840s, a New England ship called the *Don Quixote* became a familiar sight in both California and Hawai'i. In the early 1830s, it was owned and captained by John Meek, who made significant profits in the China trade. Operating out of Honolulu, where he remained an influential resident until his death in 1879, Meek bought hides and tallow in California with the *Don Quixote*, "a fast sailer, noted for her speedy voyages."[1] Trader William Heath Davis noted that in "about 1833 Don Antonio Jose Cott, a Spanish merchant of the department, chartered and loaded the *Don Quixote* with tallow, for Callao, Peru." There the ship traded its tallow, rendered fat from California's cattle, for "an assorted cargo," which it then brought to Honolulu for sale, then back to California to complete the circle. Davis, who would later work as the ship's supercargo, making the business transactions that would fill and empty its hold, bragged that "on this trip from Callao to the Islands she averaged 200 miles a day for nearly the whole distance, the quickest passage known at that time."[2] Davis went on to relate, "In the spring of 1846 she made the run from Honolulu to Monterey in ten days."[3] Speedy ships like the *Don Quixote* began to draw hubs of the eastern Pacific, like Honolulu, Callao, and Monterey, closer together, though just as important were the financial transactions that governed their journeys. These transactions began to transcend national boundaries and identities, especially as free trade replaced mercantilism as the reigning economic policy in the region in the early nineteenth century. In Davis's story, for instance, a Californio chartered a ship from a New England–born, Honolulu-resident captain for a journey that connected territories claimed by the Republic of Mexico, the Kingdom of Hawaii, and the Republic of Peru.

At the same time the *Don Quixote* transcended national boundaries, it played a role in rewriting them. It served to advance ecological imperialism, for instance. Captain John Meek received a gift of "three heifers and a young bull" from the commandante of the presidio at San Francisco early in his Pacific trading career, and these became the core of the Big Tree Rancho "thirty miles from Honolulu," which held "between four and five thousand head" of cattle in 1871.[4] More tragically, in 1841, in Valparaíso, Chile, a Hawaiian sailor from the *Don Quixote* caught smallpox. Of the seven Hawaiian crewmen on the ship, only the two who had been vaccinated survived. While most of the rest of the crew lived, many were ill, and they carried the disease to Tahiti, where there was a massive outbreak that killed 10 percent of the population.[5]

The *Don Quixote* also played a role in the more visible political contests of the day. Thomas Jefferson Farnham, who would become one of the most vocal proponents of Manifest Destiny, had sailed to Hawai'i after leading a party across the Oregon Trail in 1839. From Honolulu, Farnham booked passage to Alta California on the *Don Quixote*. Farnham arrived in California in April 1840, just days after the governor of California, Juan Bautista Alvarado, had arrested several Americans and Englishmen on suspicion that they were fomenting a revolution on behalf of their governments in an effort to seize the Mexican territory. Farnham took up the case, taking the *Don Quixote* to San Blas, Mexico, to represent the Americans, whom the Mexicans soon freed. Farnham publicized this event in his *Travels in the Californias* and used it, ironically, to justify American expansion in the region.[6] In 1842, Mexico's central government attempted to strengthen its control over Alta California in the face of increasing talks of pro-British or pro-American forces overrunning the state and seceding from Mexico. They appointed a new governor, Manuel Micheltorena. In 1845, he was ousted after a battle in the San Fernando Valley, and the rebels, led by Pío Pico, chartered the *Don Quixote* to carry him and his forces back to San Blas.[7] Thus, this American-owned Hawaiian ship played its small role in the intercolonial contests for Alta California.

Questions about the ownership of the *Don Quixote* add another layer to its adventures in the eastern Pacific. John Meek owned the ship in 1833. By 1840, John Paty, another New England merchant in the hide and tallow trade operating out of Honolulu, owned the ship. William Heath Davis, his supercargo, almost bought a share from him in 1845, but the two fell out over the price (Paty thought the *Don Quixote* was worth eight thousand dollars, and Davis, with advice from Meek, thought five thousand to six thousand dollars more appropriate).[8] There are hints of other owners in the interim between Meek and Paty. In 1846, when the American consul in California wrote to Secretary of State James Buchanan to question whether Paty's *Don Quixote* had the proper papers to sail under the United States' colors, he claimed that in the mid-1830s, some Americans bought and refurbished the ship and sold it to Kamehameha III as "a ship of war."[9] Supporting this claim is an 1839 statement by whaler Francis Allyn Olmsted, who reported, "A few years ago, there were several vessels belonging to the Hawaiian Government, manned by natives. . . . The king formerly owned a fine barque called the 'Don Quixote,' now lying in the harbor. She was under the charge of a former sailing master of the American Navy, and was conducted in man of war style, carrying an armament of light guns. On account of the expense of keeping her in order, she was sold to Peirce and Brewer, merchants at Honolulu."[10] There is little evidence that Peirce and Brewer, a powerful Honolulu firm, ever owned the *Don Quixote*, which might call the rest of Olmsted's story into question, but Larkin's statement suggests there is something to the story, and the Hawaiian government did purchase ships for trade and warfare.[11] Thus, it seems likely that this ship, which spent most of its life laden with hides and tallow extracted from the cattle of the Pacific borderlands, even served for a time to protect the sovereignty of the Hawaiian kingdom from the expanding European and American empires.

As the *Don Quixote*, and dozens of ships like it, carried goods, people, and new species back and forth across the Pacific, they furthered the colonial transformation in the region. In the nineteenth century, imperial rivalries in the Pacific were accelerating with political shifts caused by global war. Spain would be pushed out of the eastern Pacific, while new nations like Mexico and Peru appeared. England, Russia, and France continued to expand their presence, while the United States became a rising new player in this oceanic Great Game. At the same time, trade increased, as more merchants and traders from all of these nations entered into the Pacific theater, hawking manufactured wares from burgeoning industrial centers of Great Britain and New England and extracting lumber, skins, and hides and tallow from the peoples inhabiting California and Hawai'i. In a sense, these goods served as sinews, tying together an increasingly connected Pacific World. As hides and tallow became the preeminent goods produced by California, and then among the most important exported from Hawai'i, cattle became the substance of these sinews. One of the ways in which introduced cattle tied the region together was as a medium of exchange, as a paucity of specie in the recently settled frontiers of the Pacific Rim made hides the main currency and earned them the designation "California banknotes." Monterey merchant Thomas Larkin explained to a trading partner in New York that "The currency of California is Bullock hides & bags of tallow, Calf & Elk skins for small change or pocket money."[12] Cattle products were never as valuable as the mined precious metals or cash crops that often underwrote colonial efforts, but in the 1830s and 1840s, hides and tallow were the most valuable trade goods in the eastern Pacific, and these competing colonial interests utilized them to establish footholds in the region.

While the flow of goods and credit helped rewrite the loci of power in the Pacific, the production of these hides and tallow for international markets depended almost entirely on the labor of the indigenous inhabitants of both regions and the mediation of Franciscan missionaries, Californio elites, and Hawaiian chiefs. Chapter 3 examined early interactions with introduced cattle and the new labor regimes that resulted. This chapter will explore how those labor regimes developed in the context of the expanding hide and tallow trade, and how the connections made by that trade altered and advanced colonial agendas in the Pacific.

Imperial Outposts and the China Trade

The silks, spices, fine porcelain, and tea of China had always fetched high prices in the markets of Europe and its colonies and thus offered opportunities for substantial profits for European maritime merchants. Access to these goods had motivated expeditions from Columbus's voyage in 1492 to James Cook's fatal third expedition in the 1770s. None of these expeditions managed to find the Northern Hemispheric passage between the Atlantic and the Pacific for which they searched, so the long journey south around Cape Horn or the Cape of Good Hope served as the first challenge to accessing these goods. Increasingly in the late eighteenth century, as better charts became available as a result of the era's exploration, merchants began to deem the profits from this trade as worth the length and risks of such voyages.

Merchants willing to make the voyage still had to overcome the second challenge: supplying marketable goods to China.[13] Merchants from Britain, France, Russia, and Spain, and later the United States, especially from the busy port of Boston, could sail to Canton, the single port in the Chinese Empire under the Ming dynasty open to foreign trade by treaty. Traders usually paid for goods in specie, but paying with silver created a trade imbalance that drained the coffers of European states. The British would eventually solve this problem in the mid-nineteenth century with opium smuggled from their colonies in India, but the western edges of the North American continent offered another earlier solution. The pelts of the thick-fur-bearing animals of Siberia supplied the Russian Empire with a merchantable good that paid high dividends in China, but even more valuable were the pelts of sea otters that inhabited the coasts of North America from the Aleutian Islands to Baja California.

The Russians trained and often coerced native Aleuts on both sides of the Bering Strait to form a labor force of fur hunters, supervised and exploited by fur traders the Russians called *promyshlenniki*. It was the expansion of the hunting fields of the *promyshlenniki* and their Aleut laborers southward that had prompted Gálvez and the Spanish Crown to establish the Franciscan missions in Alta California. Though Cook's third expedition did not find the fabled Northwest Passage, it did publicize the rich fur grounds of the Pacific coast and chart the coastal waters. By the 1790s, British, American, and French ships plied the Pacific Northwest and traded for furs with local Indians. The Hawaiian Islands became an important point for these fur traders to rest and resupply on their way to the hunting grounds off California or on the voyage to Canton.[14] The trading ships caught up in Kamehameha's drive for supremacy in the Hawaiian Islands in 1790, such as American Simon Metcalfe's *Fair American* and Englishman William Brown's *Prince Lee Boo*, participated in this circuit from the Pacific Northwest to Canton with a winter layover in Hawai'i, as did the *Lelia Byrd* out of Boston, which introduced the first horses to Hawai'i in 1803.

Historian David Igler identifies three major trans-Pacific trade routes emerging at this time—one from New England to the Pacific Northwest to Canton, a Russian route to Sitka then California, and a third directly linking Hawai'i to California. Hawai'i, a well-developed and populous nation situated at the center of this vast ocean, was a stop in all of these routes.[15] Hawaiians took an active interest in trans-Pacific trade. In the late 1780s, an ali'i from the island of Kaua'i named Ka'iana traveled with the British captain John Meares to Canton, where he learned of the trading opportunities there (while making quite an impression on those he encountered with his large build and Hawaiian clothing). He brought weapons back to aid Kamehameha in the takeover of the islands and impressed upon the king the value of the goods available in China.[16] The rapidity and acuity with which the Hawaiians took to this trans-Pacific trade impressed European visitors. When the British merchant John Turnbull arrived at the islands in December of 1802, he found the price of the salt he needed to provision his ship surprisingly high. He explained that the "increased price was occasioned . . . by the frequent intercourse that the natives have with Europeans and Americans, from whom they have learned to affix a proper value to the productions of their country."[17] Experienced mariners, the Hawaiians had traded between islands and thus across political boundaries for centuries before Cook's arrival, and it appears from Turnbull's account that they quickly adjusted to the European and American style of commerce and currency. Turnbull noted Kamehameha's role in these adroit mercantile dealings. He described the Hawaiian monarch as "not only a great warrior and politician, but a very acute trader, and a match for any European in driving a bargain. He is well acquainted with the different weights and measures, and the value which all articles ought to bear in exchange with each other."[18] In exchange for provisioning ships in the Canton trade, Turnbull reported that Kamehameha had accumulated "fire-arms, gun-powder, hardware, and cloth of different sorts."[19]

Isaac Iselin, a Swiss-born merchant who plied the Canton trade for a New York firm, observed the dramatic effects of the trade on Hawaiian pigs. When his ship, the *Maryland*, stopped at the islands for supplies in 1807, he worried that "the supply of pork we may procure is likely to prove inadequate to our wants. The island has been much exhausted by northwest traders . . . which come here on purpose to put up pork."[20] Iselin explained the market effects of this demand, stating that the fur traders "have paid such exorbitant prices that the natives are overstocked with all kinds of commodities, and will thus not part with their live stock unless they can do it to greater advantage than we can reasonably afford."[21] The price rose high enough that even well-financed merchants could not afford necessary goods. By the 1810s, Kamehameha had monopolized the trade in pigs, so that his government could reap most of the profits.[22] Once sacred animals prized as household pets and for their roles in rituals commemorating almost every aspect of Hawaiian life, pigs had become more important as commodities in this new international market. The demand for meat also suggests why Kamehameha encouraged the propagation of the often destructive cattle and expanded their range onto Maui and Oahu during the kapu, and why Hawaiians risked their lives to capture feral animals and sell them to traders like Ross Cox in 1811, as shown in chapter 3.

In the early nineteenth century, British fur trappers who had hunted in Canada for centuries began to move west, as did American mountain men who followed Indian trails across the Rocky Mountains. By 1811, two

British firms, the Hudson's Bay Company and the North West Company, as well as American John Jacob Astor's Pacific Fur Company, had established permanent operations in the disputed Oregon country, just north of Spanish claims in California. By 1812, the Russians had moved even farther south and built Fort Ross a mere 100 miles north of the northernmost Franciscan mission at the San Francisco Bay. Alexander Baranov, the head of the Russian-American Company, had organized this southward expansion, and he had similar ambitions to move to the west and secure a position in Hawai'i. He hired a German doctor and naturalist, Georg Anton Scheffer, as his agent in the islands. Scheffer went so far as to begin construction of a fort and to raise the Russian flag on Oahu. The construction agitated the British, Americans, and French, and Kamehameha expelled the Russians from the site in 1816, when the workers violated the kapu of a Hawaiian temple. Hawaiians completed the fort for their own use under the direction of John Young. Scheffer moved his operation for the Russians to Kaua'i but maintained good relations with the Hawaiians.[23]

In many regions of the fur trade, hunters overharvested the animals to feed a large international demand. Within a few years of Fort Ross's foundation, the otter population in California had begun to decline, but the settlement remained active until 1840. The Russians continued to hunt otter and sea lions, but the colony's main wealth rested in the same introduced animals that supported the Franciscan missions: cattle. Though their skins were not as valuable, the populations of domestic livestock could be monitored and controlled much better than those of wild fur-bearing animals. The Russians managed to acquire a herd of cattle from the missions and used them to supply their northern hunting grounds with salted beef and dairy products.[24] They traded with the Spanish, who founded two missions closer to the fort in the 1810s, either to assert their claims to the territory or to take better advantage of the goods offered by the Russians, or, most likely, both. The Franciscans built their twentieth and then northernmost mission, San Rafael, in 1817 with materials obtained from the fort in exchange for cattle and probably with an eye toward continued trade with Fort Ross.[25]

Despite the benefits of new Pacific trade linkages, some Spanish officials in Alta California continued to fear that these imperial rivals threatened their position. In 1817, then president of the missions Mariano Payéras worried that the English and Anglo-American operations on the Columbia River (which, he exaggerated, stood only "80 leagues" from San Francisco) and the Russian presence at Fort Ross would undermine

Spanish efforts there, and he complained that "such neighbors" threatened the Spanish colonies by "improperly occupying those lands which are Spanish possessions and corrupting that immense heathendom with their errors and evil customs, to the great harm of religion and state."[26] Payéras also confirmed the role of Hawai'i in this trade as he further extrapolated its possible threat to Spanish possession. He explained that the activities of the three rivals to the north "also place this province and all of the coast of this South Sea in imminent danger of being successfully attacked, especially when the three nations—the English, Russian, and Anglo-American—have access, shelter, and aid in the Sandwich Islands, farther south than our San Blas."[27]

The economic development of the missions in the early nineteenth century suggests that the expansion of these commercial and imperial rivals had benefits as well as posing a danger. From their founding in 1769 until the end of the eighteenth century, the missions depended on the yearly supply ship from the port of San Blas on the Pacific coast of New Spain.[28] Even as the herds of horses and cattle rapidly grew and the fathers baptized more Indians to work as skilled and unskilled labor, the missions still generally failed to produce enough foodstuffs for self-sufficiency, and they required manufactured goods, from textiles to china to religious decorations for the mission churches, from New Spain.

Under the mercantilist system of New Spain, the missions traded with local presidios and pueblos and with Mexico through the system of arancel, in which the colonial government determined the value and the prices for all goods.[29] While the missionaries' highest priorities lay beyond commerce, they did at times resent the mercantilist system. In 1810, Payéras explained, "I have just returned from Santa Barbara and notwithstanding a thousand efforts I was unable to get a single pound of tallow loaded, although Purísima had ready for putting aboard 500 large *botas*."[30] He explained that he was unable to move this valuable product of his mission "because of the hemp business (with which San Blas is over-supplied and which is overabundant in this province) which must, by order of the superior government, be preferred."[31] Payéras saw the value in his mission's herds of cattle and complained that the viceregal government had given precedent to a less marketable product that not all of the missions produced.

New Spain did not allow California to trade with merchants from any other nation, which meant that even limited exchanges with British, American, or Russian fur traders from along the coast were illegal. Since they could not legally trade with any of the established fur companies, enterprising Spanish merchants set out to capture their own furs in trade with California Indians. In 1784, Vicente Vasadre y Vega, a Spanish fur trader, arranged to trade California otter pelts in Canton for quicksilver needed for Mexican mines. California Indians understood that they could gain brightly colored cloth, glass beads, and other valuable manufactured goods for otter pelts.[32] The demand stimulated increased hunting, and the furs made their way through networks of exchange from Indian hunters to Vasadre via presidial soldiers and mission fathers. After a three-month stay in California, Vasadre carried more than a thousand skins with him to China in 1787.[33] The Spanish remained aloof from other fur traders; the first Bostonian fur-trading ship to anchor officially off the California coast was the *Otter* in 1796, which stopped for emergency supplies on its way from the north to Hawaiʻi, then Canton. Californian officials did not allow the Americans to trade but gave them eight cattle and other provisions.[34]

The missions' participation in the otter fur trade helped equalize the balance sheet with their viceregal supplier, but it also created competition between missions and secular merchants for the furs of California Indians. When New Spain asked the Franciscans to lower the price that they paid for furs, Fray Lasuén argued that competition with secular Spanish traders and foreign smugglers like "the Frenchmen" drove prices higher. If the missions lowered their price, they would cut off their own supplies from Indians, who could find better offers elsewhere. He also claimed that the trade put the largest burden on the missionaries, "for they were being obliged to select the Indians who were to do the fishing [Lasuén's term for gathering the mammals in the ocean], to support them from the common fund, to assign them according to their ability as far as possible, to supply them with rafts, canoes, and nets, and especially with provisions."[35] As a result, Lasuén thought that "the price agreed on seemed to me to be equitable, and . . . it was quite in accord with the basic objectives of the establishment."[36] As Lasuén recognized, this earliest participation of the California missions in Trans-Pacific trade did serve an important dual function for the mission that the hide and tallow trade would also serve. The revenues from the furs kept the missions in the black with their Mexican suppliers, and it also gave the fathers an opportunity to teach the Indians a trade that would help put them on the path to becoming gente de razón.

At the same time, the conflict over prices established a precedent of rivalry with secular entrepreneurs who could bargain with Indians without the added burden of Christianizing them. Lasuén argued that the missions would "always pay the Indians for pelts, and pay in a form that suits him better and is more equitable than what the military and civilians pay. Through greed and self-interest each of these will leave much to be desired in their regard for the terms of their contract. They will cause the natives much vexation, and will prejudice and frustrate the efforts of the missionaries."[37] Lasuén resented and feared secular competition that could undermine the missions' efforts at social control through labor and, by virtue of their existence outside the missions' moral economy, pay less than the fathers. His comments suggest a lively frontier exchange economy in which neophytes, gentiles, friars, and soldiers used official and contraband maritime traders to enter into a burgeoning Pacific exchange network linking the Canton trade and the fur trade.[38]

While New Spain held the upper hand in California's commerce at the beginning of the nineteenth century, in Hawai'i, Kamehameha controlled all trade. Canton-bound merchants from the United States searched for opportunities for further freight on the island to make their visits more profitable than the resupply landings of the 1790s. The Chinese paid high prices for the fragrant wood of the 'iliahi a'loe or sandalwood (*Santalum ellipticum*) that grew in abundance on the islands and that they used in woodworking and to make incense.[39] In 1811, three Boston merchants carrying sea otter furs from California to China, Nathan Winship of the *Albatross*, Jonathan Winship of the *O'Cain*, and William Heath Davis Sr. of the *Isabella*, gained a ten-year monopoly on shipping sandalwood through agreement with Kamehameha. In return, Kamehameha was to receive a quarter of the proceeds in either specie or Chinese goods.[40] Like the Franciscans, Kamehameha had the power to marshal native labor, and he began an indigenous timber industry to collect the valuable wood. However, the Winships and Davis failed to fulfill their contract and lost their monopoly as a result of the outbreak of war between the United States and Great Britain in 1812.

Kamehameha hoped to begin an indigenous carrying trade from the islands, and to that end he often traded sandalwood for merchant ships. Just as he had previously acquired the *Fair American* to wage war, he now acquired ships like the *Albatross* and the *Lelia Byrd* in the hopes of reaping greater profits from trade with China.[41] In exchange, Hawaiian chiefs redirected the labor of their maka'āinana peasant workforce from taro plantations to the removal of large stands of native forest.[42] This was difficult and ecologically damaging labor; the wood was dense and most of it went to waste. Debts still increased, as did the intense labor levies to harvest the wood, and swaths of forest disappeared until there was little forest left to harvest by the end of the 1820s.[43] Eventually, the nascent Hawaiian navy would even embark on an ill-fated mission to colonize the New Hebrides in order to control more stands of sandalwood.[44]

Hawaiian labor moved across the ocean, as well, as the exchange of goods also prompted an exchange of people. Fur traders often took on Hawaiians as crew members or took them to the coast of North America to work in processing furs. European sailors "blackbirded," or kidnapped, the earliest Polynesian laborers in European maritime enterprises.[45] However, Hawaiians mostly volunteered for maritime work in the late eighteenth and early nineteenth centuries. On an expedition to the northwest coast explorer Gabriel Franchère stated that his crew took on twenty-four Hawaiians, twelve to work on the ship and twelve to work at Astoria. He explained that their contracts lasted "three years, during which time we undertook to feed and clothe them at the expiration of their contract, to give them goods to the value of one hundred *piastres*."[46] He also noted that "these people made reasonably good sailors, seemed eager to enter our service and we could have engaged more of them."[47] In 1802, John Turnbull also observed the work of Hawaiians in the Pacific Northwest, which he stated "was an opportunity of which they eagerly availed themselves." He explained that the Hawaiians profited through this contact work, as they "thereby acquire sufficient property to make themselves easy and comfortable, as well as respected among their countrymen."[48]

Drawn by the lure of the goods now flowing back and forth between Pacific markets and Atlantic metropoles, Hawaiians readily joined these operations, and their experience as Polynesian mariners apparently helped make them quick studies as skilled sailors on European ships. Hawaiian elites served as brokers for common laborers signing on to these ships, which may suggest an element of coercion or exploitation in the process. However, Hawaiian leaders also stimulated the labor market by legislating increased wages for their sailors, and cash advances served to induce the commoners to sign on.[49] Ross Cox noted that his ship hired twenty-six "kanakas" to take to Columbia, ten as sailors and sixteen to work there. They each received "ten dollars a month and suit of clothes annually."[50] Cox further stated that "an old experienced islander, who was called Boatswain Tom, and who had made several voyages both to Europe and America, was engaged to command them; he got fifteen dollars a month, and was to have sole control of his countrymen."[51] By Cox's 1811 voyage, a captain could hire old hands from Hawai'i who had made extensive journeys for merchants in the Pacific. More vulnerable to the diverse disease environments that transoceanic voyagers lived in and encountered, many

Hawaiians did not survive the journey, with at least a quarter perishing from various illnesses.[52] Hawaiians used the profits from this dangerous labor to buy into the upper classes of the hierarchical Hawaiian agricultural system. Peter Corney reported that "when they return, [they] give all they have earned to their chief, for which he gives them a farm, and they become great men."[53] In contrast to these industrious natives, Franchère also reported that he "found some white people who had remained on this island, to the number of about 30 of all nations, mostly weak characters who stayed on through laziness or drunkenness."[54]

As early as 1802, Europeans noticed that merchants from the United States played a dominant role in trade with the Hawaiian Islands. John Turnbull, an Englishman, explained that "the Americans in particular carry on a most active trade with these islands, supplying them with property at an easy rate in exchange for provisions."[55] Noting that "North Americans display an industry and perseverance in their commercial undertakings, which is not exceeded even by the English," Otto von Kotzebue summarized the growing American presence throughout the Pacific at the beginning of the nineteenth century.[56] He explained, "On the northwest coast of America, they barter with the savages all kinds of European trifles for the beautiful skin of the sea otter, which they sell for a high price in China." He added, "Many of the vessels take in cargo of sandal-wood in the south-sea islands, for which they also find a good market in china, where it is in great estimation."[57]

Trans-Pacific Exchange in Wartime

In the 1810s, the eastern Pacific felt the effects of the decades-long Napoleonic Wars in Europe, as they spread to the United States and Spain's American colonies. In 1808, Napoleon Bonaparte invaded Iberia and installed his brother Joseph as the new king of Spain. England sent troops to support a Spanish drive to remove the occupying French. In 1810, creoles in several of Spain's Latin American colonies, emboldened by the chaos in Iberia, revolted against Spanish rule. More than a decade of fighting followed. In 1815, after Napoleon's defeat at Waterloo, a restored Spanish monarchy invaded the rebellious colonies and put the insurgents on the defensive; however, this seeming victory only escalated the wars.

The war for independence in Mexico had direct effects on its northern frontier. The Franciscans, motivated by loyalty to the monarchy and the often anticlerical actions of the Enlightenment-influenced revolutionaries, condemned the insurgents. Since they dominated Alta California through the missions, it remained loyal Spanish territory. However, the last supply ship from San Blas arrived in 1810; Mexican insurgents captured the supplies for the 1811 ship, and it never arrived on the Alta California coast, much to the chagrin of the mission fathers. The Yuma still blocked overland supplies. The California frontier had always been isolated, but now warfare had almost completely cut it off from New Spain.

The removal of Spanish supplies led to the destruction of Spanish mercantilism. Though still technically illegal, free trade flourished along the coast of California during the wars of independence. To whatever extent the fathers resisted smuggling before 1810, they found it a necessity for obtaining manufactured goods in the following decade. In fact, California still relied on trade for basic foodstuffs, and Payéras explained the importance of illicit foreign traders in an 1820 letter in which he wrote that "until [18]15, if we of the Province were eating it was because of them."[58] Smugglers regularly anchored at some of the more secluded points along the California coast; popular stops included Point Concepción at the entrance to the Santa Barbara channel and Point Reyes near Drake's Bay. William Heath Davis Sr., one of the Boston pioneers of the sandalwood trade, collected otter furs in California on the same voyage in 1810 and 1811. His son explained that Davis would stop near Santa Barbara and "many of the wealthier Californians came to this place and purchased from the vessel choice articles of merchandise, as did also the padres."[59] In return for these goods "the rancheros and priests brought with them bags of Spanish doubloons and paid for their purchases in coin, or in sea-otter skins, which were then plentiful . . . which they [the padres] had accumulated."[60] The fathers required goods for religious services and to run the missions as acculturating economic enterprises, and they had to trade for everything from Christian paraphernalia to textiles to spices and alcohol. Indian labor produced ample trade goods, but between the wars and mercantilist policies, the mission fathers had limited access to markets. Smugglers from Britain, the United States, and other countries provided supplies between 1810 and 1820, though the wars did not prevent interception.

On June 2, 1813, a privateer named Nicolás Noé, operating out of Lima under papers from the Spanish government, captured the *Mercury*, a merchant ship from Boston captained by George Washington Eayrs, near Santa Barbara.[61] The *Mercury* had traded for otter pelts from the California missions, and Noé brought Eayrs, his crew, and his family to Santa Barbara for imprisonment as smugglers. Noé also seized the *Mercury* and all its cargo for Spain. An experienced smuggler of furs along the California coast, Eayrs had served on a similar voyage in the previous decade. He had spent years shuttling between China, Polynesian islands, the Pacific Northwest, Alaska, and California (his common-law wife, with whom he had a newborn baby at the time of his capture, was a half-Tahitian girl known as "Peggy," the daughter of one of the mutineers from the HMS *Bounty*).[62] The failure of the San Blas supply ship gave further impetus and justification to his activities. Eayrs protested the seizure of his furs and told his captors that "in general all the officials resident on the coast and at their request I have given them agricultural tools and other things that they needed."[63] He further explained that "I have provided the priests with what they required for instructing the natives and for the ceremonies of religion. . . . They have paid me with provisions and some few otter skins."[64] The wars had made smuggling a necessity, and even the loyal mission fathers bent the rules and allowed the otter trade to continue so that they could continue to receive crucial supplies without shipments from San Blas. Despite the complicity of California officials in his dealings, Spanish authorities held Eayrs and then transported him to San Blas as a prisoner. They eventually released him years later, and he settled in Mexico.[65]

Further complicating and prolonging the situation with the *Mercury* was the entrance of the United States into the conflicts of the Napoleonic era. The British blockade of France had hurt American growers in the southern states, Britain continued to support Indians hostile to the United States in the Great Lakes region, and the impressment of American sailors into the British navy to help fight the Napoleonic Wars had wounded American pride. In 1812, the United States declared war against Great Britain. This war also spilled over into the Pacific, where it disrupted American trade, as in the case of the American sandalwood contract with Kamehameha.

The Latin American wars for independence created other opportunities for those hoping to profit from the growing animal wealth from introduced species in the Pacific basin. In 1818, Kamehameha purchased his sixth ship, the Philadelphia-built corvette the *Santa Rosa*, for 60,000 pounds of sandalwood.[66] The *Santa Rosa* had sailed from Buenos Aires as a privateer under the flag of newly independent Argentina, and the Hawaiian king soon learned that its crew had mutinied. The mutineers had subsequently used the ship to raid along the Pacific coast in Peru and Ecuador, then fled to Hawai'i, where they sold the ship and scattered.[67] In September 1818, another Argentine privateer, the Frenchman Hipólito Bouchard, anchored at Kealakekua Bay following his own raids on Spanish possessions in the Philippines. When he learned the fate of the *Santa*

Rosa, he demanded that Kamehameha hand it over to him. In his account of the incident, Bouchard exclaimed, "I didn't know what to do, an armed Spanish vessel in the hands of these barbarians."[68] The king eventually sold the ship and delivered some of the mutineers to the privateer. Bouchard duly lashed them and executed one of the officers of the *Santa Rosa*.[69]

Meanwhile, Bouchard had learned from a British trader in Hawai'i named Peter Corney of the wealth of the Spanish missions in California. The far-flung frontier settlements had drawn little attention in the ongoing wars for independence, but as an otter fur trader, Corney was aware that the missions had received a significant amount of European and Chinese wares for otter furs over the past decade, and that they possessed numerous livestock. Bouchard decided to raid the California coast, and he outfitted his ship *La Argentina* and the *Santa Rosa* for the task with Hawaiian supplies and a crew of his own men, the former mutineers, and Hawaiians. Bouchard placed Corney in charge of the *Santa Rosa*, and the English merchant turned privateer related that his crew consisted of "a compliment of 100 men, thirty of whom were Sandwich Islanders, the remainder where [sic] composed of Americans, Spaniards, Portuguese, Creoles, Negroes, Manila men, Malays, and a few Englishmen."[70] In November, the ships anchored in Bodega Bay, where they took on much needed supplies from the Russians at Fort Ross. They planned to sail into Monterey Bay under the flag of the United States and then take the presidio by surprise.

However, maritime traffic from Hawai'i had already conveyed rumors of the attack to the Californians while Bouchard was still refitting his ships at Honolulu. The Californians scrambled to mount a defense against Bouchard's coming attack. Bouchard had only two ships and fewer than four hundred men, but his multicultural crew drawn from throughout the Pacific World almost outnumbered all the soldiers scattered throughout the presidios of the isolated frontier colony of Alta California. Just as the settlers and Franciscan missionaries depended on California Indians for labor, they also called on the Indians for defense. In October 1818, Mariano Payéras wrote to Don José de la Guerra, the commander of the presidio of Santa Barbara, that he had prepared "fifteen more skilled archers with 26 bows and 500 arrows" and that "ten vaqueros likewise armed with their Montezuman armor [thick cloth] will know how to perform their duty."[71] The Californians' front line of defense consisted of Indians, both archers and vaqueros, a formula that combined indigenous skills with the new skills they had acquired to maintain and manage herds of domestic animals.

The plan to land the *Santa Rosa* under the U.S. flag failed owing to forewarning of the attack. The ship and the presidio of Monterey exchanged cannon fire for the better part of a day to no decisive end. After dark, Corney and his crew raided the fort, "the Sandwich Islanders in front with pikes," but found the presidio mostly abandoned.[72] They hauled down the Spanish flag and raised the Argentine flag. The next raid on Santa Cruz found the settlement completely deserted by the retreating Californians. In early December they moved south to Rancho de Refugio, a land grant rancho near Mission Santa Bárbara run by the Ortega family.

What kinds of plunder did Bouchard hope to win? Peter Corney noted in his account of the final raid on San Juan Capistrano that "we found the town well-stocked with every thing but money."[73] In the 1810s, California's wealth lay in native fur-bearing animals and introduced livestock. The frontier economy had little currency, but the vast fur resources and the gains of the fur trade were ripe for the maritime raiders to take. Bouchard focused on Ortega's rancho because of its numerous cattle and horses and because of its status as a center for smuggling. Payéras had apparently used the rancho's illicit trade connections to move some of the product of his nearby Mission La Purísima. During the preparations for Bouchard's arrack, he noted that "I have hired Tapia to go tomorrow to Ortega's rancho with the *requa* [mule train] and remove my tallow from danger."[74] Goods like tallow or warehoused furs or hides made for profitable targets, as did the European and Chinese wares for which Californians traded these goods.

Payéras recounted the raid on Rancho de Refugio as an Indian vaquero named José Andrés related it to him. He said that Bouchard's men "scattered among the canyons in gangs of three or four," and they went after cattle "like hungry wolves."[75] According to Payéras, José Andrés also helped protect the valuable livestock, as he explained that "knowing that they were looking for horses, he took away five that he found."[76] The vaqueros also managed to strike back at the raiders. Peter Corney stated that at "about noon [on December 5, 1818] a lieutenant and two seamen having strayed a short distance from the town, a party of horsemen rushed on them, threw the la's-aws [lassos] over their heads and dragged them up a neighbouring hill, before we could render any assistance."[77] Payéras explained that three "insurgents have been taken prisoner, among them an American lieutenant, a Negro, and a Quiteño."[78] Bouchard responded by shelling the pueblo of Santa Barbara. He then bargained to exchange the prisoners for a Californio prisoner he had taken in Monterey (Molino, the town drunk) and a promise to end his raids on the California coast. The exchange occurred on December 10, and Bouchard promptly broke his promise and raided San Juan Capistrano on December 16 before moving on to the Pacific coast of Mexico. As at Monterey and Santa Cruz, Bouchard met only token resistance to his looting at San Juan Capistrano. Bouchard's raids on California illustrate the growing trans-Pacific connections of the nineteenth century and the value of California's livestock, as well as the isolated and undefended nature of the colony due to its weakening connection to the Spanish empire.

Hides and Tallow in California

The end of Spanish hegemony in Latin America that began in the Napoleonic Wars offered new opportunities for imperial powers in the Pacific, especially Great Britain and the United States, and changed the complexion of Pacific colonial rivalries.[79] While otter pelts remained the most marketable products from North America's Pacific in Canton, the herds of California's missions represented a larger and more easily replenished source of wealth, and while the populations of fur-bearing animals rapidly declined, the herds only continued to grow. Ranchers could transform a cow's body into several products and commodities. The animal's meat and most of its internal organs were edible. Although unrefrigerated beef spoils rapidly, dried and salted it could provide provisions for ships and food for the workday. The animals also produced useful products when boiled in large vats. The Californios called the rendered fat from the animal's front parts manteca, or lard, and used it locally for cooking and baking such as lard rendered from pig fat. Californians also marketed this lard to the Russians.[80] They rendered the fat from the animal's back and stomach and boiled it into tallow, which they used primarily to make candles, though tallow was also a key ingredient in soap and served as a good lubricant. The hides were even more versatile, as leather was a major material for clothing, especially shoes, and made up bags, ropes, and belting for new industrial machines in Europe and New England. The cattle's horns served as containers or as a source of keratin, and the bones could be ground into gelatin for cooking.

With such a reservoir of readily producible, merchantable goods, the California missions had a clear desire to participate in international markets for the products of cattle; however, the mercantilist system of New

Spain remained a major stumbling block until the 1810s. In 1814, a Spanish naval officer, Don Francisco de Paula Tamariz, estimated that Californians slaughtered 19,000 cattle each year to feed settlers and neophytes, and yet they sold almost no hides because of the lack of a legal market. Thus, 19,000 hides, worth as much as 40,000 pesos, went to waste every year in California.[81] The Rancho Ortega stores of tallow that Payéras had to protect during Bouchard's raid suggests that the missionaries did not always abide by these rules, especially after the official Spanish presence faltered during the Latin American wars for independence.

Legitimate trade, though sporadic, also picked up after 1810. The productive gold and silver mining operations of Peru, which included Potosí, consumed significant amounts of tallow. Tallow candles served as the main light source in mine shafts in the early nineteenth century, and the viceroyalty of Peru was one of the most heavily mined regions in the world and also one of the most remote from the eighteenth-century ranching centers of the Mediterranean, northern Europe, and eastern North America. Latin American cattle populations in Mexico, Chile, and Argentina helped feed the Peruvian demand for tallow, and in the 1810s, California joined these suppliers. Peru, like California, remained loyal to Spain throughout the decade, and when the Peruvian ships *Tagle* and *Flora* (Noé's ship) arrived off the coast in 1813, they legally purchased mission tallow in exchange for much needed goods and supplies like sugar, rice, spices, clothing, medicines, and religious items.[82] California's isolation put the missionaries at a disadvantage. The *Tagle* initially offered only 8 reales per arroba (25 pounds) of tallow, about half the going rate, and demanded high prices for their goods in exchange.[83] More ships arrived from Lima in 1814, but traffic again stopped as an insurgency in Cuzco disrupted shipping in 1815 and 1816.

This new demand for tallow from Lima stimulated more production from the missions. In their 1814 *Respuesta* to questions concerning mission Indians, the fathers of San Buenaventura noted, "At this mission every week there are slaughtered sixty, fifty, or at least forty-five head of cattle."[84] They noted this fact to testify to how well they fed the neophytes, but they also mentioned another reason for slaughter, explaining that "in the season when the cattle are very fat, the slaughter of sixty cattle takes place twice a week in order to increase the amount of tallow for sale so that necessary goods may be procured. Large portions of meat are taken in carts to the field and burned because there is no one to take it away."[85] While the padres explained that they took part in this commerce to obtain "necessary" goods, the massive slaughter leading to a waste of excess meat signaled a new set of priorities for the missions. Whereas the fathers had previously focused on management in trust of animal and agricultural resources for converted Indians, necessity now drove the mission to an emphasis on production for the limited but growing international tallow market. In his memoir of Mexican California, rancher and customs agent Antonio María Osio recounted that "when ships from Peru or San Blas came to purchase some tallow, they would offer to pay one peso per *arroba*, which was practically nothing"; however, despite these low prices, "the cattle owners . . . would rush out with their vaqueros and helpers to round up the animals."[86] Osio also noted the inefficiencies of this drive to market tallow, stating, "They would kill the cattle on the spot, cut open their bellies to take out the fat, and leave the rest behind as food for other animals. It was not worth the effort to carve up the animals, stretch the hide, and take out the rest of the fat."[87]

In 1818, the Californians still faced unreasonable prices offered by their few legitimate trading partners. In 1818, Father Payéras complained to José de la Guerra, "The people of the ship want to take advantage of us too much. Last night I received a letter from Illas asking for the tallow at 10 ½ reales, and if refused, he wanted to cash in to pay for the orders."[88] Gaspar Illas of the frigate *Hermosa Mexicana* used California's isolation against Payéras in their negotiations, as he asked for a low price for the tallow (which averaged a price of 2 pesos, equal to 16 reales) and threatened to rescind the credit granted to the missions. In the cash-poor economy of Alta California, such a move could be devastating. Because of the continuing trade restrictions and the lack of interest in cattle products by American and English traders, the missionaries had little choice but to trade at these low prices. Osio noted that "American ships that called on the coast would sell their wares only in exchange for silver or for otter pelts."[89] Within a few years, however, the British and Americans would come to see the value of hides and tallow, and the Spanish would no longer be able to monopolize California's trade.

In 1821, the Californians received the news that New Spain had declared its independence from Spain, and the region had become a northern territory of the empire of Mexico under Agustín de Iturbide. Trade increased dramatically. David Igler's survey of the 953 vessels known to have visited Alta California before the gold rush shows that only 20.1 percent visited in the thirty-five years before Mexican independence with the other 80 percent in the twenty-eight years of the Mexican period.[90] British and American traders were first among those who took advantage of the liberalization that followed this political change. The

United States would eventually make up the plurality of shipping to Mexican California, serving as the national origin of 45 percent of the ships, with Britain a distant second with 13 percent.[91] As Spain finally began to cede its South American colonies in the early 1820s, John Begg, a British merchant, conducted business along the west coast of South America. He worked out of Santiago and Valparaíso before establishing an office for his firm of Begg & Co. in Lima in 1821. Two of Begg's clerks, the English William Hartnell and the Scottish Hugh McCulloch, had heard of the animal wealth of the California coast, as well as the independence and likely trade liberalization in Mexico. They contracted with Begg to form their own firm McCulloch, Hartnell, and Company, to exploit these newly available resources.[92] In exchange for five-eighths of all profits, Begg & Co. financed the operation and chartered them a ship, the *John Begg*, at $1,200 a month. They loaded $22,000 worth of cargo on the ship.[93]

The partners would travel to California, where Hartnell would remain to establish the firm there in order to obtain a steady supply of California goods. Their focus was always on hides and tallow. José Cavenecia, the Lima-based owner of the *Tagle*, had freely shared his thoughts on California with Hartnell. The otter population on the coast had declined, and Begg, Hartnell, and McCulloch were all well aware of the market for tallow in Lima and the value of hides to manufacturers in Britain and New England.[94] London and Boston were centers for the manufacture of leather goods, including clothing and shoes, and these two hubs of early industrial production had a seemingly bottomless demand for leather in the 1820s. Begg's "Note of Produce," which informed Hartnell which products to seek in California, focused on hides and tallow, though it also asked him to seek other products of old-world animals, specifically butter and horsehair.[95]

On December 13, 1821, the junta then in charge in Mexico City had declared California's ports open to trade. The *John Begg* arrived in San Diego Bay in June 1822, and thus William Hartnell and Hugh McCulloch became two of the first traders to take advantage of California's newly opened door. They made plans to establish a permanent store in San Diego, as well as a warehouse for the goods they would export from the territory; then they traveled to Monterey to meet with the governor, Pablo Vicente de Solá, and Fray Mariano Payéras, who had taken over as father president of the missions. Solá acceded to the firm's permanent establishment in San Diego, and Payéras welcomed a three-year contract with McCulloch, Hartnell, and Company that gave the new firm a monopoly on the missions' hide and tallow for three years. The firm would pay one peso per hide and two pesos for each arroba of tallow, better terms than those of the earlier Lima traders, especially for tallow.[96] Payéras wrote a circular letter for distribution to all of the then twenty missions, which gave them the power to negotiate their own deals. He explained, "By the authority of the Governor, Messrs. Hugh McCulloch, a Scotchman, and William Hartnell, an Englishman, both Protestants and partners of the English merchant, John Begg established in Lima, presented themselves before me. The object of the aforesaid gentlemen is to enter into a commercial contract for three years with all this Province; the provisions give promise of advantages to both contracting parties. . . . Every mission is free to accept or reject this agreement."[97] Such a contract with two Protestant Brits marked a sea change for the missionaries, and this dramatic shift from mercantilistic relations probably led to the extreme latitude that Payéras gave to the individual missions. Payéras also reported the deal to Mexico, explaining that "especially for leather" the Englishmen would pay "a good price either in money or in the goods that are requested and ordered either from Lima (where they have their principal office) or from London."[98] He noted the benefits that the deal entailed for all the missions, some of which had struggled during the isolation of the 1810s, and he explained, "For our greater good they have decided to go to all points along the coast with their ships, so that everyone will be provided with necessities."[99] As a result, he predicted, "If things go as planned the poverty of the Province will disappear and the Missions will be provisioned."[100]

McCulloch acted as the supercargo for the *John Begg*; with contract in hand, he traveled from north to south down the camino real that linked the missions and negotiated the monopoly with each of them. San Antonio de Padua and La Purísima agreed to the monopoly without reservations. The rich missions of San Gabriel negotiated a separate three-year contract. San Carlos would sell 250 arrobas of tallow and 100 hides a year for the next three years. San José offered 30 arrobas of tallow and at least 600 hides a year for three years. San Francisco offered 500 arrobas of tallow in the next year. Santa Clara could only supply 25 arrobas of tallow a year. La Soledad could offer no tallow.[101] These numbers show that not all the missions were equally wealthy or equally prepared for commercial production, but for the first time the California missions could sell agricultural products from their own animals on their own ranches to broader international markets. Hides and tallow would provide significant wealth from introduced livestock and Indian labor.

Since the largest markets for hides remained in the Atlantic, distant political occurrences affected the trade. Continuing conflicts in Brazil and

Argentina and the lingering political struggles following independence increased the value of the hides that McCulloch, Hartnell, and Company obtained from the distant but relatively stable California market, and soon the profits on hides outstripped the profits on tallow, which remained "next to hides, the most valuable local commodity."[102] Lima continued as almost the exclusive market for mission tallow, as mining operations still required large numbers of tallow candles, and Peruvian miners used tallow to lubricate machinery in the mines.[103] Ships that collected both hides and tallow would trade one of the products to another ship along the coast, so that hide ships could sail straight to Boston and tallow ships to Callao.[104] A single cow, if slaughtered while fat in the spring, could provide three arrobas of tallow with each arroba, like each hide, selling for between one and two pesos.[105] Duflot De Mofras, a French agent and explorer, noted that deer tallow sold for much more; however, beef tallow made up almost the entirety of the trade, due to the convenience of and Spanish control over the domestic animals.[106]

Although Hartnell complained of higher prices than anticipated for the hides he purchased from the ranchos, Hartnell and McCulloch made a large profit from these dealings.[107] Antonio María Osio took time to note in his memoirs, "The agreement was quite profitable for the company."[108] Other firms followed their example and transferred their attention from the diminishing otter fur supply to the reservoirs of hides and tallow in the vast herds of cattle.[109] Traders like William Gale of Boston anxiously awaited the end of the monopoly. In 1822, the most active American firm in the fur trade, Bryant & Sturgis of Boston, sought to make deals with the missions and independent ranchos that had not joined Payéras's contract with Hartnell and McCulloch.[110] Antonio Osio explained that "the agent of the Sturgis Company of Boston, the American Don Guillermo A. Gale, established trading relations by offering to pay twelve reales per cattle hide."[111] With new competition between foreign traders, the price of hides increased, and Gale established a longtime trading presence in the province by offering prices ahead of this curve. By 1827, trans-Pacific merchant William Dana had a difficult time selling his goods for otter furs because Californians preferred to trade hides and tallow.[112]

Payéras died in 1823, months after concluding his contract with McCulloch, Hartnell, and Company, but the new market that he helped create flourished after his death. By 1828, just six years after this contract, and only three after the monopoly ended, the British Arctic explorer William Beechey described a thriving trade in hides and tallow that greatly benefited the missions. He noted that the missions "cultivate large portions of land, and rear cattle, the hides and tallow of which alone form a small trade, of which the importance may be judged from the fact of a merchant at Monterey having paid 36,000 dollars in one year to a mission, which was not one of the largest, for its hide, tallow, and Indian labour."[113] He later explained that "hides and tallow constitute the principal riches of the missions and the staple commodity of the commerce of the country," and he used one mission as an example, stating that "San Jose, which possesses 15,000 head of cattle, cures about 2000 hides annually, and as many botas of tallow, which are either disposed of by contract to a mercantile establishment in Monterey or to vessels in the harbour."[114] Bryant & Sturgis had several ships operating along the coast at any given time, including the *Pilgrim*, the *Alert*, the *California*, the *Plant*, the *Roxana*, and the *Lagoda*.[115] William Heath Davis counted 1.25 million hides exported from California between 1826 and 1848, and another visitor estimated that in the early 1830s, California exported 200,000 hides annually.[116] Another estimate for total exports in this period is 6 million hides and 7,000 tons of tallow.[117] Mofras recorded figures for California exports in 1841. Out of total exports with a total value of 280,000 piasters (roughly equivalent to American dollars at the time), $210,000 was in hides and $25,000 in tallow.[118] Not including the fairly marginal values of salted beef, horns, and other cow products, 84 percent of California's exports came from cattle in 1841. Ships left the California coast on their way to Boston "carrying nothing but hides," and Richard Henry Dana noted that in sleepy California towns like Santa Barbara, "there was not a sound to be heard, or anything to be seen, but Sandwich Islanders, hides, and tallow-bags."[119] Portions of the California coast were suddenly bustling with various labors of processing and transporting hides for broader Pacific markets. In 1828, Begg & Co. permanently stationed a ship, the *Young Tartar*, in California to transport hides from port to port within the territory.[120]

Until the mid-1830s, the missions made up a significant portion of this trade. The fathers took care not to slaughter enough animals to halt the herds' natural increase. One observer noted that the missions' production "could have been doubled without diminishing the base."[121] The mission herds generally grew throughout the 1820s, as the fathers invested in maintaining this vast biological resource. Although the official counts of the cattle owned by all of the missions never rose over 150,000, Osio estimated that actual holdings, including the unbranded cattle that the missions claimed, numbered over 430,000 at their peak. He claimed that former mission mayordomos were the source of his statistics and methodology.[122] There is a debate among historians as to whether the missions began to focus more on commercial enterprises during this period. As they made more money in trade, production in other areas, especially in grains, began to fall, and the implication is that they began to focus less on providing for the Indians' spiritual and bodily needs and began to see them more as an exploitable labor force in the lucrative hide and tallow trade.[123]

The marketability of beef products served as an added impetus for the expansion of private ranchos, which began to eclipse the missions in the 1830s and spawned a debate over the control of mission lands, which culminated in secularization in 1834 (the subject of chapter 6). In 1827, however, private ranchers owned less than 10 percent of the cattle in California.[124] These ranchers utilized the same methods for managing and harvesting bovine wealth as the missions, including Indian labor. In fact, missions often further subsidized their profits by hiring out Indian vaqueros to private ranches.

Merchant firms soon developed a system for the hide and tallow business in California. The long Pacific coast of California offered several favorable locations for trading. Monterey was the capital and the location of the customhouse, and all legitimate traders stopped there first to unload their cargo and pay the customs duties. Ships could then move freely up and down the coast, trading their wares for hides and tallow with missions and, increasingly, independent ranchos. In 1828, William Beechey declared San José, Santa Clara, San Juan Bautista, and Santa Cruz the richest of the missions, though he overlooked the substantial herds of San Gabriel, which were probably the largest.[125] Ships could sail through the Golden Gate to the large and well-sheltered San Francisco Bay to trade with the first two. Monterey Bay granted access to the bovine wealth of San Juan Bautista and Santa Cruz. San Pedro, near the Pueblo de los Angeles, was near San Gabriel and some of the early large ranches, like that of the de la Guerra family. Traders often visited the southernmost port, San Diego, last. The mission at San Diego remained relatively poor, but most firms located their warehouses there. Another popular stop, the Santa Barbara channel, granted access to the herds of the missions of Santa Bárbara, Santa Inés, and La Purísima. Strong winter southeasters threatened to wreck ships in this less sheltered bay from November to April, however, forcing ships to anchor miles offshore.[126]

Hide-trading vessels would anchor in each of these bays, where they would exchange goods for the promise of hides. The trade grew quickly enough that demand soon outstripped supply, and this fact, coupled with the natural rhythms of California's climate and the natural life spans of cattle, necessitated long stays to fill up a cargo hold. When George Simpson scouted California for the Hudson's Bay Company in 1841, he explained, "The provincial exports of hides do not exceed at the utmost, the number of 60,000; and though such a vessel as our neighbour the *Index* has room for two-thirds of the whole, yet there are, at present, on the coast, fully sixteen ships of various sizes and denominations, all struggling and scrambling either for hides or for tallow."[127] A full cargo hold is the most efficient, and thus the most profitable, way to move goods, but as the trade along California's coast expanded, the province could not produce hides quickly enough to serve all of the coasting ships in a year. Summer drought complicated the problem, as cattle grew skinny and thus produced inferior hides and far less tallow. Instead of slaughtering these hungry and thirsty cattle, the Californians held an annual slaughter, or "matanza," at the end of the wet season in the spring, when the cattle grew fat and the animals born two or three summers previous had matured. Indian vaqueros participated in massive rodeos in which they gathered the large wandering herds and killed thousands of cattle, skinned them, and rendered their fat. Coasting ships had to stand on the coast through two or three matanzas to fill their holds with 40,000 hides before sailing for Boston or London. The Boston merchant Faxon Dean Atherton satirically described the desperation for cow products among these traders. He said that when a vaquero slaughtered a beef "it now, as if by miracle, gets sounded abroad to the distance of from 60 to 100 miles that there has been a B[ullock] killed. . . . Immediately that it is known on board, away starts the hide chaser of one vessel by land one way, off goes the tallow hunters another way, while perhaps some 3 or 4 launches, 5 or 6 surfboats, gigs, and cutters start off in the direction where it was heard of as having been seen."[128]

John Girdler, a merchant from Marblehead, Massachusetts, complained in a letter to his family that this process represented "a very slow and tedious way of loading a ship."[129] Richard Henry Dana noted that he had expected a voyage of eighteen months on the *Alert*, but "here was a gloomy prospect before us. The *California* had been twenty months on the coast, and the *Lagoda*, a smaller ship, carrying only thirty-one or thirty-two thousand, had been two years getting her cargo; and we were to collect a cargo of forty thousand beside our own, which would be twelve or fifteen thousand; and hides were said to be growing scarcer. . . . Hints were thrown out about three and four years."[130] George Simpson noted that the *Alert*, "belonging to the oldest and most experienced houses in the trade, has already spent eighteen months on the coast, but is still about a third short of her full tale of 40,000."[131]

In the meantime, the ships worked to secure future hides. A supercargo, in charge of the ship's wares for sail in California, would sell the items to the missions and the ranchers. While in harbor, the supercargo could bring hide suppliers to a display room, which showed what the ship had to offer. In Richard Henry Dana's widely read account of his journey on a hide ship to California, he described such a room on the *Alert*. He explained that this room "consisted of everything under the sun."[132] He then listed the available products: "We had spirits, of all kinds (sold by the cask), teas, coffee, sugars, spices, raisins, molasses, hardware, crockery-ware, tin-ware, cutlery, clothing of all kinds, boots and shoes from Lynn, calicoes and cotton from Lowell, crapes, sills; also, shawls, scarfs, necklaces, jew-elry, and combs for the ladies; furniture; and in fact, everything that can be imagined, from Chinese fire-works to English cart-wheels—of which we had a dozen pair with their iron rims on."[133] Californians remained dependent on the outside world for almost all manufactured goods as well as the usual luxuries brought by traders with access to goods from Eastern markets. Calico, plain cotton cloth produced cheaply in abun-dance in the textile mills of Britain and New England by the 1820s, was the most common good purchased by the Californians.[134] The majority of merchants' profits in the hide and tallow trade apparently came from the markup on these items, and not from the commodities obtained in California, which served mainly as the basis of exchange.[135] John Girdler noted that "the prices people pay for goods on board the ship is enor-mous."[136] Dana used this as evidence to conclude that "the Californians are an idle, thriftless people, who can make nothing for themselves."[137]

A French trader, August Duhaut-Cilly, learned a great deal about the workings of the hide and tallow trade when he arrived in California in 1827 hoping to sell his cargo for silver. He had been sent as a merchant to the Pacific by Jean-Baptiste Rives, who had exaggerated his connections in Hawai'i and his understanding of California's market. Upon making the California coast, Duhaut-Cilly met a mission father who helped set the fel-low Catholic straight. Despite his mistakes, Duhaut-Cilly stated, based on this information, "I decided that I could profit from the advantageous prices offered in this market."[138] However, he also noted that he would have to backtrack to Peru because "the scarcity of money allowed no other means of exchange but cow hides and tallow; the second of these could be converted only in Lima, where it sold very well, I knew."[139] He also traded his goods for hides and resold them to "the American captains who were in California to obtain them."[140] To Duhaut-Cilly's frustration, hides and tallow were the sole means of exchange in California. However, the markets locally and in other regions of the Pacific for these goods remained active enough that his venture could still succeed.

Supercargoes also moved up and down the coast, carrying wares to missions and ranchos. The American explorer Charles Wilkes noted in 1841 that "the mode of conducting business in this country is peculiar."[141] He explained that the "supercargo or traveling agent" was "some person well known throughout the country, who visits all the pueblos, missions, and estancias, as a traveler, passing from place to place without any apparent object of business."[142] According to Wilkes, the wandering supercargo assessed who had the richest herds and needed the most goods, and was thus likely to run up a debt with the visiting merchant but who would also be able to settle that debt with hides or tallow. Wilkes also stated, "Because currency was extremely rare in California, these merchants tabulated all of these sales and deliveries as exchanges for hides or tallow."[143] As Dana explained, "They have no credit system, no banks, and no way of investing money but in cattle. They have no circulating medium but silver and hides—which the sailors call 'California bank notes.' Everything that they buy they must pay for in one or other of these things."[144] So it was that products from this introduced species became the main medium of exchange in California's economy. Since matanzas were generally annual events, most of these sales were conducted on credit. A mission father might buy a hundred pesos worth of cloth for Indian laborers on his mission. He would then owe the selling supercargo's ship at least fifty hides (depending on individual negotiations) after the next spring's matanza came. The missions paid their debts more reliably than independent ranchers did.[145] Girdler explained, "It is the custom on the coast, of selling goods to the traders and most of the Rancheros (farmers) at one year's credit."[146]

Selling on credit was risky business in California.[147] Larkin complained, "The payment of debts are horrible. It appears as if every one had come to a conclusion that it was not necessary to pay old debts."[148] Because the trade so heavily depended on cattle, the inconsistent climate of California exacerbated the typical problems of credit-based business. Drought years inevitably led to nonpayment and the extension of debt. The two largest droughts during the heyday of the hide and tallow trade were in 1820–21 and 1840–41; the first killed tens of thousands of cattle.[149] In December of 1841, an American rancher apologized to Larkin: "I am sorry I cannot send you hides. I have none nor do I know whare [sic] I can get them till next summer. You know last season very bad; the farmers made no matanzers [sic] with one or tow [sic] exceptions & of course few hides came into the market."[150] Earlier that summer, another rancher had explained, "My Catell [sic] I Cant [sic] kill their [sic] so poor."[151] Duflot de Mofras explained, "If the season is dry and pasturage unavailable, the live stock cannot graze and the rancheros, in the belief that they will not produce much tallow, kill as few as possible."[152] Merchants, hoping to fill their holds in the next matanza, continued to sell goods on further credit, and "debts thus accumulate indefinitely and become increasingly difficult to collect, not only on account of diminishing live stock, but also because of the increased consumption of merchandise, particularly spirits."[153]

Anglo-American Capital, Native Labor

Anglo-American capital dominated in the region, and merchants from the United States and Britain gave their respective nations distinct advantages in the imperial contest for the Pacific frontier. As the wars for Latin American independence pushed Spain out of the eastern Pacific (though its major colony in the western Pacific, the Philippines, remained an important Spanish possession for the remainder of the century), the fur trade opened the door to the Russians, and the larger hide and tallow trade increased the regional power of the British and the Americans. Economic relationships were potential imperial relationships, and the importance of supply and credit also made them personal relationships. Before the institutionalization of risk management through insurance, personal arrangements sustained transoceanic merchant communities.[154] Merchants in California allied themselves with prominent ranching families through marriage and conversion to Catholicism.[155] William Hartnell married María Teresa de la Guerra, a member of the prominent Santa Barbara ranching family in 1825. Alfred Robinson, who worked for McCulloch, Hartnell, and Company's American rival, Bryant & Sturgis, married another de la Guerra sister, Anita. Abel Stearns married Juan Bandini's daughter Arcadia. Henry Delano Fitch married Josefa Carillo of a San Diego ranching family, and British trader Henry Dalton married María Guadalupe Zamorano, the fourteen-year-old daughter of California's governor. William Heath Davis Jr., known as "Kanaka Bill" in California, was the son of William Heath Davis Sr. and a half-Hawaiian woman, and he married María de Jesús Estudillo, the daughter of the owner of the San Leandro rancho.[156] Similar familial alliances to mission ranches were obviously impossible, and this may have contributed to the growing power of independent ranchers through the 1830s. Historian Andrés Reséndez has made a compelling argument that commercial ties and the more personal links of marriage led to layered and shifting identities in Texas and New Mexico during this time period, and many of the same processes occurred in Alta California with the hide and tallow trade.[157]

American traders outnumbered the British in California. The Hudson's Bay Company caused a brief stir in the early 1840s, when they established a store in San Francisco under William Glen Rae. They planned to trade goods at this store for hides and tallow, which they could ship with their other Pacific ventures, and they also reportedly planned to buy 100,000 cattle to create their own herd and thus ensure a steady supply. One American complained to Thomas Larkin that the British company was "playing the devil with the California Cattle, if not with California itself," as their efforts would dramatically raise prices for cattle and cow products.[158] But in 1843, George Simpson, believing that the California venture had been run poorly, ended the operations in San Francisco, and thus ensured the ascendancy of the American interests in the hide and tallow trade.[159]

The new scale of commercial production, and the labor that the trade required, necessitated training the California Indians in new skills regarding the management and use of European animals. The missions now employed more Indians for longer hours in the rendering of animal fats and the cleaning of hides; Mariano Vallejo called California an open-air slaughterhouse.[160] In *Two Years before the Mast*, Richard Henry Dana presented a detailed account of the hide-curing process, which he had to participate in while working at the San Diego hide house for Bryant & Sturgis. After the vaqueros slaughtered cattle, usually in the annual matanza, they would skin the animals and cut holes around the edges of each hide. They then tied the hides to stakes through these holes and stretched them out to dry. Drovers then took the dried hides to the beaches, where ships took them to San Diego. At San Diego, according to Dana, "the hides, as they come rough and uncured from the vessels, are piled up outside of the houses, whence they are taken and carried through a regular process of pickling, drying, cleaning, etc., and stowed away in the house, ready to be put on board. This process is necessary in order that they may keep, during a long voyage, and in warm latitudes."[161] Pickling required that every hide soak in brine for forty-eight hours—often Saturday through Monday, which left the Sabbath free for the workers. Cleaning was a crucial part of the process, as workers had carefully to cut away all meat and fat and thoroughly scrape the hide. Stray pieces of meat could play host to decomposing bacteria, and, on a ship, a single rotting hide could ruin an entire shipment because of the close proximity and length of storage.[162] Before the ship's departure, after two or three years on the California coast, the crew cleaned out and smoked the hold and carried the tens of thousands of hides on board, sometimes in wheelbarrows but often in the "California fashion," with two hides carried on one's head.[163]

Rendering fat to produce lard and soap had been an important activity at the missions since their foundation, but now the scale increased significantly. Commodified cattle fat required that mission Indians carefully butcher the animals; fat for manteca had to be separated from sebo, the fat around the kidneys used to make tallow, and both had to be separated from muscle and bone. Laborers "tried" each fat, or boiled it until it turned into a waxy solid, in separate "large pots brought by the American whaleships—such as are used to try out their blubber."[164] Workers had to carefully monitor the trying, especially the manteca, which could burn if overcooked. The workers staked out hides next to the vats, and when the trying was complete, they poured it onto the hide, which they then tied up into a bag "each containing twenty to forty *arrobas*."[165] Even the Indian expertise in the making of these simple hide bags was important to the commerce of California. A merchant named John Foster wrote to another merchant, Abel Stearns, and requested, "If you should have an Indian in your employ that understands making tallow bags, I wish you would send him down for a few days to put up the tallow that is in rotton [*sic*] bags."[166]

Cleaning and preparing animals skins was another familiar duty to the California Indians, who had long hunted and prepared game animals, but the international market required an unfamiliar uniformity and level of production. Except those (usually gentiles) who had hunted otter furs, California's Indians were not used to dealing with animal skins as commodities. McCulloch, Hartnell, and Company occasionally had to struggle with this unfamiliarity. Their customers claimed that the Indians stretched the hides too thin. James Brotherson & Company complained, "It is not the size of the hide that is looked to but its weight and the smaller compass this is in so much the better."[167] The Indians may have preferred thinner leather, which would be easier to work into personal tools, as opposed to the industrial-strength hides demanded by European and American markets. Archeological evidence from Mission La Purísima suggests that the Indians did work the hides with familiar bone and stone tools, suggesting "native agency in preference in action."[168] Accounts are vague about the gender of the Indians doing this work, though there are specific references to women working at the rendering vats.[169] Working skins was traditionally gendered as female labor in California Indian societies; the missionaries may have seen this as a male activity and reshaped the gender division of labor, signaling another shift in Indian societies linked to cattle. Or the European writers of accounts of the trade may have simply overlooked the gender dynamics among the Indian laborers.

Many of the missions constructed their own ships to help transport their stores of hides to the foreign traders. Dana explained, "Large boats, manned by Indians, and capable of carrying nearly a thousand hides apiece, are attached to the missions, and sent down to the vessels with hides, to bring away goods in return."[170] Osio noted that "the padres not only taught the Indians to build vessels and boats, but instructed them also in their management, and made sailors of them. They were sometimes employed as such by myself and other merchants at Yerba Buena . . . in the delivery of goods and collecting hides and tallow."[171] The Indians at Mission San Gabriel constructed a ship on the mission grounds, then carried it in pieces to be reassembled in San Pedro Bay, fifteen miles away.

Hawai'i in the Hide and Tallow Trade

Alongside American and British sailors and California Indians, the labor of native Hawaiians, which had become common in Pacific trade with the Oregon territory, also became crucial in the hide and tallow trade. Hawaiian mariners had already played a significant role in the fur trade earlier in the nineteenth century, and they continued to crew ships in the hide and tallow trade. For instance, four Hawaiians signed an 1846 contract to work for William Leidesdorff, a California rancher and merchant from the Danish West Indies, on a hide ship for ten months at twelve dollars a month. Each took a Western name for the purpose of the contract— thus "Keo ni ma" was also known as "Johny Wine."[172] Another contract from 1848 dubbed "Kimikolo" as "'Jim Crow' Marsh."[173] The reference to a popular American minstrel show song hints at the racial construction of these Polynesian workers.

Many other Hawaiians worked onshore in California. While Richard Henry Dana toiled at Bryant & Sturgis's San Diego hide house, he befriended several of the "Sandwich Islanders" and was impressed with their skill at loading heavy hides and tallow bags onto ship-bound boats in rough surf.[174] Several Hawaiians had settled in San Diego to work at the hide houses, and they occupied a building that the Russians had supposedly built as a large oven to bake bread. The sailors called it the "Kanaka Hotel" or the "Oahu Coffee-house" and Dana spent much of his free time there.[175] He explained that, between jobs, the Hawaiians "lived there in complete idleness—drinking, playing cards, and carousing in every way."[176] However, perhaps because of their hard work on the beaches, Dana did not condemn the Hawaiians for this behavior (in contrast, he often complained of the laziness of the Californios). He also noted, "They bought a bullock once a week, which kept them in meat."[177] While beef may have never passed pork in Hawai'i as the native food of choice, in cattle-rich California, the Hawaiians consumed the animal as their main source of protein.

Hawai'i served as a major hub for the California hide and tallow trade. Vessels brought hide and tallow cargoes to Hawai'i on their way to South America and New England, or sold these cargoes to Hawaiian merchants, who transported them to Callao and Boston. Several Hawaiian firms also entered into the trade themselves, sending their own ships, like the *Don Quixote*, to collect hides and tallow on the coast. The Paty brothers, John Coffin Jones, Alpheus B. Thompson, William French, William Hinckley, and Peirce & Brewer were important participants in this trade.[178] Increasingly throughout the 1820s and 1830s, these merchants looked to the growing bovine resources on the islands to supplement their Boston- and Callao-bound cargoes, while Hawaiian leaders hoped to profit from the animals as the sandalwood trade diminished.

According to a nineteenth-century native Hawaiian historian, though Kamehameha readily exploited Hawai'i's sandalwood resources, he also worked to conserve stands of the tree.[179] When Kamehameha died in 1819, however, his successor, Liholiho (also known as Kamehameha II), increased the harvesting of the plant.[180] Even more than the Californios, the Hawaiian chiefs began to purchase a variety of luxury goods and alcohol from Europe and the United States on credit and to incur debts as a result. They sold sandalwood, the most marketable good on the island, to service their credit lines. Missionary-trained native Hawaiian historians noted, "In former times, before Kamehameha, the chiefs took great care of the people. But from Liholiho's time to the present, the chiefs seem to have left caring for the people. Their attention had been turned more to themselves and their own aggrandizement."[181] In a history of Liholiho's reign, one of these native historians said, "The public debt . . . is a moth which eats up Hawaii. It is plain that rum is a poison god, and debt is a viper."[182] By 1823, easily harvested sandalwood was rare on the islands, and the trade had greatly diminished. In 1826, an American naval commander, Thomas ap Catesby Jones, pressed the Hawaiian government to pay the extensive debts that the chiefs and royals had racked up during the sandalwood trade. A group of merchants, led by John Coffin Jones, claimed the Hawaiians owed them $500,000. Commander Jones lowered the number to $200,000.[183] Among the concessions Jones received from the king in subsequent treaty negotiations was a promise to protect Americans on the islands and most-favored-nation trade status for the United States.[184] In 1827, the Hawaiian kingdom's first written law commanded Hawaiians to deliver a quota of sandalwood to the government to help pay off these debts.

After this destruction of the sandalwood forests and before the rise of cash crops like plantation-grown sugar and pineapples after 1850, Hawai'i's main assets were its location and the feral herds of cattle descended from Vancouver's introduction. With or without sandalwood, Hawai'i would always be an ideal stop for Pacific traders who needed provisions, and salted beef was a staple food. The development of the Pacific whaling industry increased foreign maritime traffic in the islands and thus created a new market for beef products from the wild cattle. Whale oil was an important source of illumination as sperm oil burned more cleanly and brightly than any other fuel widely available at the time. Clean and clear illumination became even more important as industrialization in Europe and the United States required illumination for labor divorced from the limits of solar rhythms. Whaling grew rapidly over the early nineteenth century, especially in the Pacific, which had many more whales and a shorter history of exploitation of the resource. The first whaling ship stopped in Hawai'i in 1819, but by 1821, more than a hundred had anchored in the islands' various bays. Before population declines caused by overhunting, whales were abundant throughout the Pacific Ocean. Whalers moved in a circuit around the ocean, taking advantage of the migrations of whale pods along the Pacific coast of North America and through the seas around Japan. Hawai'i's central location between these whale fisheries made the ports of Honolulu on Oahu and Lahaina on Maui ideal locations for ships to stop for provisions and repairs. By 1835, Hawai'i "had become the Pacific Basin's principal whaling station and held this position until the demise of the industry in the 1870s."[185] This also coincided with the overall peak in Pacific whaling between 1835 and 1855.[186] The overwhelming number of whaling ships that stopped in Hawai'i for reprovisioning in the mid-nineteenth century created a hefty demand for salt beef that the feral cattle populations of Hawai'i could help supply. In 1846, William French explained that the "large number of whale ships visiting these islands . . . causes a good demand for salt provisions. Beef sells readily at 12$ per barrel—1500 barrels were sold last year from 12$

to $14 per barrel."[187] French was a Honolulu merchant who had established himself buying sandalwood but later purchased and gathered a herd of cattle at Waimea to feed this growing trade. One Hawaiian cattleman remembered him as "the first person that got a good private herd at Hawaii."[188]

Before French began his herd, there had been previous attempts to tame Hawai'i's feral cattle and harness them as a resource. As discussed in chapter 3, Russian explorer Urey Lisianski reported that Kamehameha had penned cattle in 1806, and the king had sold Ross Cox, a participant in the Canton trade, a pair of bullocks in 1811. In 1819, when Ka'ahumanu, one of Kamehameha I's wives, took charge of the kingdom as kuhina nui following his death, she increased utilization of the feral cattle herds. On June 16 and 17, 1821, she slaughtered cattle to distribute among the captains of visiting ships.[189] She used the animals to maintain her relationships with the foreign traders, and she helped encourage the sale of provisions. One newspaper article noted that Waimea's wild cattle "have afforded no inconsiderable revenue to the chiefs for some years past."[190] The islands did gain a reputation as an excellent source of beef provisions. One of the members of the United States Exploring Expedition explained that they obtained good provisions in Honolulu and that "the beef comes chiefly from the Island of Hawaii, and is fat and well-flavored."[191] Edward Belcher, an English naval officer and provision connoisseur, was particularly fond of beef from Kaua'i. He said, "I am certain that our men derived more nourishment from the cattle we embarked there [Hanalei on Kaua'i] than from any previous diet," and he even went so far as to claim that the "noble animals" yielded "meat as fine as in England."[192]

Despite these Hawaiian uses of the animals, domesticated herds in Hawai'i remained rare before the 1830s. A few foreigners had private herds in the environs around Honolulu in the 1810s and 1820s. The Spanish Don Francisco de Paula Marin, known as "Manini" to the Hawaiians, deserted an American ship called the *Lady Washington* in 1793 or 1794. Like John Young and Isaac Davis, he became an adviser and translator to Kamehameha, who in turn granted him usufruct rights to land on Oahu. Several visitors reported that Marin gathered a herd there. In 1824, after Liholiho and his queen, Kamamalu, died of measles on a visit to England, the British navy sent a ship, HMS *Blond*, to return the bodies to Hawai'i. The voyage's commander, Lord Byron (George Anson Byron, successor to the title from his cousin, the famous poet George Gordon Byron), wrote an account of the journey, in which he took note of Marin. He explained that "Marini had . . . reclaimed some of the cattle which

Port d'Hanarourou, by V. Adam after Louis Choris
(note the cattle in the left foreground and the busy port in the background;
courtesy National Library of Australia)

had become wild by the operation of the ten years' tabu, imposed after
Captain Vancouver landed the parent stock, and had taught the arts of
dairy; a considerable profit was also derived from the salting of beef for
ships."[193] The Dutch merchant Jacubus Boelen claimed that "Don Francisco Marini . . . possessed about a thousand cattle" in 1828.[194] In 1822,
Gilbert Farquhar Mathison, after noting that "wild cattle . . . roam in
prodigious numbers through the woods [of Mauna Kea] . . . but the inhabitants make no use of them, and they are now absolutely ferae naturae," admiringly discussed "Menini's [*sic*]" vineyard of introduced grapes
and "his farm-yard, and grounds adjoining, stocked with a wild herd of
fine cattle."[195] While Marin engaged in selling the products of his herds to
ships, he also looked to them to make further introductions of nonnative
species, some of which proved invasive. His garden was famous, and most
European and American travel narratives on Honolulu commented on it.
Marin brought the first pigeons to Hawai'i, and the first dandelions, which
he may have encouraged as forage or medicine.[196] He introduced rabbits
to Moku'ume'ume Island in Pearl Harbor, which they soon overran. The
Hawaiians began to call Moku'ume'ume Rabbit Island, or Little Goat,
because they thought the rabbits resembled small goats.[197] In November
1824, Marin also received a few cattle and horses from California on a
Hawaiian ship.[198] It seems odd that he would purchase a few cattle when
his herd numbered in the hundreds. Perhaps this was a breeding cow or a

cabestro, one of the trained cattle California vaqueros used to break wild cattle.[199] He appears to have received far more horses, which were less numerous in Hawai'i, than cattle from the mainland.

In 1810, Anthony Allen, an African American and a former slave, arrived on an American ship. Working in the Canton trade and serving as a steward on one of the *Lelia Bird*'s trips to China, Allen earned enough wealth to trade "a bar of Russian iron" with a chief for the rights to a few acres of land near Waikiki.[200] English visitors in the 1820s noted, "His grounds are extensive, well cultivated, and lie within a ring fence. . . . His present flock of goats amounts to two hundred, having been lately reduced one half below the usual average by the demand, from ship-captains, for provisions of this kind; he sells animals to them at prices according to their size, from half a dollar to three dollars a head."[201] One of the missionaries commented that "he owns large flocks of goats, and a few cattle; and supplies the tables of many of the residents with milk."[202]

Hannah Holmes Davis was another intriguing owner of cattle near Honolulu. She was the daughter of Oliver Holmes, a sailor from Plymouth, Massachusetts, who had won favor with Kamehameha I in the 1790s and had taken Isaac Davis's place as one of the king's chief foreign advisers after Davis's death in 1810. Holmes married Mahi Kalanihooulumokuikekai, a member of the royal family and thus attained an official position among the ali'i; Hawaiians addressed him as "Ali'i Homo."[203] Hannah was the second of their two children, and she and her sister Jane acquired notorious reputations among Christian missionaries for their beauty and their associations with various men in the community. Hannah had a daughter with the merchant John Coffin Jones Jr., though the two never formally married. She then married New England trader William Heath Davis, who had made the failed sandalwood deal in 1811. They had two sons; William Heath Davis Jr., who would serve as supercargo for the *Don Quixote*, was the second. William Heath Davis Sr. drank himself to death before his second son reached his first birthday. This left Hannah Holmes a widow, but, as the daughter of royalty and the wife of a prominent, if struggling, merchant, she had resources to draw upon. William Heath Davis Jr. noted in his biography that in 1845, "My mother was living in Honolulu and was wealthy, owning a large number of cattle, which were good property, as they were always in demand by the ships of war, whalers and other vessels visiting the Islands."[204] Unfortunately, we don't know a great deal about this half-Hawaiian widow's circumstances, but her son's account shows both the general profitability of cattle and her ability to take advantage of them. New England customs and laws had influenced

Hawai'i for decades, and in 1845 legislators enshrined the concept of coverture, which forbade women from owning property, in the law of the Hawaiian kingdom to the detriment of many female ali'i who had owned property.[205] Holmes, as a widow, would have been exempt from this new legal imposition.

Despite attempts by Hawaiians to control and profit from cattle, foreigners continued to mediate their relationship with the species and acted as the main managers of the animals. Cattle husbandry required special skills and practices, a cattle culture that Vancouver did not import with the animals. Hawaiians used beef to service debts as sandalwood production declined, but they still required foreign labor to do so. Marin reaped most of the profits from his domestic herd, but he paid taxes or tribute for the use of Hawaiian land. Anthony Allen would have as well. Hawaiians slaughtered wild herds, known as the cattle of the king or the cattle of the government, but they had to utilize foreign labor. The government engaged foreign bullock hunters to capture the wild cattle by offering a monetary award for each hide gathered. It could then resell these hides to ships in Hawaiian harbors.[206] Many of these bullock hunters came from Europe, the United States, or Australia, and they did not use the traditional methods for wrangling wild cattle associated with cowboys. Most had deserted ships or escaped from the Botany Bay penal colony. Dealing with the feral Hawaiian cattle remained dangerous work, and Charles Wilkes noted that "bullock-hunting seems to partake somewhat of the dangers of the chase of wild-beasts, and has much of its attraction. Many stories are related of natives having been tossed, gored, and carried on the animal's horns for hours."[207]

Chief Kuakini, also known as "John Adams" to the foreigners, had some bullock hunters on his payroll, including one William Hughes. The governor of the Big Island, home of Hawai'i's largest herds, Kuakini harvested cattle to provide beef for whaling ships and hides to hide and tallow traders. Levi Ha'alelea, who grew up in Kuakini's household, reported that Hughes worked for the governor. The king still had ultimate control over the wild cattle on Hawai'i, even as Kuakini managed the herds and foreigners did the hunting. In 1823, for instance, the king granted ten cattle to a chief named Paalua, who then wrote to Kuakini explaining that "our whitemen are coming to you to shoot cattle in Waimea; they are to shoot ten heads, the 1st whiteman is the blacksmith and the second whiteman is the cooper, they are to shoot the cattle. The blacksmith will do the shooting and the copper will do the salting and is to bring the beef back to me. There are all the cattle I got from our king, ten of them."[208]

Ha'alelea also noted some of the other men who hunted bullock on the slopes of Mauna Kea; he testified that "the people that killed wild cattle I know from my own knowledge was Parker and Ao and Davis."[209] George Hueu Davis was the half-Hawaiian son of Kamehameha's British adviser Isaac Davis. John Palmer Parker, a sailor from Massachusetts, had jumped ship in Hawai'i in 1808 and started a small farm in Kohala on the Big Island.[210] A San Francisco newspaper correspondent described Parker in 1853 and explained that "for some years he ranged the woods after wild bullocks, and became a second NIMROD, 'a mighty hunter before the Lord.' He showed me a rifle with which he had shot twelve hundred head of cattle."[211]

Ao's identity is not as clear. We do know from a missionary's journal that a Chinese settler on the islands was also hunting bullock in the vicinity of Bill Hughes by the 1830s. H. O. Knapp reported entering a house at Waimea "belonging to Mr. Hues [*sic*] formerly occupied by him, now occupied by a Chinaman."[212] Knapp explained that Hughes was "a Beef catcher. . . . Hides and tallow are the things for which they are caught" and that the hunter "said he had taken 5 or 6000 cattle in six or seven years, & the Chinaman as many more."[213] Since Ao is a Chinese surname, it is reasonable that he may have been the man occupying Bill Hughes's former house.

Ha'alelea's testimony and Parker's rifle suggest that these hunters usually shot cattle. However, many of Hawai'i's bullock hunters worked by setting elaborate traps for the dangerous longhorns. One visitor explained that "the greater number procured in their wild state are shot . . . but many are caught in pits. A hole is dug large enough for a bullock to fall into. This is then concealed and covered with fresh hay, till the sweet scent attracts the wild animals, which fall in."[214] Wilkes added that hunters usually dug them near watering holes and with "the hoofs of cattle imprinted on them, to deceive."[215] These pits were rather dangerous, and the famous botanist David Douglas died after falling into one and being trampled by a bull. Douglas worked as a collector for the Royal Agricultural Society, and he had collected several specimens along the Pacific coast of North America, including the Douglas fir, named after him. In 1832, he visited Hawai'i on a voyage from California to the Pacific Northwest, and he returned on a second visit in December 1833. He sailed to the Big Island and ascended its volcanic peaks to collect more plant specimens. On July 12, 1834, he was found dead and mangled in a bullock pit with a trapped cow.[216] It seemed that he had stumbled into one of the concealed pits where an angry bullock had already fallen.

A group of concerned foreigners, Protestant missionaries, and the British consul, Richard Charlton, first assumed that he was a victim of this method of hunting, though their suspicion soon turned to one of the socially marginal hunters taking hides on the volcano's slopes. Douglas had ten gashes on his head that were deep enough to prove fatal, but, in the judgment of those examining the slaughtered cow from the pit, not deep enough for the animal's horns to have caused them.[217] Douglas had breakfast the morning of his death with Ned Gurney, one of the Botany Bay convicts who had taken up bullock hunting. Decades later, at the turn of the century, some native Hawaiians from the region testified that Gurney had been seen following Douglas on his way to the fatal bullock pit and that Gurney had killed Douglas to rob him, though the temporal distance of this testimony from the event makes it suspect.[218]

Many of the hunters, including Ned Gurney, took native wives, and evidence suggests that these native women played important roles in supporting the foreign hunters. As a result, the bullock hunter culture did represent a hybrid cattle culture in itself. For instance, an archaeological survey of one region inhabited by bullock hunters found no signs of the stone-walled houses most foreigners built in Hawai'i, suggesting that they built thatched huts in the native Hawaiian manner, probably with the input of their wives.[219] Like American Indian women in the North American fur trade, these native Hawaiian women certainly played essential roles in supporting their husbands' endeavors to supply colonial markets. Unfortunately, also like those women in the fur trade, most bullock hunters' wives' names and activities were not recorded in written sources or even remembered in extant oral traditions.[220]

By 1837, cattle hides were Hawai'i's most valuable export. That year, George Washington Bates estimated hides accounted for $50,000 of Hawai'i's almost $200,000 worth of goods shipped. Thirty thousand dollars or 60 percent of these hides had been purchased from California for resale to Atlantic markets, and the remaining 40 percent, worth $20,000, came from Hawaiian animals. Sandalwood had fallen to just 5 percent of Hawai'i's total exports.[221] These numbers did not take into account the considerable amount of beef sold as provisions to visiting ships. In 1844, the demand of visiting whaleships prompted William French, an important Hawaiian merchant who controlled a domestic herd, to write to Parker and remind him that "we wish to have a good supply [of beef] always kept at Kawaihae [a harbor on the Big Island] as whaleships may call there for it."[222] Merchants like French increasingly moved cattle from port to port within the islands to serve different markets. In 1844, French also shipped sixty-five cattle from Kawaihae, the main port of the Big Island at the time, to Honolulu on the American brig *Lafayette*. As in Cook's and Vancouver's days, shipping live animals remained difficult and uncertain work. When the *Lafayette* foundered on a reef, the crew had to jettison the animals. All the cattle swam to shore, but thirteen died shortly thereafter from the stress, prompting French to sue the *Lafayette* in Hawaiian admiralty court.[223]

As the economy switched from sandalwood to hides and tallow, ali'i continued their increased tributary demands on the commoners. In September 1834, New England missionary Lorenzo Lyons decried "the burden of taxes heaped upon these people!" He then went on to note that "to carry beef, hides, and horns to the shore to ships sent by the king, requires much of the time of the natives and interrupts our schools."[224] Ali'i continued to use their position in Hawai'i's quasi-feudal economy to command common labor for their own interests. At the same time, this quasi-feudal system began to break down, as Hawaiian commoners moved away from the agricultural systems that it was based on. Lyons noted that the Hawaiian farmers he saw carrying beef and hides, "when they find they can procure beef for food by carrying certain quantities of it, they neglect to cultivate the ground."[225] As Hawaiians joined ships, sailed to work on the Pacific coast of North America, left their farms to cut down sandalwood, or carried hides and beef across islands, they moved away from traditional agricultural roles. Some, to Reverend Lyons's lament, compensated for time away from agricultural work by eating some of the provisions they carried. Thus divorced from traditional agricultural activities, it would be a short leap to take up wage work for foreigners in a town like Kawaihae, Lahaina, or Honolulu.[226]

Trans-Pacific Links

Mofras's and Bates's hide and tallow trade statistics reveal how close the links between California and Hawai'i and to the United States had become. In 1838, almost two-thirds (65 percent) of Hawai'i's $207,000 in imports came from the United States or California; $73,000 came from the United States and $61,900 from California. China came in third with $30,000 in imports, while Mexico and "Chili" ranked fourth and fifth, respectively.[227] Mofras noted that California sold $150,000 of its $280,000 in exports to American firms, of which $110,000 went to firms in Boston, and \$40,000 to firms in Hawai'i.[228] Overall, 45 percent of ships traveling to California in the Mexican period hailed from the United States.[229] Forty-two percent of ships that visited California in the first half of the nineteenth century also visited Hawai'i, which was, by far, the most common shared destination. Lima's port of Callao was second with 22 percent of ships that visited California also stopping there.[230]

The government of California earned all its revenue from customs duties, which forced the hide and tallow ships to unload their entire cargoes of manufactured goods at Monterey to pay tariffs on them before coasting to San Francisco, Santa Barbara, San Pedro, and San Diego.[231] Smuggling, according to one American visitor, "is very common."[232] Antonio María Osio, who served as California's customs agent, explained that he had to worry about fraud by "a number of wretched vessels which would arrive from Callao, Lima, the Sandwich Islands, and Central America."[233] In the 1840s, the Monterey customhouse averaged revenues of \$86,000 a year, according to Larkin.[234] Ships also had to pay customs and pilotage fees in Honolulu. Kamehameha started requiring these fees after his own ship carrying sandalwood had to pay a great deal to do business in Canton.[235] Hawaiian elites also worked to participate directly in shipping. As mentioned earlier, Kamehameha developed his own fleet of Western ships, mainly for interisland trade, though he also hoped that some ships would allow direct participation of ali'i in trans-Pacific trade. A ship called the *Becket* sold in 1821 to Kaumuali'i, the semi-independent king of Kaua'i, with the express purpose of participating in the California trade, which it did for the next several years.[236] Of course, purchasing ships drove Hawaiian leaders deeper into the dangerous debt that threatened their sovereignty; it was a calculated risk to take on more short-term debt in the hopes of reaping more of the profits of trans-Pacific trade in the long term.

Honolulu merchant Henry Peirce summed up the typical Pacific merchant voyage in a letter to James Hunnewell suggesting a specific plan for trade in the Pacific market. Peirce advised Hunnewell:

> I think from my present information that a vessel of about 300 tones should come out from Boston with such a cargo as I could pick out. . . . The voyage I should recommend would be for her to come to the Sandwich Islands first . . . from thence to Nootka Sound and down to the coast of California selling all she could at each place; if a cargo of hides could be obtained on freight for America she of course would take them and proceed home round Cape Horn + with such funds as would realize on the cargo brought out from home = if freight could

not be obtained on California—the vessel would in that case proceed to the islands again and from thence to Canton where a freight is always to be got at some rate or other.[237]

Peirce's advice reveals the linkages of the Pacific World and the opportunities they presented. There were ample markets for New England goods in the Pacific, and to fill his hold for the return voyage, Peirce advised Hunnewell to look to California before Canton.

These trade networks extended up the Pacific coast, as well, though not to the same extent. In 1831, for example, the *Ganymede* left Fort Vancouver with a shipment of beaver furs. The ship's next stop was Oahu, where it was to deliver a consignment of timber. John McLoughlin, the chief factor of the Hudson's Bay Company's operations out of Fort Vancouver, instructed the *Ganymede*'s captain that "Mr. Charlton writes me he has a cargo of Hides to send to England. You will take it or any freight Mr Charlton may put on board providing it is not of nature or in the way to injure the Furs."[238] These hides probably came from the British consul's own herds, which often caused trouble grazing on others' property in Honolulu.

Credit also stretched across the ocean in this interlinked Pacific World. Monterey merchant Thomas Larkin's correspondence contains several instances of his use of hides to settle debts with Peirce & Brewer in Honolulu.[239] In February 1842, Larkin sent hides with John Coffin Jones to pay off his debt to an English firm in Mazatlán, Parrott & Co. Larkin asked Jones to buy further merchandise on credit but added that if Jones failed, he would ask John Paty, who planned to take a load of hides to Oahu, to acquire the merchandise.[240]

These emerging international trade networks had profound repercussions on the Pacific World of the early nineteenth century. Lines of credit created social networks built on trust and exchange that connected Hawaiians, Indians, Californios, Englishmen, and Yankees across great distances. A merchant like John Coffin Jones in Honolulu had to depend on a Henry Dalton in San Gabriel, who in turn depended on native laborers and Spanish rancheros like the de la Guerra family. The economies of California, Hawai'i, Mexico, Peru, and Boston all had stakes in these trade networks to varying extents. Lines of credit stretching across the Pacific served to cement the interconnections in the region. If, in America, "the pervasiveness of commercial indebtedness meant that the economic fortunes of antebellum proprietors were inextricably bound up with one another," then transoceanic indebtedness could expand the binding ties of risk.[241]

Trade networks also tied these individuals together in a common cultural world as a shared set of goods from the older Atlantic World, mostly of British (or, increasingly, American) manufacture, served as the basis for the material culture of the entire Pacific region. Historians have demonstrated that trade leads to transformations within a polity, by changing a sense of national identity or personal alliance.[242] Archaeologists often use the presence of trade goods as evidence of cultural change, and most sites in California and Hawai'i demonstrate the heavy influence of foreign material culture.[243] A dig of one early nineteenth-century Southern California ranch showed ceramics from China, Mexico, France, the United States, Scotland, and England alongside native pottery. Paul Chace argued that "the ceramic inventory recovered reveals the international potpourri of material culture on a thriving, early California cattle ranch."[244]

Conclusion

European explorers planted old-world organisms in the eastern Pacific where local pastures and climates fed and watered them. In the 1820s, the harvest of these goods began in earnest. British, American, and French ships participating in the Canton trade became frequent visitors to both areas in the late eighteenth century. Hawai'i's abundant sandalwood became an important product in the trade, and European and American traders rapidly depleted the sandalwood forests in the first two decades of the nineteenth century to supply Chinese markets with lumber and incense. Meanwhile, the California missions utilized their cattle herds to supply international markets with profitable hides and tallow, while revolution and the creation of a politically independent Mexico decreased trade restrictions. As observed by Richard Henry Dana, Hawaiians often signed on as sailors on ships plying the Pacific in the hide and tallow trade, and communities of kanakas developed along the California coast. When the supply of sandalwood began to diminish on the islands and Kamehameha's kapu on cattle came to an end, Hawai'i became another supplier in the hide and tallow trade. As California and Hawai'i became important depots for whaling ships, beef also became a marketable product to crews in port or to whaling ships seeking to replenish their stores, and whaling circuits that included stops in both California and Hawai'i further served to connect the two regions. Because of the opportunities presented by new markets in the Far East and new resources in the eastern Pacific, European powers became increasingly involved in the eastern

Pacific in the nineteenth century, and imperial competition increased between England, the United States, France, Spain, and Russia.

The products of booming cattle populations were the most merchantable product out of California before the gold rush, and the same was true in the Hawaiian Islands between the sandalwood trade and the eventual rise of plantation agriculture. Commercial exchange advanced the power of the United States in the Pacific and laid the groundwork for its imperial expansion to the region. Commercial links promoted international relationships and even shifted local identities in the changing frontiers of California and Hawai'i. Flows of credit, which favored the manufacturing centers over the pastoral peripheries, put more and more power in the hands of creditors from the Anglo world. By offering a viable trade good for the broader world economy, Hawai'i and California gained access to useful and desirable goods, but it was often a Faustian bargain.

While Californio ranchers, Franciscan missionaries, Anglo merchants, and Hawaiian chiefs made many of these deals that would determine the fate of the Pacific, indigenous people always remained at the center of the trade. Some, like Indian vaqueros in California, managed the ranging cattle. Others harvested them, including the Hawaiians who braved charging longhorns to gather animals for Ross Cox. Indians processed the animals in missions, and native Hawaiians loaded them onto merchant ships on California's beaches as well as on their own. The labor of native peoples husbanded, then harvested, these hoof-bound resources at the behest of the mission fathers, rancheros, and Hawaiian chiefs who were all motivated by British and American capital. Thus, Californios, Indians and native Hawaiians underwrote the creation of a Pacific World, united by the ecological imperialism of old-world livestock. The continuing drive for hides created by this international market would lead to the evolution of native labor and the creation of new cattle cultures that utilized the trans-Pacific linkages created by the capital of rival imperial powers.

CHAPTER FIVE

Labor

On December 19, 1850, Fray Filomeno Ursua at the former mission church of Santa Cruz recorded the burial of a man named Joaquin Armas who had died of "morbid cholera."[1] Armas had been born forty-two years earlier to an artillery soldier named Sebastián Armas, and he was baptized on February 28, 1808, at the presidio in San Diego. The officiant recorded his name as Juan Juaquin Nester and noted his ethnicity as razón; Sebastián, who was from Vera Cruz in Mexico, was not a converted Indian.[2] Though his father was a soldier, at some point, Joaquin Armas began to work with the cattle in California, alongside neophytes trained at the mission and sharing in the techniques the fathers had taught them over five decades of colonization, as well as some methods that they had developed themselves. In the 1830s, Armas began to work with another group of indigenous cowboys, harvesting another introduced herd. His will included among his assets (perhaps with some hyperbole) "the work I did for the king of the island of S Dich" amounting to 65,000 pesos.[3] Armas spent much of the last years of his life working to get this money from the royal Hawaiian government; he felt he had earned the money catching cattle on the Big Island in the 1830s. Many people had gathered hides and tallow in Hawai'i over the decades, but Armas was part of a new effort by the ali'i to use vaqueros from California to train Hawaiians how to work with cattle; native Hawaiians were to have their own cowboys.

For months at a time, Joaquin Armas plied the slopes of Mauna Kea, living in primitive shelters exposed to the cool temperatures of the volcano's high altitudes. He worked with a team of native Hawaiian helpers and trainees, and he complained about them in letters to representatives of the government he served; according to Armas, they fired their guns incessantly, damaging the hides of the rare cattle they did hit while scaring away the rest. Despite Armas's complaints, they accomplished much. They gathered some of the hardy feral longhorns into makeshift corrals, so they could harvest them at their leisure. They had to skin the animals as they shot them, and preparing the hides, which was not a part of most vaqueros' duties in California but rather given over to an entirely different set of Indian laborers there, probably took up much of their time. Royal officials demanded that Armas meet high quotas of hides, and he and his assistants had to keep up a fast pace. By 1840, the herds had diminished in size, and Armas's assistants had become quite skilled. Hawaiian officials relieved the Californio of his duties, leaving him with a grievance that he would nurse for the rest of his life. Reading his letters, one gets a sense that Armas was never entirely happy with the working conditions on Mauna Kea, which did not seem to equal the temperate environs of San Diego, where Armas probably learned his trade. He also did not seem to have a great love of the native Hawaiians who either employed or assisted him. Nonetheless, Armas represented a significant transformation in the Hawaiian relationship with cattle and a deepened connection between California and Hawai'i.

While the increasing profits made possible by cattle products in the Pacific encouraged new industries and new connections, the scale of this new production required considerable labor. The European and European-descended populations of Hawai'i and California were not large enough, nor particularly inclined, to supply this labor. The native peoples of Hawai'i and California did much of the work with introduced livestock, and indigenous methods of herding cattle evolved through the ongoing interactions with the animals and through cultural exchanges across the Pacific Ocean, exemplified by the work of Joaquin Armas. Vaqueros created their own native cattle culture in California.[4] As the vaqueros perfected and adapted methods for handling cattle transferred from Mexico, they then transferred these practices to Hawai'i, where they evolved to conform to yet another new physical and cultural environment. The adoption and transfer of cattle cultures created new opportunities for these indigenous peoples to participate independently in cattle-based economies. The ali'i could reap a greater share of the profits from the feral cattle of Hawai'i, and California Indians beyond the narrow band of Spanish colonial control in the region could harvest the animals for their own needs.

However, the majority of cattle harvested in the eastern Pacific in the 1830s and 1840s still entered into the booming hide and tallow trade, a trade dominated by the capital of English and American traders with bases from London and Boston to Callao and Valparaíso to Honolulu, San

Diego, and Monterey. As a result, most of native Hawaiian and California Indian cattle culture served, either directly or indirectly, colonial regimes that controlled native labor. California Indians still served the mission fathers in a paternalistic system, though, increasingly, many worked on independent ranchos for low wages.[5] Many of the Hawaiians still worked in a quasi-feudal system under the command of ali'i who were, in turn, heavily indebted to foreign merchants. In California, both the mission fathers and the rancheros found that they owed increasingly large sums to many of the same hide and tallow traders as the ali'i. Thus, California Indians and native Hawaiians stood at the center of the emergent economic and ecological orders in the eastern Pacific, attempting to use livestock resources to strengthen their positions in the colonial order. Meanwhile, Great Britain and the United States rose to economic ascendancy in the region and gained a significant advantage in the ongoing colonial contests there with the necessary help of native labor.

California Indian Cattle Culture

Before laborers could process cattle into commodities for maritime shipping, work was required to gather and claim animals from the open range. With much of California's economy dependent upon the hide and tallow trade by 1830, Indian labor in the Mexican-controlled coastal areas took on a new annual rhythm. Whereas flowering plants and maturing acorns had previously ordered Indian time, the seasonal rhythms of bovine bodies and market activity now structured vaqueros' lives. The greening pastures that fattened cattle during California's rainy winters foreshadowed the rodeos for the summer matanzas, while summer calving led to rodeos required for the fall herraderos, during which vaqueros branded calves. These annual rituals required native peoples to work closely with animals once completely foreign to the region. With cows and horses spread out over a vast amount of unfenced land, unmonitored for much of the time, these animals were far from tame or docile. Thus, vaqueros required great skill and carefully developed techniques to herd them.

The existence and availability of Indian vaqueros undergirded California's pastoral economy throughout the Spanish and Mexican periods. During the 1830s and 1840s, Indians still made up most of California's vaquero labor force. In 1834, 31,000 vaqueros tended almost 400,000 cattle and more than 60,000 horses.[6] An unknown number of the vaqueros, probably a majority, were converted California Indians or their descendants, while many others were the products of Mexico's mestizo past. Californios did distinguish the Indian vaqueros, especially converts who worked at the mission. While discussing a matanza at Mission San José in 1840, Antonio Osio related that the vaqueros slaughtered two thousand cattle, which exceeded the typical ratio that had led to the rapid increase of the herds in California. He explained that "the missions did not give so much attention to these matters as the regular ranchmen. The vaqueros of the missions were always Indians, who were more careless in the management of stock."[7] Osio explained the reckless slaughter by pointing to the race of the slaughterers. Of course, the amazing multiplication of cattle on mission ranches in the preceding decades challenges this explanation, and a decline of the missions following secularization is a more likely cause for the excessive slaughter. Osio's remarks do reveal, however, the preponderance of Indian vaqueros in the missions and even suggest that these Indians had a managerial role in deciding the number of cattle slaughtered. "Baquero" was not an uncommon surname among the mission neophytes in the early nineteenth century, as this mode of labor apparently defined the converts to some of the fathers and became a central part of their Christian identity.

By the height of the hide and tallow trade, California vaqueros had developed their own uniform and unique repertoire of equipment, based in large part on the cattle culture of northern Mexico. According to California vaquero aficionado Jo Mora, this outfit included a wide-brimmed and low-crowned hat worn over a kerchief and held on despite often violent riding by a chin strap, or barbiquejo. Vaqueros also sported loose colonial shirts, short vests or jackets, red sashes, "long drawers" under knee-length pants, "buttoned up the sides, and . . . open for six inches or so at the bottom."[8] Leather botas, or leggings, covered the vaquero's legs below the knees. They wore low-heeled buckskin and leather shoes with large iron spurs and "a tirador" (a heavy, wide-at-the-hips belt).[9] Vaqueros carried a blanket called a sarape that they could wrap around themselves for protection from the elements. The reata allowed the vaquero to lasso animals and restrain them from a distance. The hilly terrain of California soon prompted an evolution in the saddle; Mora explained that Californios "adopted the center-fire rig. In this rigging the leathers led from the bow and cantle to a point on a vertical line with the center of the saddle, where the látigo ring (rigging) was placed."[10] Vaqueros also sought a woven blanket called a tiruta to make their seats more comfortable. A group of Indians in the Colorado basin wove these blankets from wild introduced sheep that had gone feral in Sonora.[11] Armitas, strips of cowhide hanging from either side of the saddle, protected the vaquero's legs from spiny or clinging vegetation; they replaced the larger armas of cactus-filled northern Mexico and Baja California.[12] Almost all of this equipment, and much of the vaqueros' clothing, consisted of leather or rawhide.

The most important event in the vaqueros' year was the matanza. When Alfred Robinson, working for Bryant & Sturgis, visited a mission in the spring of 1829, he explained that "we found the Indians busy at their annual 'matanzas' or cattle killing," and that "the vaqueros, mounted on splendid horses and stationed at its entrance, performed by far the most important part of the labor."[13] Antonio Osio depicted the matanza as a gathering of bustling workers laboring to process large amounts of the animals for the hide and tallow trade. From July through October, after the vaqueros gathered the cattle, they selected the fattest and slaughtered them on the rodeo grounds "fifty to one hundred at a time."[14] He further explained that "about two days would be occupied in killing fifty cattle, trying out the tallow, stretching the hides and curing the small portion of meat that was preserved."[15] When the herd was gathered, some vaqueros known as nuqueadores would range around the animals and deliver killing blows by cutting the animals' necks with their long knives, sometimes while galloping at full speed.[16] Peladores would skin the animals, and tasajeros would sometimes cut away edible meat to make jerky or salt beef.[17]

Indian women would gather up the animals' fat into sacks to be rendered into tallow, and workers had to watch over the trying vats, which operated at high temperatures and could catch on fire.[18] The missions, ostensibly focused on instilling European cultural norms among the Indians in their effort to Christianize the gentiles, usually had strict gender divisions of labor, though these did fall by the wayside in the name of productivity at times.[19] In the case of the hide and tallow trade, women worked in processing, especially in processing tallow, but they were not allowed to work as vaqueros. Thus, the cattle culture that the Spanish brought to the Indians was highly gendered.

While vaqueros herded and slaughtered the cattle and other workers skinned the animals, dried the hides, or worked the trying vats, buzzards scavenged the rest. Osio estimated that hides and tallow (as well as manteca and other secondary products) made up about 200 pounds of each animal.[20] An adult would yield 75 to 100 pounds of tried tallow and 40 to 50 pounds of tried lard; the rest rotted on the rodeo grounds, and many visitors to California noted the cattle bones strewn about California's ranches. Guadalupe Vallejo recalled, "Every Mission and ranch in old times had its calaveras, its 'place of skulls,' its slaughter corral, where cattle and sheep were killed by the Indian butchers."[21] He added that "grizzly bears, which were very abundant in the country—for no one ever poisoned them, as the American stock raisers did after 1849—used to come by night to the ravines near the slaughter-corral where the refuse was thrown by the butchers."[22]

Of all of these labors, the rodeo itself required the most skill and represented the greatest adaptation to California's new faunal regime. The semiferal nature of the unfenced, free-ranging cattle ensured that the rodeo would remain a vital part of California pastoralism throughout the Spanish and Mexican eras. Osio explained, "Although the cattle that belonged to the various ranchos were wild, yet they were under training to some extent, and were kept in subjection by constant rodeos."[23] Upon the establishment of a new ranch, vaqueros would frequently drive the cattle from the nearby pastures to the rodeo ground to get the animals acquainted with the journey, then allow them to disperse after a few hours. These drives occurred two or three times a week, and then less and less frequently, until the cattle "came to know" the rodeo ground. Osio explained that once the cattle were familiar, "Then, whenever the herd was wanted, all that was necessary for the vaqueros to do was, say twenty-five or thirty of them, to ride out into the hills and valleys and call the cattle, shouting and screaming to them, when the animals would immediately run to the accustomed spot."[24] Farmers, who began to increase production and landholdings in the 1840s, had to find creative ways to deal with marauding cattle. In the Livermore and Napa Valleys of northern California, Anglo-American farmers like John Marsh and Robert Livermore hired Miwok Indians as "human fences" that would walk in a line and sweep cattle out of their land.[25] Vaqueros also used other bovine social behaviors to aid in further taming the animals. They employed specially trained cattle, called cabestros, to help calm the more recalcitrant animals. To make a cabestro, vaqueros took an especially tame and calm specimen of cattle and drilled holes in its horns, which they strung a strip of leather through. After capturing a wild animal with the lasso, vaqueros could attach the unruly animal to the cabestro with the strip and allow the cabestro's calming influence to take hold.

Establishing and maintaining ownership was a paramount challenge among the free-ranging cattle. The Californios utilized brands and earmarks to this end, and each mission or rancher put these marks on record with local administrators. Thus, this ritual herradero, or branding each September or October, complemented the matanza, as vaqueros rounded up the cattle in an annual rodeo and marked the young calves with a hot iron.[26] Osio remarked that rancheros would notify their

California Method of Roping Cattle, 1839 (from Forbes, *California*;
courtesy C. C. Pierce Collection, the Huntington Library)

neighbors when they held a rodeo so that they could send vaqueros to cut
any of their own stray cattle from the gathered herd.[27] Some municipalities, such as San José in the 1830s, mandated community participation
in rodeos.[28] This expanded the labor base that rancheros could draw on
for the most taxing gatherings of animals and allowed all the ranchers to
separate their cattle at once.

Visitors to the missions testified to the skills that Indians utilized in
managing their cattle. When the famed mountain man Jedediah Smith
visited one of Mission San Gabriel's ranches in the fall of 1826 during his
overland trip to California, he noted that he was "was kindly received by
an elderly man an Indian who spoke Spanish and immediately asked me
if I would have a Bullock killed."[29] After he accepted the offer, "away rode
two young Indians in a moment. . . . In a short time the Indians returned
bringing a cow as fast as she could gallop. She was held between the two
horsemen by ropes thrown over her horns and having the other end fast
to the Pomel [*sic*] of the Spanish Saddle . . . she was forced along without the power of resistance."[30] Alfred Robinson described the skill with
which the Indians captured animals to be slaughtered for hides, stating
that "when the mayordomo pointed out the animal to be seized, instantly

a lasso whirled through the air, and fell with dexterous precision upon the horns of the ill-fated beast."[31] Indian vaqueros also demonstrated their technique in handling horses and cattle and their familiarity with the animals in games. One common game, carrera del gallo, challenged a rider to grab a live rooster buried to its head out of the ground at a full gallop.[32] Vaqueros also roped large and dangerous grizzly bears and sometimes pitted them against bulls; roping a bear posed severe risks as the roper had to contend not only with a large and powerful predator but also with a very frightened horse. In 1837, the hide trader Faxon Dean Atherton witnessed a bullfight at Mission San Rafael to celebrate the anniversary of the mission's founding. The participants engaged in the Spanish tradition of provoking a bull by waving a cloth, and then avoiding the dangerous longhorn's charges; in California, the participants often challenged the bull while on horseback. As he watched the spectacle, Atherton noticed that "the Indians showed much greater courage and dexterity than the whites, they taking a blanket and going on foot would shake it [in] the bulls [sic] eye, and as he rushed toward them would throw it over his horns and jump onside with an agility truly astonishing notwithstanding which some three or four got thrown down and trampled upon pretty severely."[33]

Bullfights were not the only context in which vaqueros faced danger from the animals that they managed; wrangling cattle offered a variety of potentially deadly hazards. Mission records note that a neophyte vaquero with the Christian name of Gil died from "a bad fall from a horse" on July 4, 1824, at Mission San José.[34] Another neophyte vaquero, Viador, died in 1836 when he "fell riding too violently through the countryside."[35] José Antonio, a neophyte from Suisun, "died suddenly . . . without sacraments" shortly after saddling his horse for a ride to Napa. The cause of death is unclear, but he "spent his last hour in the presence of some other vaqueros."[36] This notation hints at the camaraderie of mission vaqueros and the comfort they may have provided in the absence of a priest, even if it fails to explain what happened to the victim.

Horses played a central role in the management of large herds of semi-feral animals that could outrun or seriously injure a laborer on foot. In 1837, a visiting U.S. Army officer, Colonel Phillip Edwards, stated, "Everything possible is here performed on horseback. If a man drive oxen he must ride."[37] Jedediah Smith noted that it was "the custom in this country as I have since learned to keep a horse or horses . . . constantly tied at the door Saddled and Bridled and of course ready to mount at a moments [sic] warning."[38] Horses had quickly become abundant in California, and some of the largest herds ran wild in the interior. Osio explained that "there were large bands of wild horses in the valley of the San Joaquin . . . frequently during summertime, young men, the sons of the rancheros, would go in companies of eight or ten or twelve to the valley on their best and fleetest steeds to capture a number of these wild horses and bring them to the ranchos."[39] The interior served as a reservoir of animal wealth for rancheros and Indians alike (and as a reservoir of animal wealth for Indians outside the coastal Spanish colonial sphere). According to Osio, on the ranches, "horses were never stabled. They were broken for the saddle only and were used almost wholly for herding cattle."[40] In the labor-scarce world of California ranching, horses existed mainly as tools to manage the mobile wealth of cattle herds and did little labor as draft animals. Vaqueros left them relatively wild. Californians "used up [the horses] very fast," as "they were numerous and cheap, and the owners placed no restraint upon the vaqueros, who rode without a particle of regard for the horses."[41]

Despite this well-developed culture for using one old-world animal, horses, to transform another old-world animal, cattle, into a commodity for Pacific trade, Anglo-Americans critics saw missed opportunities in the Californians' management of cattle. Alfred Robinson observed that there were few dairy products in California despite the large population of cattle and the dominance of cattle ranching. In his *Life in California*, Robinson related that "it may be supposed they are totally ignorant of its [dairy products'] value: not so; for since the introduction of foreign settlers, they have been well instructed in the art of making both butter and cheese; and it is only from sheer indolence that these articles are not more plentiful."[42] There was waste at several points in this harvesting process, from the overgrazed grasslands to the mountains of skulls to the lack of a dairy industry. This was not the product of indolence, however. The cattle industry in California was extensive rather than intensive; it used scarce labor to provide a narrow range of products with international demand.[43] A few skilled laborers worked to turn thousands of cattle into the most valuable goods, and they did not have the spare industry to develop these secondary products. Robinson saw a missed opportunity, but really he was viewing the extraction of a colonial commodity. Internal dairy markets were unlikely to develop under these circumstances.[44]

California Indians and Rancho Labor

For the ranchers and merchants of California, a chief concern was managing and controlling the skilled Indian laborers, including Indian vaqueros, who made their engagement in Pacific cattle economies possible. When a farmer named James A. Forbes established a ranch near Santa Clara in partnership with Thomas Larkin in 1844, he complained that he could not complete a transaction for seventy-four mission cattle at three pesos a head because "at the present time it is not possible for the Mission to deliver these cattle for want of horses, and 'vaqueros' who are at the Tulares on their accustomed liberty."[45] "Tulares" refers to Indian-controlled land, and Forbes's quote demonstrates the close connection many Indian vaqueros maintained to these lands and lifeways. These Indians, at least, were at ease crossing back and forth between the coastal world of Spanish settlement and the interior world of the Indian Tulares, even as their work centered around animals that had been unknown two generations earlier.

The free movement of these Indians between their mission work and the Tulares raises questions about how the Spanish organized and controlled Indian labor. Most historians of Spanish and Mexican California have emphasized the unfree nature of Indian labor in nineteenth-century California, and not without good reason. One economic historian has described the ranching regime on California's ranches as "a combination of slavery, peonage, and free labor."[46] Californios made extensive use of convict labor; Indians arrested by presidial soldiers had to work without pay.[47] Mission Indians also rarely received remuneration as they were theoretically working for their own good and the benefit of the entire mission community.

Anglo-American laborers were quick to seize on the exploitation of Indians in California, and more than one compared California's labor regime with their own South. American fur-trapper James Clyman observed, "The Mexicans do not labor themselves the native Indians perform all the labor and are kept in slavery much like the Negroes of the Southern states."[48] Wilkes argued that "the Californians, as a people, must be termed cruel in their treatment to their wives, as well as to the Indians; and in a still greater degree, of course, to their slaves and cattle."[49] He continued this analogy between the treatment of Indian laborers and livestock later in the account, stating that "the Indian's life in the eye of the rulers scarcely exceeds that of one of the wild cattle."[50] Alfred Robinson explained that in a typical mission, "in the interior square might be seen the various tribes at work, presenting a scene not dissimilar to some of the working departments of our state prisons."[51] Richard Henry Dana stated that outside the missions "the Indians . . . do all the hard work, two or three being attached to the better house; and the poorest persons are able to keep one at least; for they have only to feed them."[52]

Some Anglo-Americans' admiration of mission productivity suggests that they believed that forced labor regimes served to motivate the otherwise indolent Indians. In 1837, the hide and tallow trader Faxon Dean Atherton complimented Don José Jesús Vallejo, a new Californio administrator of Mission San Juan Bautista, for improving one of the poorer missions. Among Vallejo's accomplishments, Atherton noted that at the mission "the Indians are now kept at work, the cattle are kept tame."[53] Despite Anglo-American comparisons of California's labor regime with slavery, their own ideas about the employment of Indian laborers shared many of its characteristics.

Many Indians were subjected to forced labor regimes in California, but others willingly labored for wages or accepted work within the supposed communal system of the missions.[54] Indian vaqueros had incredible mobility and had gained valuable equipment from the missions. They could escape to the interior on horseback if they felt mistreated, and, in fact, some Indians did so, like the Yokut rebel Estanislao. The Indians from Santa Clara who took their seasonal liberty in the Tulares need not return. These Indians did return, and they did so because they profited from, and maybe even enjoyed, their work as vaqueros. Increasingly, they could work at independent ranches and get paid, and many probably made informal arrangements to get compensation for their labor. They probably traded goods received in compensation with Tulares Indians, and thus became important bridges between California's two worlds with their own identities shifting as they moved back and forth. The mere fact that they could ride horses set them apart from other neophytes in the early nineteenth century. A Luiseño Indian named Luis César recalled that the only converted Indians allowed to ride were "alcaldes, corporals, and vaqueros." These Indians went on horse or "a caballo" like the Californio gente de razón.[55] Vaqueros, because of their skill sets and mobility, received more in payment for their labor and linked interior Indians communities to the wider world of Pacific exchange.

Some Indian vaqueros stepped into a more mercantile role. As California became more commercially oriented, vaqueros began to work closely with merchants alongside their traditional work on ranches. Some supercargoes had vaqueros on permanent retainer to care for and transport their horses as they traveled back and forth between California's ports. These vaqueros helped develop networks between the supercargoes and the rancheros, and Osio remembered that the supercargo's vessel's "approach was sometimes announced by the vaquero." This phrasing suggests that the vaquero played an intermediary role in the ongoing trade between rancheros or managers of mission herds and hide and tallow merchants.[56]

Indians increasingly worked outside the mission system, which began to decline in the 1830s as independent ranchos flourished. In the 1840s, foreigners, most of whom encountered California's cattle economy through the hide and tallow trade, increasingly gained their own land grants and started cattle ranches. Since they established many of these newer ranches in California's interior, where Indians made up an overwhelming ratio of the population, foreign ranchers depended on Indian labor to manage their ranches and their animal resources as much or even more than the Californios.[57] One of the first foreigners to establish a major ranch, New Englander Abel Stearns, founded his Rancho Los Alamitos near the pueblo of Los Angeles in 1840. He includes several "baqueros" in an 1843 "cuenta de los sirvientes" for April 1843, including "Alejo, Fortunato, Fernando and Servino."[58] The fact that Stearns referred to most of these workers solely by a first name gives some clue to their ethnic origin, and the fact that he kept a monthly roster suggests that his workers were often transient.

While missions utilized communal work, these independent ranchos theoretically operated under capitalistic forms of labor. However, in cash-poor California, as in many frontier societies, rancheros often paid for services in goods, and most found ways to make the accounts settle in their favor. Many Indian laborers found that they had squandered their wages in trade for hard alcohol sold by their employers. They labored under a form of debt peonage as they found it impossible to stay ahead of the debts they accumulated in the form of room, board, supplies, and drink. The London-born and Peru-based hide trader Henry Dalton established the Rancho Azusa in the San Gabriel Valley in 1843 and kept detailed records of the ranch's operations for the next forty years.[59] While the daily recorded activities often included killing a bullock, or driving the herd to or from pasturage, Dalton's records also show the constant presence of Indian laborers, including "Jose Viejo—indio," "Juan Pablo—indio," and "Francisco—alcalde indio," the last showing a carryover from the mission system of choosing Indians as alcaldes or overseers.[60]

His balance sheets also reveal that these Indians acquired significant debts that they had to work to repay.[61] Alcohol served as one of the main causes of such debt. For instance, liquor like "aguardiente negro" appeared on the balance sheets against the earnings of one "Hipolito" at seven reales a bottle—more than a day's wages.[62] On Sunday, he typically wrote "Indios borrachos" in his notebook to indicate that his resting laborers were drunk.[63] The laborers abused alcohol to the extent that it occasionally led to violence. On July 26, 1845, Dalton noted that he sent two "bacqueros [*sic*]" to find some missing steers, but "Juan Bautista fell in with another Indian, they both got intoxicated and the result is that Juan Bautista killed the other in fighting."[64] Dalton's description is vague, but it appears that one of his Indian vaqueros had killed another Indian, perhaps while drunk on the job or after becoming drunk upon returning to the ranch.

In 1840, the Swiss immigrant Johann Augustus Sutter obtained a large land grant near the junction of the American River and the Sacramento River in Alta California's Central Valley. There he built New Helvetia, one of the largest and most famous of the foreign-owned ranches. Though Sutter focused on establishing agriculture in the Central Valley, he also ran a large ranching operation to feed his laborers and subsidize his agricultural pursuits.[65] In 1841, Wilkes observed that he had built "extensive corrals" and "the extent of his stock amounts to about one thousand horses, two thousand five hundred cattle, and about one thousand sheep, many of which are now to be seen around his premises, giving them an appearance of civilization."[66]

Sutter had to depend on native labor to run his operation at New Helvetia. He had visited Hawai'i before establishing himself in California, and he had networked with hide traders there, meeting herder William French and merchant William Sturgis. He received a letter of introduction from John Coffin Jones, another major player in the trans-Pacific hide and tallow trade. He arrived in California with eight Hawaiian men and two Hawaiian women.[67] They helped build his fort, and they remained in the area. He also drew heavily from the nonmission Indians of the central valley.[68] Isidora of the Suisuns later recounted to a researcher working for Hubert Howe Bancroft that Sutter sent Indians to "trade liquor for hides, pelts, and dried fish."[69] Along the way, Sutter also accumulated cattle for his ranch through suspect business deals, as Isidora also claimed that "my compadre Peralta and friend Bernales had many cattle. Sutter tricked them and took everything but paid for nothing."[70]

Sutter used brute force to control Indian labor. He utilized corporal punishment, including flogging, to compel labor from recently converted Indians, and he pursued and imprisoned runaways.[71] At the same time, he relied on trade goods to compensate Indians for their labor. Wilkes stated that at New Helvetia "labour is paid for in goods."[72] Sutter sometimes paid Indians with glass beads, a common trade good on American frontiers for centuries, but, in isolated California, even this simple good could run scarce. In an 1846 letter, Sutter complained, "I have to pay the Indians with something else as I cannot get beads."[73] When glass beads were scarce or insufficient, Sutter utilized other goods, including alcohol.

Sutter's herds required vaqueros, and he had a significant supply of skilled cowboys at New Helvetia. Many of the Indians in the Sacramento Valley were not mission Indians, and it is unclear how these vaqueros received their training. Did Sutter hire Indian vaqueros from the coastal missions or did he train local Indians to manage the cattle? Records do not indicate the origins of his vaqueros, though he probably would have needed at least a few mission Indians to train his workforce. We do know that he had a large enough reservoir to hire out his vaqueros. An undated bill from Sutter to the businessman William Leidesdorff included the services of Sutter's "baqueros" at one peso a day.[74]

As the settlements in California spread inland from the coastal camino real, cattle and vaqueros again led the way in opening up frontiers. As Sutter took control over new territory to the east of existing settlements around San Francisco Bay, the Vallejos established ranching operations to the north. Mariano Guadalupe Vallejo and Salvador Vallejo were the sons of a Spanish officer in Monterey who rose to the position of alcalde of San José. Mariano Vallejo established the Rancho Petaluma near the northern mission of San Francisco de Solano in Sonoma in 1834. Shortly thereafter, his brother Salvador Vallejo extended this frontier ranching empire northeast into what is now Lake County. Around 1840, Salvador Vallejo took ten trained vaqueros into the Indian-controlled territory with a herd of cattle, and at Clear Lake they constructed the housing and corrals needed to run a working ranch.[75] An early historian of Lake County noted that by the late 1840s "the stock had multiplied until the valley was full to overflowing with cattle, which had long since become as wild as deer, and about as hard to handle."[76] He also explained, "The Indians did all the work about the place. They constructed the corral, built the house, and did the vaqueroing."[77] Thus, the Vallejos extended the influence of the Californios by replicating the biological introductions that had underlain the foundation of Alta California while relying on the labor of Indians who had adapted cattle culture in the region to manage the animals. These frontier ranches continued to connect to the hide and tallow markets of the eastern Pacific, accessed by the relatively close San Francisco Bay. Charles Wilkes observed these operations in 1841 and recorded, "Salvadore [sic] Vallejo is engaged . . . particularly in raising cattle, which, under the governor, he has especial privilege of supplying to vessels, which he does at prices that ensure a handsome profit."[78]

In 1849, Salvador Vallejo turned his Lake County operation over to two Anglo-Americans, goldminers Charles Stone and Andrew Kelsey, who utilized Pomo Indian laborers, including vaqueros, "as slave labor of the worst kind."[79] An account by Agustín, one of their Indian vaqueros, noted that "they had always had good food in abundance when working for the Spaniards," but under Stone and Kelsey, the Indians starved. They soon grew rebellious, and the vaqueros conspired to kill their new overseers.[80] Nearby Anglo-American settlers attacked and killed sixty to one hundred (or more) of the Indians in retribution.[81] This violent incident demonstrates that vaqueros had received better compensation in the past, but their economic position became more tenuous as Anglo-American capital began to assert its control over these borderlands.

Vaqueros and Paniolo in Hawai'i

Herman Melville's 1847 novel *Omoo* dealt mostly with a fictionalized account of the author's time in Tahiti, but he digressed for a chapter to discuss cattle in Hawai'i. After a brief overview of feral longhorns in Tahiti, where "the natives stand in great awe of these cattle; and for this reason are excessively timid in crossing the island," Melville changed his focus to the "vast herds" of these "useful quadrupeds" on the Big Island of Hawai'i.[82] He explained that upon "learning the value of the hides in commerce, [Hawaiians] began hunting the creatures that wore them; but being very fearful and awkward in a business so novel, their success was small."[83] He then noted that "it was not until the arrival of a party of Spanish hunters, men regularly trained to their calling upon the plains of California, that the work of the slaughter was fairly begun."[84] Finally, he painted the vivid picture of these "showy fellows. . . . Mounted upon trained Indian mares, these heroes pursued their prey up to the very base of the burning mountains; making the profoundest solitudes ring with their shouts, and flinging the lasso under the very nose of the vixen goddess Pelee."[85] While Melville played up native Hawaiian superstitions and ignored the diverse array of people profiting from cattle in Hawai'i before and during this time period, the central idea of this account is true. Vaqueros from California played a crucial role in the harvest of Hawaiian cattle beginning in the 1830s.

When King Liholiho died from measles while visiting England in 1824, his eleven-year-old brother ascended the throne and took the name Kamehameha III. Kamehameha's wife, Ka'ahumanu, served as queen regent until her death in 1832, but Kamehameha III ruled Hawai'i longer than any other monarch. He served during a period of increasing foreign influence and the continuing erosion of traditional Hawaiian society, but he also worked to retain sovereignty and wrest the Hawaiian economy from its spiraling debt to European and American merchants.

By the 1830s, Kamehameha III sought to profit more directly from the resource of feral cattle now roaming in the tens of thousands across the islands. The cattle population had continued to expand, and the forward-looking king was not satisfied with the royal and chiefly dependence on transient foreign laborers to harvest this resource. Furthermore, the same mounting debts to foreign traders that had driven Hawaiian leaders to harvest the islands' sandalwood now drove them to expand their participation in the hide and tallow trade. Maritime traffic with California had alerted the king to the existence of the California vaqueros' facility with horse and lasso, and their ability to gather and slaughter large numbers of the animals to feed the hide and tallow trade.[86] Hawaiians, like those who worked with Richard Henry Dana in the hide houses of California near the mission herds, probably brought this news themselves.[87] It seems that he actively sought word of skilled California vaqueros on ships from the North America coast, or perhaps even sent word for some to come over to the islands for work.

Whether the king wanted more native involvement in the management of cattle, more expertise, or simply more laborers to exploit the feral herds is unclear, as are most of the details of this transaction with California. Joseph Brennan, a historian of Hawai'i's largest ranch, related the oral tradition that "knowhow was at a premium, and it was fortunate that the three celebrated Mexican-Spanish cowboys—Kossuth, Louzeida, and Ramon—had been brought over from the mainland to work the ranges and break Hawaiians into a more efficient way of handling cattle, horses, and all the equipment essential to the business. The newcomers first started working out of the Hanaipoe on the slopes of Mauna Kea just twelve miles east of Waimea."[88] These vaqueros completed unfinished business begun by Vancouver in 1793. The British explorer had introduced an alien species of domestic animal and encouraged the Hawaiians to let it run wild. He failed to import the cultural traditions related to the longhorn cattle that populated California, which included methods for capturing wild cattle and managing herds. This failure created another avenue of "escape" for the animal that encouraged its invasiveness. With the importation of California's cattle culture, native Hawaiians gained their own cultural expertise in handling the animals. The Hawaiians referred to the vaqueros as españoles—or "paniolo" in Hawaiian—despite their origins in the Americas. This term eventually encompassed all cowboys working in the Hawaiian Islands.

Few, if any, contemporary records for the activities of Kossuth, Louzeida, and Ramon exist, though accounts agree that they came from California and they arrived in 1832.[89] Brothers James and Isaac Louzada were active on the islands during this time, and James Louzada became involved in ranching in Waimea decades later. "Ramon" may refer to the Ramon family from northwestern Mexico, including Frederico Ramon Baesa, who had a Yaqui Indian wife named Vincenta Romero.[90] Kossuth remains a mystery.[91] On April 27, 1833, an American merchant in Honolulu named Stephen Reynolds noted in his journal that the "Brig Neo sailed for Hawaii [the Big Island] with horses & Spaniards to catch bullock for the king."[92] Some accounts claim that it was the governor of the Big Island, John Adams Kuakini, and not the king, who requested the service of vaqueros from California, and it is clear that he supervised efforts to rationalize the management of the herds on his island.

The early Hawaiian vaquero of whom we know the most is the aforementioned Joaquin Armas, whose grievances against the Hawaiian government provide a paper trail of his activities on the islands.[93] A passport application to return to California from Hawai'i in the fall of 1848 (perhaps to look for gold) referred to Armas as a "native of San Diego" and described Armas as five feet and eight inches tall with "black" eyes and hair and a "dark physiognomy."[94] Armas related, "In the month of May 1831 I came to Oahu in the British whale ship *Harriet*. The King hearing from the Captain of his having a man in the ship who was expert on catching wild bullock came on board and conversed with me on the subject and asked me to go on shore and live with him."[95] Armas explained that he had planned to sail on to England, but the king promised "to give me imployment [*sic*] his friendship and protection," and "thinking this would be a good opportunity of getting a livelihood and having the King's promise to befriend me I assented and went on shore with him."[96]

Armas, whom the Hawaiians knew as "Wokine" or "Huakini Paniolo," worked for the king for nine years, capturing bullocks, gathering hides and tallow for the world market, and training his native Hawaiian assistants. He stated that after seven months on Oahu, he journeyed to the Big Island "to catch wild Bullock which work I continued to perform for nearly nine years being in the mountain for four or five months at a time exposed to cold and hunger."[97] He also noted that the king placed pressure on him to meet deadlines and quotas, as he was "frequently pressed by the king for a specified number of hides which was to be at Oahu by a stated time," and thus he "was frequently obliged to work at night running the risk of my life in capturing wild bulls and receiving great injury in body from the many falls I had from horses."[98] Nevertheless, Armas had great success in the harvesting of the wild cattle at Waimea on the Big Island. He claimed that "in this dangerous work . . . I returned him [the king] cattle hides and tallow to the amount of sixty thousand six hundred dollars which I can prove by receipt and documents from other hands and other individuals."[99] Correspondence shows that Armas remained under the king's close supervision, and the vaquero notified his royal employer of the numbers of animals gathered and traded with foreign merchants.[100]

Training Hawaiians to do the work of vaqueros was the most lasting facet of Armas's work for the king, and, according to Armas, the most frustrating. Armas claimed that the Hawaiians were overzealous, and he complained in an 1838 letter to the king that "I should particularly wish to see you concerning the Kanakas shooting, they go all about Pens shooting and frightening the Bullocks away. If there is not a stop put to it I shant be able in a short time to get any this side of the mountain."[101] Guns, which could disperse herds and damage hides, were not a part of the cattle culture that Armas brought with him, in contrast to the practices of some of the bullock hunters who had harvested cattle on the islands before. Despite these complaints that Hawaiians acted recklessly, they made clear progress managing the cattle. By the end of Armas's career on Hawai'i in the early 1840s, native Hawaiians threatened to displace him. In his 1843 letter, Armas claimed that "some time ago there was a man sent by the king to Hawaii for the purpose of working with me [but] I objected to it as he knew nothing of the business and as he was a native of these islands."[102] He resented the native intrusion into his realm of cattle management, and his raising the man's ethnicity as a rationale for his refusal adds context to Armas's earlier complaints about Hawaiian workers. Armas explained that his objections "offended the king, for in a short time afterward Kekauluohi [Ka'ahumanu III, the kuhina nui, or prime minister] came to Waimea and took everything from me Cattle I had tamed Oxen I had broken into work and Horses I had purchased with my hard labour and left me penniless." The intervention of the prime minister herself suggests the importance of Armas's operation to the government.

Armas subsequently wrote to the British consul to arbitrate a return of some of these assets, and he noted the "fidelity with which I served the King after spending a great portion of my life in inriching [*sic*] him and injuring my constitution in his service to be turned adrift as a vagabond in poverty."[103] He also noted that Kekauluohi had not even paid the "people I had imployed [*sic*] to do the King's work," and that "had it not been for Governor Adam's kindness in giving me employment with which he paid me handsomely for, I should have been destitute."[104] Armas revealed in passing the close oversight of the ranching industry by the aliʻi nui and the royal family through his description of John Adams Kuakini's involvement in his work. This passage also suggests that Armas paid the native workers for their labor, although it is unclear if they received a portion of the profits, part of the increase of the herd, or wages. In any of these cases, Kekauluohi's seizure of his animals would have prevented Armas from making good on his promises to pay.

Armas as "Huakini Paniolo" received land in the whaling stop of Lahaina on the island of Maui, and he worked in Lahaina as a clerk in a liquor store with his brother Felipe Armas in the 1840s. As mentioned, he returned to California at the start of the gold rush and died of cholera two years later. While Armas may have felt frustrated by his employment as a cowboy in Hawaiʻi, he and the other California vaqueros left a lasting impression on native Hawaiians by transferring a cattle culture that would better equip them to deal with the multiplying exotic species.

Anglo-American residents and visitors to Hawaiʻi noted that the vaqueros introduced to help manage the wild cattle had a dramatic effect on Hawaiian culture. In 1892, Curtis J. Lyons (Lorenzo Lyons's son) presented a paper to the Hawaiian Historical Society in which he fondly remembered the presence of the vaqueros, "whom I saw in my boyhood."[105] Addressing the Historical Society on these early memories, Lyons remarked that "I may be pardoned for recounting a number of instances of the introduction of Mexican and South American ideas and habits amongst Hawaiians," before launching into a romantic description of the vaqueros he saw in his youth.[106]

He begins with the vaqueros' tools and equipment, stating that "he brought with him the Mexican saddle in all its rich adornment of stamped bull-hide leather and stirrups broad winged. He brought the jingling spur with bells of hand-wrought steel. He brought the hair-rope in strands of alternate black and white, and the hand-whirled wheel for twisting it; also the hand-wrought bit, not so crude as it looked to be, and a necessity in bullock-hunting."[107] Lyons moved on to discuss the vaqueros' clothes: "Do not I remember him well, this Spaniard, the red bandanna handkerchief tied over his head under the broad flapping hat with rim upturned in front? Did not the serape . . . commend itself to our common sense as a defense against the rain?"[108]

These descriptions admittedly do more to convey a heroic, archetypal character recalled through the lens of decades of memory (Lyons remarks that "all this . . . back in the thirties, long before the birth of the modern cow-boy") than to trace the subtle interaction or influence of a foreign culture.[109] However, Lyons's reverent and laudatory phrasing illustrates the importance of the vaquero figure in his own view of the Hawaiian past. He ended this description of "Spanish influence" by asserting, "These Spaniards are the men that taught the Hawaiians the conquest of the wild herds of Mauna Kea. Not tens, but hundreds of thousands, of skeletons have bestrewed the sides of that old mountain."[110] Lyons equated the immense success of bullock hunting, and thus the cattle industry and the marketing of beefs, hides, and tallow, with the vaqueros' teachings. The costumes and equipment of the Spanish cowboys filtered through to their Hawaiian students and enabled the "conquest" of vast wild herds. The first introduction of cattle was incomplete until accompanied by the vaqueros' material culture.

Lyons did not stand alone in his appreciation for the vaqueros' equipment and techniques, or their overall appearance. In an earlier account, nearly contemporary with the vaqueros' 1832 arrival, Francis Allyn Olmsted prefigured some of Lyons's observations. Olmsted came from a wealthy background and was the son of a professor; however, shortly after graduating from Yale in 1839 he took passage on a whaling ship bound for the Pacific as therapy for a chronic illness. He recorded his travels and eventually published them in *Incidents of a Whaling Voyage*. While visiting the "Sandwich Islands," Olmsted recorded a hike in Waimea. His account includes a picturesque description of vaqueros that is more immediate than Lyons's:

> Here a novel scene presented itself to us. In front of the door, a bright fire was blazing in a cavity in the earthen floor, displaying in strong light the dark features of the natives congregated around it in their grotesque attitudes. Immediately back of these, a group of fine looking men, in a peculiar costume, were leaning against the counter of the store. Some of these were Spaniards from California, and they were all attired in the *poncho*, an oblong blanket of various colors, having a hole in the middle through which the head is thrust. The pantaloons are open from the knee downwards on the outside, with a row of dashing gilt buttons along the outside seam. A pair of boots armed with prodigiously long spurs completed their costume. They were *bullock hunters*, employed in capturing the wild bullocks that roam the mountains.[111]

Olmsted showed a great deal of admiration for the bullock hunters, especially in contrast to the "grotesque" natives arrayed on the floor beneath them. The hunters, meanwhile, were "fine looking" and "dashing." Perhaps Olmsted was also relieved to see fellow Europeans amid the "savages" he perceived in Hawai'i, but he does remark that "some," not all, of the bullock hunters were "Spaniards of California." We can only speculate on the ethnicity of the remaining "fine looking men." A variety of Anglos from Britain, the United States, and Australia were active bullock hunters in Hawai'i before this time, but it seems that Olmsted would have commented on such a presence. They may also have been native Hawaiians already trained by the vaqueros: observing a group of hunters striking out the next day, Olmsted commented on the differing riding styles of "natives" and "cavaliers."[112] Either way, the skill of these cowboys in lassoing the wild cattle impressed Olmsted as much as their appearance.

He also noted that the Spaniards had already made an appreciable difference in suppressing the dangers posed by feral longhorn cattle. He explained that "the bullocks of the mountains were till within a year or two, very numerous and savage, so that traveling among the mountains was attended with great danger."[113] The vaqueros also utilized similar techniques to those used in California for taming wild cattle. Olmsted stated, "The bullocks to be marked were driven into a pen towards which we directed our steps. They were noble animals, and had been tamed by tying them singly with tame cattle for a time."[114] These vaqueros used cabestros in Hawai'i as in California, and they also gathered the animals for branding. "The skill with which the lasso is thrown" impressed Olmsted, who narrated that "one of the bullocks was selected from the herd, and in an instant, the lasso was firmly entangled around his horns or legs, and he was thrown down and pinioned. The burning brand was then applied, and after sundry bellowings and other indications of disapprobation, the poor animal was released."[115] On the day of Olmsted's observances, the vaqueros branded forty cattle that they would then drive to the coast and embark on a ship bound for Honolulu.

In 1845, Walter Colton, an officer in the U.S. Navy, observed paniolo at work on Oahu while stopping over on a voyage to California. In the "deep, green valley" of 'Ewa, he noted that "herds were seen cropping the grass or ruminating in the shade."[116] In the "bosom" of the valley, Colton observed "a spacious enclosure, into which the cattle, horses, and sheep are driven at night—to protect them, as one would suppose, from ravenous beasts; but there are none in the island: the object is to keep them from straying off among the mountains, and becoming too wild for domestic purposes; for every thing here runs instinctively to wildness."[117] The labor-intensive method of corralling the animals represented a dramatic change from typical cattle operations in California, but the pastoralists in ʻEwa, despite the lack of predators, apparently drove the animals in every night to prevent them from going too feral. The nightly drive may have been a response to the long wildness of the longhorn cattle, although it may also have represented an attempt to prevent further incursions into the nearby taro plantations of which ʻEwa's residents had complained in a petition (discussed in chapter 2). Either way, it demonstrates the new and more intense management of Hawaiʻi's bovine resources following the training of the paniolo and the existence of a labor force capable of effecting such management.

Colton also witnessed the paniolo's use of some of the California vaqueros' techniques. He stated that as his party rode through the valley, they "soon fell in with a herd of cattle, which two or three noisy kanackas [sic] on horseback were driving to their enclosure for the night. When a beast attempted to break away, one of these started in pursuit; and instead of heading off the animal, brought him up with the lasso, which he threw, with surprising dexterity, over his horns."[118] A protestant missionary on the islands, E. B. Robinson, wrote to his family back in the United States about the work of vaqueros on Maui. He described lassoing in detail, as the practice would have been unfamiliar outside the realms of Spanish American cattle culture, and he added, "Some natives are skilled at this. The day we were out, in two cases, when the Spaniards' lasso missed, a native right behind him secured the bullock."[119] American naval medical officer William Ruschenberger, who visited the islands in 1836 on a voyage to East Asia, explained, "Though few years have elapsed since the introduction of horses, which are now numerous on the principle islands of the group, the Hawaiians have become dexterous horsemen, and have learned to wield the lasso with a precision only excelled by the gauchos of Buenos Ayres."[120]

The Hawaiians also added their own innovations to adapt California vaquero cattle culture to the islands. Paniolo developed their own folk art traditions, including distinctive music, and introduced their own touches to standard vaquero dress and equipment, including the addition of the lei. Paniolo used Hawaiian materials like koa wood to make saddles and developed an extra-lightweight design to deal with high-altitude riding and the absorption of water in high rainfall areas.[121] They also utilized ornate rawhide rigging, ʻaweʻawe, for their saddles that was waterproof for drives to ships that often forced paniolo to work in ocean water.[122]

One of the better accounts we have of mid-nineteenth-century paniolo at work is from an anonymous article written in 1859 for an English-language Hawaiian newspaper called the *Pacific Commercial Advertiser*. After discussing the disappearance of California vaqueros from the islands, the story related, "In their place has sprung up a class of Hawaiian mountaineers, equally as skillful horsemen as their foreign predecessors, but leading a vagabond sort of life, alternating between hardships and privation on the mountain and plenty and lavish expenditure upon their return to the settlements."[123] The privations included poor shelters that did little to protect their inhabitants from the cold winds of Mauna Kea's slopes and that were partially made of flea-infested hides. The work itself still involved a fair amount of danger, as the anonymous writer tells a dramatic story of the most skilled paniolo, named Komo, or Tom, surviving a charge from a longhorn. These paniolo were rounding up some of the last of the wild cattle on the slope under contract by driving them into pens with horses and lassos. Apparently, they still made a decent profit, receiving $1.25 for each bull hide and $1.00 for each cow hide, money that they spent "lavishly" on entertainments when off the mountain, in the grand cowboy tradition. This signals a shift, at least in relation to the royal or feral herds, away from feudal command of labor. The government paid the paniolo, at least in this narrative, with bounties as it had the foreign bullock hunters.

The account also described the paniolo outfits, stating, "An odd looking company it was. The men wore mostly flannel shirts, as did the women, but while some few had hats, the majority were bareheaded, with thin, long elfin locks, confined by a gay-colored handkerchief, and streaming behind in the wind, gave them a wild Indian-like appearance." The direct connection to American Indians is an intriguing element. Probably intended mostly to emphasize the wildness of these figures, it also underlines the fact that the workers were indigenous people and draws a connection to the indigenous roots of the vaqueros themselves.

This anonymous account adds another interesting detail as well. The author noted that he "found them to the number of thirty or forty, including three native women, ready mounted for the start." It is unclear why women joined the workers, though economic motivations are the obvious answer. They may have been wives of some of the other workers, though in this case, the fact that they were "ready mounted" to ride out with the men on a drive leaves it unclear whether they were going to engage in the more supportive roles usually ascribed to wives in the nineteenth century. As noted in chapter 2, women did work alongside men to meet the agricultural needs in many regions of Hawai'i, especially when not restrained by kapu against handling sacred materials. As mentioned in chapter 3, Hawaiian women also rode for recreation. A patronizing letter to the editor in an 1849 issue of the English-language Hawaiian newspaper the *Polynesian* complained, "Hawaiian women who once labored in beating kapa, now lounge and sleep, or ride on horse back, displaying their gay apparel."[124] Assuming there is some truth in the fact that the making of kapa cloth was in decline, it seems that while many men moved away from traditional agricultural labor, Hawaiian women, at least in Honolulu, were no longer as involved in their traditional roles of making clothing, which could now easily be acquired from trade. Perhaps some took to paniolo work against the typical gendered construction of such labor.

Women on the islands rejected the Anglo ideal of riding sidesaddle and instead developed another Hawaiian variation on horse culture, an elegant, voluminous, pantaloon-like divided skirt called a pā'ū.[125] The name derives, quite simply, from the Hawaiian word for a woman's skirt, which suggests the logic of the adaptation; rather than adapting a Western style of women's riding outfit, Hawaiian women would adapt their own clothing to riding. The outfit would be impractical for the sort of work the women did in the *Pacific Commercial Advertiser* account, but they did extend Hawaiian cattle and horse culture away from the pastures and cement it as part of broader Hawaiian culture. Pā'ū play a significant role in modern parades, for instance.

Many of these accounts highlight the surprising presence of heroic vaqueros on the island, but the Hawaiians clearly began to further adapt cattle culture for the islands. This began with the use of Hawaiian names for equipment and terminology for the methods derived from vaqueros, such as kūpe'e for hog-tie and alaka'i for leading a bullock.[126] Although paniolo culture was based on an exotic animal and the incursions of American and European imperialism on the islands, the Hawaiian language has persisted in the daily operations of ranching. Hawaiian cattle culture would further evolve after vaqueros like Armas had left as the ali'i continued to attempt to use cattle as an economic resource to protect the islands' sovereignty.

Hawaiian Management of Animal Resources

In the 1830s and 1840s, the labor system in Hawai'i still functioned on the principle of royal and chiefly ownership. Paniolo and vaqueros worked for the royal government or local governors and chiefs. However, individual owners increasingly gained control of animals and pasturage, and some employers paid for labor transactions with currency. Jack Purdy, rodeo winner Ikua Purdy's grandfather, was an Irish bullock hunter on the Big Island who earned a dollar and a half for each head of wild cattle he captured.[127] John Simmons, an Anglo-American lumberman on the Big Island, reported that John Adams Kuakini paid for two years of work with "bullock out of his flock."[128] In turn, Simmons hired a group of native drivers, perhaps paniolo, to move the cattle to his residence on the east side of the island at Hilo for forty dollars.[129] These transactions demonstrate the growing commercialization of the animals and related labor on the islands.

In April 1834, a surgeon on a whaling voyage that stopped for supplies in Honolulu, Frederick Debell Bennett, noted the changes that had occurred in the management of the animals on Oahu. He explained that "the cows are quiet at the pail, and yield an abundance of milk, applicable to all the purposes of a dairy," and that "a few of the oxen are trained to yoke, and employed in drawing carts on the roads of Honoruru [sic]."[130] Milking and drawing carts required tame animals and human supervision. Bennett went on to explain that "the majority, branded with their owner's mark, range the country in a half-wild state until required for slaughter, when they are pursued by the bullock-catcher, mounted on his active well-trained horse, and secured by the lasso, or noose and thong cast over their horns, in the South American mode."[131] Paniolo, or perhaps foreign vaqueros, operated on Oahu and managed wild bullock as on the Big Island. Bennett's description also provides evidence that individual owners branded the cattle and allowed them to forage on the open range in a manner reminiscent of California. Certain landholders branded these animals and accumulated herds.

The potential employers for paniolo included not only the royal government, chiefly land managers, and aspiring ranchers gathering herds but also the Protestant missionaries on the islands. While cattle raising undergirded the Franciscan efforts in California, the Protestant missionaries merely utilized cattle to supplement their operations. In 1846, the Reverend Dwight Baldwin searched for "a large pasture in the neighborhood of Lahaina to find a place to build a pen for the cattle."[132]

As such operations proliferated on the Hawaiian Islands, the royal government stepped in to regulate them. During Kamehameha III's reign, the government passed laws to further rein in the threat the abundant cattle posed to agricultural pursuits. This "law for protection of persons who wish to cultivate and persons who wish to raise livestock" ordered "all persons who wish to engage in cultivating the soil" to "first construct a fence of seven feet high around the land."[133] Thus, the law put the impetus to protect crops on agriculturalists and forced them to expend significant labor, which suggests the importance and favor granted to the hide- and tallow-producing livestock industry. However, pastoralists had to prevent their animals from impinging upon fenced fields or face fines of a dollar a head for cattle and horses, fifty cents for swine, and twenty-five cents for goats.[134] It also stated, "All persons who raise livestock are required to keep said livestock in a pen during day and night. If the livestock are turned out during the day, a person must accompany said animals."[135] Still, the law forbade farmers from killing trespassing animals, and it seems that animal owners' rights remained paramount.

By the middle of the 1840s, Hawai'i's legislative House of Nobles had passed another law establishing pounds for stray animals in the islands' municipalities. According to the statute, all animals "found at large in any of the islands of this kingdom, or doing damage therein to the property of private persons, or to the property of government shall be denominated an estray, and may be taken up and lodged in pounds."[136] The governor of each island established a pound to hold the offending animals, which owners could reclaim at the price of one dollar for every day held in the pound, payable to the government. The owner also paid damages to those affected by the loose animals. The government reserved the right to auction off unclaimed animals. The law also required that owners brand all of their animals with a personal mark. Pounds were to confiscate unmarked animals over the age of six months and auction them.[137]

These new laws ushered in a new age of fence building, including extensive public works to manage the increasingly rationalized and controlled ranching operations on the island. While the laws mandated that farmers fence their fields, municipalities like Honolulu and Waimea built their own larger fences. Levi Ha'alelea recalled "the people at Waimea joining together and constructing a wall to keep them [cattle] out. The wall . . . extended a long distance [and] was made of stone in most parts of it but where it struck into the wooded country, it was constructed of posts and stand wood. The wall was built as a general protection there for the people from these Beasts in order that the people might be able to cultivate his lands."[138] Lorenzo Lyons dated this construction to 1837, when he reported that "a great portion of Waimea is being surrounded by a stone wall."[139] This fence building began the process of circumscribing areas that had once been part of the larger feudal ahupua'a, which bridged resources. Now, areas set aside as rangeland with clearly

Stone wall on the Big Island (photograph by author, 2005)

staked out boundaries foreshadowed a world of smaller, individually held plots of land.[140]

Native Hawaiians did take it upon themselves to adjudicate disputes involving trespassing animals. Civil court records demonstrate, for instance, that a Hawaiian named Kamaina living in the Kona district of the Big Island sued another named Piena "for the trespass of five bullocks, one mule, and one jackass on his cultivated land . . . with damages laid at $45."[141] The two Hawaiians had attempted to resolve the dispute themselves, as Piena had given a chicken to Kamaina in exchange for past damages, but apparently continued damages escalated the confrontation into the legal system.

With the advent of the paniolo as an indigenous labor force capable of managing cattle, the 1830s and 1840s saw increasing rationalization of cattle industry on the islands and concerted efforts to regulate the animals on the part of the Hawaiian government. Trained Hawaiian cowboys drove cattle onto ranches, where hopeful ranchers branded them. The government expected these ranchers, through their trained laborers, to contain the animals in pens and prevent them from trespassing, though it also required farmers to fence their crops and promoted public works to keep livestock out of agricultural spaces. Hawaiians increasingly directed the once untamed, dangerous, and relatively unconstrained cattle into narrower domestic and commercial channels, and those channels echoed Anglo-American ideas about property and economy.

This new relationship with the cattle in Hawai'i had rapid and dramatic ramifications for the animals. It seems that the paniolo were extremely successful in the management of the feral cattle population. The resulting changes in human-cattle relationships could be read in the animals' behavior, according to Charles Wilkes. In 1841, while visiting Waimea for an ascent of Mauna Kea, Wilkes noted, "Small herds of cattle were seen, but at a great distance apart: these have now become shy, from having been hunted by Spaniards with horses from California, which were imported for the express purpose of carrying on systematically the business of killing the cattle for their hides. These hunters would soon have exterminated them."[142] Levi Ha'alelea corroborated Wilkes's observation of the decline in the cattle numbers. He testified that "the cattle were very much reduced in numbers and the cattle were pretty nearly all cleaned out on the west side."[143]

The islands' English-language newspaper, the *Polynesian*, reported in 1841 that the government had decreed a new kapu to preserve some of the feral cattle population. The article noted that 1,500 bullock hides had been exported in the last year at two dollars apiece and stated that "owing to the kapu on killing wild bullock laid by the king for five years, from 1840, to enable their number to increase, the amount of hides exported this year was small, and will be still less while the kapu remains in force. Heretofore from 3,000 to 9,000 hides have been exported annually."[144] An impressive number of hides flowed out of Hawai'i in the decade following the vaqueros' arrival, and it seems that wild bullock hunting may have gone almost too well, as the lucrative animals seemed threatened enough to warrant a second kapu. Wilkes learned that "the cattle have been tabooed for five years, from the year 1840, in consequence of the slaughter that had been made among them. Upwards of five thousand hides, I was told, had been procured in a single year, and when this became known to the government, it interdicted the hunting of the animals."[145] Gerritt Judd, an American missionary who had great influence in the royal government and eventually became the king's minister of finance, claimed credit for the new kapu. Citing declining hide prices on the islands from a glut in the market and the declining cattle population, he later stated, "In 1842 I advised the King to put a stop to the catching of the cattle and he did so, it might have been 1843. . . . The receipts from the hides did not pay the expenditure on work."[146] Despite the key role claimed by an American missionary, the new kapu represents yet another attempt by Hawaiians to manage and control the cattle population.

Wilkes noted a decline in Waimea's economy resulting from the new kapu. He observed that "since the taboo has been laid, the place is comparatively deserted; and unless the cultivation of the soil be resorted to, it will, before many years, become a barren waste."[147] He explained that the Hawaiians had gained from the horses and cattle and that at the hide trade's peak "many of the habitations of the natives were improved, and they advanced much in civilization. Some of them own horses and cattle, and are industrious; but the mass, who have lived on this precarious employment, and found their subsistence in that way, have become, since it ceased, more indolent than before."[148] The kapu did not end the hide and tallow trade, but it greatly restricted access to the profits of that trade to those who had established herds in the 1830s and those with connections in the royal government.

However, some Hawaiians defied the kapu, which did not hold the religious weight of the first Kamehameha's original ten-year kapu. Since the prime minister and Queen Regent Ka'ahumanu had abolished most religious injunctions in 1819, the kapu was merely a royal decree.[149] During their ascent of Mauna Kea, Wilkes's party observed "some huts occupied by natives who had been bullock-hunting. In this illegal practice they seem to have been extensively engaged, judging from the quantities of jerked meat they had on hand."[150] Wilkes left no more details about this illicit operation. The poachers clearly utilized bullocks as a food resource, though they likely would have sold the hides as well. Despite the lack of an indigenous hunting culture, natives had developed their knowledge of cattle to the point that they could capture and skin the wild animals outside the purview of the government or its hired vaqueros.

Hawaiians also illicitly hunted or stole from Hawai'i's increasing reservoir of branded cattle. A native named Naipualoha faced prison for cattle rustling in the 1850s. George Sherman purchased a cow from Naipualoha in exchange for a Spanish leather saddle, and after he slaughtered it and his native workers dressed it, a rancher named H. King with eighty head of cattle near Kona claimed that the animal's hide bore his brand. A Hawaiian court sentenced Naipualoha to six months in prison with a fourteen-dollar fine, but Naipualoha appealed. When three other Hawaiian workers in the cattle industry, friends of Naipualoha named Kaikuahine, Hama, and Kukile, noted that Naipualoha's parents owned cattle with an apparently similar brand to King's, and that they had seen Naipua-loha "catch the bullock to take it to sell," the appeals court overturned the guilty verdict.[151] While the courts eventually concluded in this case that no theft had taken place, the proceedings indicate the commonplace nature of such thefts and accusations, as well as the increasing Hawaiian familiarity with ranching.

Indian Banditry and Independent Livestock Cultures

While Hawaiian leaders and paniolo used a mixture of vaquero training and traditional authority to rationalize the management of cattle on the islands and participate more efficiently in the trans-Pacific trade in bovine products, California Indians increasingly used that same training to create their own animal economies outside the mission and rancho system. When Isaac Iselin, a New Englander involved in the Canton trade, visited California in 1807, he experienced this native cattle economy firsthand. He stated that while riding to Sunday mass on horseback "a naked Indian, at full speed, ranged alongside me. I was not aware of his intentions, but putting the spurs to my horse, which was an excellent one, I endeavored to outride him. But he pressed close to me. In casting my eyes back, I perceived that he had got hold of my horse's tail, and . . . I was thrown." By the time he had recovered from his fall, "The Indian and my horse had disappeared."[152] This rapid assault is a brazen example of a phenomenon that was becoming more common in nineteenth-century California.

The theft and destruction of livestock had plagued California since the establishment of the missions. In early revolts, like the revolt at Mission San Diego and the Yuma Revolt (both discussed in chapter 2), Indians often attacked livestock as threats to indigenous subsistence or as symbols of Spanish power. After decades of familiarity, however, the Indians began to see horses as a tool to protect or recapture their own sovereignty. In February 1824 Indians in the Chumash Territory around Mission Santa Barbara, Mission La Purísima, and Mission Santa Inés erupted in revolt after a severe beating of a young neophyte. The Chumash fighters captured many of the horses in the region, causing panic among the Spanish.[153] Eventually, as the worst violence died down, Mexican authorities enlisted mission vaqueros to help gather horses and guns from the Chumash rebels, who had retreated into the backcountry after a series of largely successful attacks.[154] Oral traditions of the revolt suggest that the Chumash saw the horse as central to their success and even possessing supernatural powers of transportation that linked the animals with older mystical traditions.[155]

Horse and cattle thieving escalated in the 1830s and 1840s, and became one of the province's greatest enduring problems. These economies often underlined the fluid situation on California's frontier. The settled coast contained thousands of missionized Indians, who shared many characteristics with the Spanish but retained connections with Indians of the interior. Spanish soldiers had conducted raids, for pacification and neophyte recruitment, into the interior for decades that led to the diffusion of goods and culture, and runaway Indians from the missions often fled into these areas. The penetration of settlers like the Vallejos and Sutter into California's interior created a new group of Indians connected to European cultures. Finally, many of California's interior Indians continued to avoid consistent contact with settlers, but even these peoples remained connected by trade and migration.

The easy availability of animals like horses facilitated easier movement between these worlds. In 1819, Fray Mariano Payéras noted that the interior Tulares region served as a continuing base from which Indians could prosecute raids. He also noted that the "Tulareños" often came to the missions to be baptized but quickly left, taking Spanish horses with them. He complained that "with such visitors no animal is safe in all the northern valley."[156] Indians could also profit by bridging the coastal and interior worlds and removing livestock from the former. In a subsequent letter, Payéras lamented, "Any small altar boy grabs horses; kills cattle; goes about the mission chain terrorizing; steals tame and castrated herds, taking them and selling them in the *Tular*."[157] Now Indians were introducing old-world animals into their own territory, controlling the distribution and incorporating the animals into their subsistence strategies. In the process, they promoted the spread of the ecological change that came with introduced species; the new grazing mammal probably promoted the spread of old-world plants ahead of the slow Spanish advance from the coast. Cattle remained relatively rare in most of the Central Valley until the 1840s, and one researcher has speculated that this was because Indians killed and ate strays.[158] Horse populations, on the other hand, they favored, and wild horses were common in the interior by 1805, when they were observed by a Spanish military expedition.[159]

By the 1830s, American and British traders and trappers were active in California's interior, and they began to link California to New Mexico via the 1,200-mile "Old Spanish Trail" (as the Americans knew it) that linked Santa Fe to Los Angeles.[160] This trade route followed, in part, the trails blazed by Juan Bautista de Anza in the 1770s. The Spanish settlements in New Mexico suffered from a shortage of livestock and ongoing raids from powerful Indian groups while California had tremendous herds upon which to draw. The Indians in California's interior could trade their own stocks for manufactured goods that flowed into New Mexico from the United States. They were developing their own long-distance trade networks based on animal resources. Once engaged in this trade, the incentives to raid along the coast only increased.

Mariano Guadalupe Vallejo remembered an Indian vaquero named "Martin, who was stationed in Amador Valley and became a leader of the hill vaqueros, who were very different from the vaqueros of the large valley near the Missions. He and his friends killed and ate three or four hundred young heifers belonging to the Mission before he relented and confessed his sins to a priest."[161] The Vallejos and Indian allies, including Chief Solano in an 1835 attack against the "Yolos," conducted military operations against Indian cattle raiders in their northern territories, but also allowed an illicit trade network of captives and livestock to operate in the area.[162] As the problem escalated in the 1840s, American businessman Thomas Larkin stated that "the Indians tame & wild steal several thousand head of Horses yearly from the Ranchos."[163] Wilkes observed that raiding Indians had become "so daring . . . that they not unfrequently [sic] take them out of the enclosures near the pueblos."[164]

Even neophytes could be in danger. In November 1826, Mission San José records indicate that a vaquero named Francisco de Sales was "killed by the gentiles" while "on a ride" ["en el paseo"].[165] The lack of a specific date suggests that the details of his fate were not known, but his ride was probably part of his regular duties. Sixteen years earlier, Francisco de Sales had been a nine-year-old boy named Yaspay, one of many from the Miwok village of Anizumne on the lower Sacramento River baptized around the same time.[166] He had risen to the status of vaquero and become the target of other Indians in the region. The fathers recorded no details as to why the gentiles killed him, though taking his horse or cattle he watched is one obvious possibility.

Many of the interior Indians kept and utilized the stock that they pilfered. The British fur trader George Simpson visited a village of "free Indians" inland from Santa Barbara. He called the group "miserable" and noted that "they were engaged in that wretched expedient of making bread of acorns."[167] Simpson seems to have mistaken a gastronomic cultural tradition for an unpleasant survival strategy, and he had trouble reconciling acorn consumption with the Indians' significant animal resources. He explained that they had "enclosures of land, with a few cattle and horses," and that they "appeared . . . to be, on the whole, more comfortable than General Vallego's [*sic*] serfs."[168] These Indians in the Tulares had developed their own contained livestock resources. French explorer Abel du Petit-Thouars likewise observed that by 1836 Indians "thirty or forty leagues from the coast . . . have begun to domesticate animals procured by stealing from the mission."[169] While descending the western slopes of the Sierras in his 1826 overland journey to California, mountain man Jedediah Smith had his horse stolen by the local Indians. He tracked the animal in hopes of recovering it, and came upon an Indian encampment complete with horses. He noted, "As they have no fences what few horses they have are kept constantly tied by a long halter and at this season are fed on Pumpkins and melons of which they appear very fond."[170] These semisedentary Indians, perhaps related to the Yuma, adapted local materials to prevent the horses from wandering away and traditional crops as feed.

Tulareños could draw on vast wild herds of horses in the interior valleys. Simpson claimed that one such valley near the San Gabriel "contains multitudes of wild horses, which are even seen in bands of several thousand each. . . . These enormous troops indicate their approach chiefly by making the ground tremble beneath their tramp."[171] However, these Indians still valued the tame horses of the coastal Spanish settlements. Puzzled observers noted that they would raid horses from the coast despite living among vast herds of wild horses, but it was clearly more economical to raid and trade domesticated livestock than to put the labor into the difficult task of taming wild horses.[172]

Indians throughout California focused their livestock rustling efforts on horses. Charles Wilkes explained that "the Indians at present rarely steal any thing but horses. . . . Their reason for confining themselves to this description of property is, that with them they are able to avoid pursuit, which would not be the case if they took cattle."[173] The Indians valued horses for the mobility that the animals conferred. The animals' speed combined with the Indians' riding skills made possible the sort of daring raids that Wilkes described or to which Iselin fell victim. Despite the appropriation of old-world animals, the Indians did not consistently follow old-world patterns of usage. For instance, California Indians developed an appetite for horses. Larkin explained that Indians would only steal "fat" horses, and he elaborated that "as the Indians eat their horses, they don't steal a poor one."[174] Antonio Osio flatly stated, "The Indians preferred eating horse meat over beef."[175] William Ruschenberger pointed out that "they plunder the farms of the colonists if horses, which they eat in preference to beef, though horned cattle are more abundant: this fact contradicts the assertion . . . that no people eat horse flesh through preference."[176]

The Indians developed new traditions around horses and even around the practice of taking the animals. Osio noted that "when a tribe obtained a share of horses, it would invite neighboring Indians for a banquet. The gathering and the dance afterward would last as long as was needed to finish off the stolen animals."[177] This account suggests that, at times, Indians consumed stolen horses in a ritual manner with other tribes, perhaps to cement alliances and certainly in the hopes of some form of reciprocity. They also showed expertise in the animals' behavior in their raids, allowing the horses to move out of rancho corrals at their own rate and then gathering and driving the animals once they had moved about half a mile away. They sometimes used specially made arrows that would hurt the animals without doing permanent damage to keep them from straying from the herd during a drive.[178]

Observers also noted that the Indians violated typical Western gender conventions in their riding. The skill with which a female Indian rode her horse surprised Walter Colton when he encountered "wild Indians" in 1846. He noted that a man with a bow and "a squaw and a papoose" rode, "dashing ahead in the wake of their dogs, which were in hot chase of a deer. The squaw stuck to her fleet animal as firmly as the saddle in which she sat, and took but little heed of the bogs and gullies over which she bounded."[179] Colton found the Indian woman's skill on horseback worthy of note, but he does not provide more context. It would have been a major shift in gender roles for the woman, with her child, to be actively participating in a hunt. That is unlikely, but she was, it seems, accompanying a male rider for some reason, and she seemed very capable of keeping pace, demonstrating a high level of familiarity with the animal. It is likely that women found their traditional roles devalued by the emerging horse-raiding cultures. In the horse cultures that developed among the plains Indians, raiding was male work, horses became male property, and women took on new duties in the care of livestock without gaining the same level of prestige that men gained.[180] It is likely that many of the same dynamics existed in California's interior, and any impacts that introduced livestock had on plant life that harmed female gathering activities may have compounded the problem. Certain male leaders did seem to benefit from the power and prestige that came with raiding and trading, and observers noted a political restructuring that included more male brokers in these communities.[181] Colton's story at least suggests that Indian women also found greater mobility through the animals. Colton's scene is also noteworthy for revealing that Indians incorporated horses into their traditions of hunting indigenous animals. William Robert Garner, a former British whaler and longtime resident in California, also claimed that Indian bandits made special use of the "fleetest hoses, which they keep for the purpose of hunting the elk, which abound in the Tulare valley."[182]

Despite their preference for, and skill with, the horse, Indians did continue to take cattle from the ranches as well. Juana Machado, the daughter of a soldier from the presidio of San Diego who eventually married a New England hide trader, remembered an Indian attack on a rancho near San Diego in which the Indians kidnapped two young Californio girls. She remembered, "Before leaving, they ransacked the rancho and took all the horses, cattle, and other items of value."[183] She added that "when the fathers were still at Mission San Diego, it was very common for the Indians to steal horses and cattle."[184] Duflot de Mofras noted that raiding Indians would steal all a ranchero's horses, and then take his cattle when he could no longer pursue.[185] In 1835, the ayuntamiento, or town council, of Monterey tasked José de Jesús Vallejo, another of Mariano Guadalupe Vallejo's brothers, with "an expedition to the tulares against Indian cattle thieves."[186] Monterey's commission of such an expedition under an experienced commander suggests that cattle theft posed a significant problem to the capital of Mexican California. Sutter also sought retribution when local Indians preyed on his livestock. Wilkes noted that at a site on the banks of the Feather River "had been an Indian village, which was destroyed by Captain Sutter and his trappers, because the inhabitants had stole cattle."[187] Sutter and his Indian allies had killed one from the thieving tribe and captured twenty-seven others to serve as laborers.

According to Larkin, Indian laborers for the Spanish even stole horses to move around within the Spanish settlements along the coast. Larkin described Indian "Cooks and Stewards" who spent much of their time moving from drunken imprisonment in one settlement, like San Diego, to another, Monterey in his example. Expelled from each town in turn, Larkin stated that the offending Indian workers "find their own horses on the road, which are easy borrowed with a larzo [sic]."[188] While Larkin probably exaggerated the drunken exploits of these Indian laborers for racist and comedic effect, his story still highlights the ubiquity of horse theft and the Indians' pervasive ease and familiarity with both the animals and the lasso. Of course, what Larkin and rancheros viewed as theft, interior Indians saw as harvesting a vast, readily available resource for their own subsistence at the expense of a threatening colonial power.[189]

By the eve of the U.S.-Mexican War, California residents considered Indian livestock raids a major problem. Larkin reported that "farms are being vacated by the Californians, from fear of further depredations of the wild Indians, who yearly steal thousands of Horses, even out of enclosed yards near the dwelling houses."[190] Duflot de Mofras observed, "Unfortunately the supply of horses is now diminishing in California, for the Indians carry on endless raids, and almost every night hundreds are carried off to the Tulare valley."[191] Another British visitor, Edward Belcher, anxiously noted that California's "hour is approaching" because the Californians were "harassed on all sides by Indians, who are now stripping them of their horses, without which their cattle are not to be preserved."[192] The weakening effects of horse raiding probably did not lead directly to Mexico's loss of California, but it did fit nicely into American rhetoric that the Mexicans could not control their frontier.[193]

Conclusion

Hawaiians and California Indians utilized the tools and the techniques of the Mexican vaqueros and the fluid situations of the trans-Pacific frontier to develop independent cultural and legal practices to manage and control once exotic animals. Cattle work in both regions acquired unique rhythms and practices, and these could cross the Pacific because of the connections created by the hide and tallow trade. That trade funneled wealth harvested from the pastures of California and Hawai'i into the hands of European and American traders. Nevertheless, the Hawaiian government attempted to relieve its debts through efficient indigenous management of the animals. Paniolo labor became an integral part of the royal government's efforts to protect its sovereignty in the dangerous context of these debts. California Indians did not have an equivalent sovereignty, but they still controlled vast areas of Alta California's interior, and they utilized introduced animals to move back and forth between these spaces, while furthering their own introductions inland. Paniolo and vaqueros are enduring symbols of the ingenuity and relative independence with which these indigenous people dealt with colonial introductions of commercial species.

The success of the hide and tallow trade and the Pacific World that it helped to tie together necessitated labor, and the demographics and power dynamics of the region demanded a key role for indigenous peoples in those labor regimes. The nature of cattle work gave native laborers more latitude than in most extractive colonial economies, and the lack of colonial dominance by any single power created even more possibilities. Native cowboys could move relatively freely, had some control in negotiating the terms of their labor, and developed their own traditions and styles for managing the ranging cattle in their lands. The connections of the hide and tallow trade made the transfer of indigenous knowledge possible. California Indians could create livestock-based economies on the fringes of Mexican power, while Hawaiian elites could take control of the livestock economies developing on the islands. There were clear limits in these possibilities, however. The freedom of cowboys was only relative—many still worked at the command of mission fathers or ali'i, and the rest received only a portion of the value of their work or faced the unfair accounting of debt peonage. At the same time, interior Indians and Hawaiian elites would find the protections of their sovereignty that cattle could grant fleeting. The possibilities cattle provided served many indigenous peoples' interests in the fluid Pacific borderlands, but California and Hawai'i fell increasingly under political and economic influence from Great Britain and, especially, the United States. Anglo-American economic dominance would soon yield political and legal dominance, and the variety of arrangements that existed for the management, working, and ownership of cattle would be restructured under Anglo-American ideals at midcentury.

CHAPTER SIX

Property

Despite the capitalistic nature of the lively trans-Pacific hide and tallow trade, the livestock economies of 1830s California and Hawai'i still operated within forms of communal property ownership. The missions ostensibly managed their large herds in trust for the benefit of Indian neophytes as they made the transition to become gente de razón, while Hawaiian lands remained under quasi-feudal control. Hawai'i had no provisions for private landownership, and the king ultimately owned all lands, while hereditary chiefs, or ali'i, officially held them in trust for laboring commoners who worked specific plots. Each chief's land, or ahupua'a, stretched from mountains to sea in radial strips built around watersheds and ideally suited to the geography of Hawai'i's small islands.[1] European bullock hunters and then paniolo killed and processed animals for ali'i and the royal government. Indian vaqueros processed cattle at mission ranches, but the fathers paternalistically reinvested the profits into the maintenance of Indians and their religious education. Thus, at the height of the hide and tallow boom fueled by indigenous labor, indigenous peoples could claim some rights to the land, even if there were strong limits to those rights. Increasingly in the 1830s, however, private capital encroached on the profits of eastern Pacific cattle. Private ranches proliferated in California as Mexican governors made large land grants and began to dismantle the missions, and foreigners increasingly leased ranch lands for their own herds in the Hawaiian Islands. These shifts culminated in parallel land reforms in both regions that fundamentally changed the basic systems of land tenure in these important Pacific frontiers. Cattle ranching and hide and tallow profits drove these land reforms, which, in turn, furthered imperial processes and granted control over Pacific pastoral economies to Euro-American interests.

In Hawai'i, the transition to European notions of bounded, alienable plots of land may have begun with the building of fences to protect Hawaiian agriculture from marauding cattle. The way that Europeans in Hawai'i saw their property reveals a great deal about how colonialism affected the development of ideas about land. Richard Charlton was the British consul to the Hawaiian kingdom from 1825 to 1843; in fact, he was one of the main correspondents that Joaquin Armas wrote to try to claim back pay from the Hawaiian government. During his time as consul, Charlton caused many controversies among Hawaiians and the foreign community. He leased some land in Honolulu and ran a small herd of cattle there. He refused to control these cattle, which often violated Hawaiian agricultural areas, but when Hawaiian cattle trespassed on his land, he shot them on sight. In October of 1829, a native Hawaiian shot one of Charlton's cows that had wandered onto kapu land. Charlton asked the Hawaiian government to punish its subject, and when they refused, he and the American consul John Coffin Jones retaliated by tying a rope around the Hawaiian's neck and dragging him through the streets of Honolulu. Charlton then gathered signatures for a petition from the haole community in Honolulu asking for the defense of foreign property rights, and he threatened to create an international incident by getting the British government involved.[2] While Europeans expected Hawaiians to adopt the concepts of Western civilization, they often felt that they did not have to abide by these rules in their own relations with people whom they regarded as inferior. Charlton hypocritically ignored Hawaiian property while advancing Western property interests in the islands. Racial prejudice probably played a significant role in Charlton's double standard, but his concept of property also shaped his responses. Hawaiian ownership did not count to Charlton because Hawaiian property law lacked the formal titles and individual ownership of European property. Instead, ali'i controlled property on behalf of communal interests by custom and tradition rather than by title. The feral cattle belonged to the king and his government, as did the land they grazed on. This extended, of course, to the land on which Charlton lived and grazed his cattle, but Charlton asserted a greater control over his property by calling on the haole community (which controlled a large portion of the kingdom's capital) and through direct physical violence.

As discussed in chapter 4, John Coffin Jones, the American who helped Charlton mete out his punishment, was a prominent hide trader himself. By the late 1820s, this put him at the center of Hawaiian commerce, which is why the Americans chose him as their commercial agent in the islands. Less than a decade later, another prominent hide and tallow trader found himself responsible for enforcing transformations in landownership in the eastern Pacific. The British trader William Hartnell had opened California to foreign hide and tallow firms in 1821. His own trading firm had failed, and Hartnell had married Teresa de la Guerra and taken control of a ranch near Monterey. In the late 1830s, as the missions were closed by legislative action and the land distributed to the neophyte residents, Governor Juan Bautista Alvarado asked William Hartnell to serve as visitador to the missions and investigate claims that Indian property rights were being abused. As a naturalized Mexican citizen and respected ranchero with marital ties to one of Alta California's most prominent families, Hartnell was a respectable, if not entirely disinterested, choice to investigate the dispensation and maintenance of the secularized missions.[3] It fell to him to investigate and decide the individual property rights of converted mission Indians in Alta California. In the process, he would bring his own assumptions about landownership into the process, just as Charlton had in Hawai'i.

The early nineteenth century witnessed dramatic changes in land tenure throughout the Pacific under the influence of British and American imperial power. These reforms occurred within a shared ideological context that gave primacy to the individual ownership of alienable fee simple property.[4] European colonial powers treated some regions as *terra nullius* or unoccupied land, while elsewhere they acknowledged indigenous land rights and acquired land through treaty or sale. This differentiation depended on whether native peoples practiced agriculture, the level of indigenous political organization, and the rapidity of white settlement. The Spanish, the Mexicans, and eventually the Americans treated California, with its politically diverse and nonagricultural Indians, as *terra nullius*, while the imperial powers jockeying for influence in Hawai'i, an agricultural region united under a single monarch, acquired indigenous lands more slowly and through land reform.[5] Despite these differences, both regions saw large foreign-owned ranches rise to primacy after 1848 at the same time that American influence gained ascendency in the eastern Pacific. The chronological proximity of these developments in interconnected Hawai'i and California suggests the connected culmination of Westernizing processes throughout the region.

Mission Secularization and Rancho Dominance

Governor Pedro Fages made the first private land grants in Alta California to presidial soldiers who had acquired their own herds of cattle and horses. In 1784, Juan José Domínguez, Manuel Nieto, and "the sons of the widow of Ignacio Carillo" received sitios de ganado mayor, or ranching lands, near Mission San Gabriel.[6] In exchange for these generous land grants, the grantees were to maintain a herd of at least a thousand head of cattle with enough vaqueros to maintain the animals.[7] While these initial grants set the pattern for the large ranching estates that governors of California handed out during the next six decades, private land grants remained relatively rare during Spanish rule. Spanish-appointed governors of California made only twenty land grants between Fages's 1784 gifts to his soldiers and the advent of Mexican rule in 1821.[8] Like the Hawaiian royal family at the time, the king of Spain claimed ultimate title to all of the lands in his realm, including in distant California. All land grants ultimately consisted of only usufruct rights; grantees could use the land and even pass it to an heir, but they could not always sell it and had no rights against the revocation of the property. Thus, land grants in California were little more than open-ended grazing permits in designated areas.[9]

The Mexican government liberalized land policy in Alta California. The Republic of Mexico no longer had a monarchical ruler to claim ultimate power over all lands, which allowed for a transition to fee simple property. Influenced by the Enlightenment, Mexico's new leaders believed in individual landownership. In California, laws like the Colonization Act of 1824 and the Reglamento of 1828 reflected this new ethos. With these laws, the Mexican government hoped to encourage settlement and agricultural development in their most far-flung outpost. Under the Colonization Act, governors could issue grants to new settlers in fee simple title from any "vacant lands" in the "territories of the republic."[10] The act also allowed naturalized Mexican citizens access to land grants. The Reglamento of 1828 clarified the Colonization Act and created mechanisms for its implementation by vesting in the governors the power to grant lands and requiring petitions that included a map of the claim, called a diseño, which emphasized landmarks over exact dimensions.[11]

Despite this simplification in land titles and these new inducements to settlement, many residents of Mexican California complained that the missions remained a major obstacle to reforms of land tenure in the region. Liberal reformers championed the movement to secularize the missions and place their lands under the same property rules that now governed land grants. This agenda resonated with Enlightenment ideals by again emphasizing individual property ownership while also appealing to anticlerical currents among Mexican liberals. Proponents of secularization argued that the missions had served their purpose, namely, converting California's Indians to gente de razón. Even under Mexican rule, the missions did not hold fee simple property rights in California; theoretically at least, they held land in trust for neophyte Indians. The mission fathers claimed that they utilized all that they gained from the produce of the missions for the Indians. The fathers of Mission San Antonio reported in 1814 that "Whatever they [mission Indians] sow and harvest and whatever the mission acquires from the sale of tallow and hides all goes into a common fund of the mission for the maintenance of these Indians."[12] However, proponents of secularization argued that California had become a civilized territory, and the Indians within the purview of the mission system had come as far as they would within the Franciscan institutions. That the missions remained, and continued to utilize Indian labor and large landholdings to reap significant profits in the flourishing hide and tallow trade, now stood as an obstacle to the further development of the social and economic institutions of Alta California. It would better serve Indians to enter the economy as wage laborers, and private ranchos would do more to take advantage of the market opportunities that cattle presented. The missions did control millions of acres of the most valuable land in California.[13] Most had several subsidiary ranches in which neophyte vaqueros ran the large mission herds. Indian workers had already constructed the minimal infrastructure necessary for California ranching, including corrals, stables, and housing, as well as irrigation projects.[14] The missions also encompassed some of the best pasturage and sat at ideal locations near coastal ports.

Debate raged through the 1820s and into the early 1830s as the Franciscans attempted to maintain the institution of the mission in opposition to liberal reformers. Foreigners also weighed in on the debate. After his 1828 visit to California, British explorer William Beechey thought that "an order to liberate all those converted Indians from the missions who . . . had been taught the art of agriculture" was "of some importance."[15] Alfred Robinson believed there was another downside to the existence of the missions in that their productivity further encouraged indolence among the Californians. Robinson stated that "the bountiful distribution" of the missions' "yearly productions by the missionaries, rendered any exertion on the part of the Californian unnecessary for his support, and but few persons cared for the means of independence, preferring idleness to industry and improvement."[16] Robinson believed that the missions and their Indian labor provided enough to support Californians, making it unnecessary for them to work, which fit in with his racialized view of the Californios. He implied that another group of people may have used the riches of the missions as an opportunity to expand, but the Californians' indolence resulted in their refusal to make use of the opportunity. With the secularization of the missions and the transfer of their lands to rancheros in 1836, Robinson saw this situation changing. He stated that despite fears that these events would be "disastrous to the prosperity of California . . . individual enterprise, which succeeded, has placed the country in a more flourishing condition."[17] The end of the missions forced the Californians to work for themselves, and Robinson saw this newfound independence as creating more wealth in California.

Mission Indians also expressed their opinions in the mission debates. Governor José María de Echeandía received petitions from mission Indians asking for a release from the system. The petitioners were Indians who had learned marketable trades that they could use outside the mission system. Among them were vaqueros.[18] The advent of secularization also saw an increase in delinquency from the missions and rumors of new revolts, as mission Indians "voted with their feet" and helped influence the policy change.[19] However, Echeandía's successor Governor José Figueroa visited missions in Southern California and made speeches to the Indians to try to sell them on the idea. Apparently, some were skeptical that secularization would really represent the emancipation that it promised, or they were unhappy that they might be asked to move to new pueblos, preferring communities they had formed within the missions even if they resented the padres' control.[20] Unfortunately, few sources record the Indians' true opinions of secularization, but these varying responses indicate that mission Indian views likely varied by mission, by position within the mission, and perhaps by other factors, including gender and time in the mission. Many Indians seem to have preferred secularization primarily as an escape from Spanish colonial influence. Indians more integrated into Spanish society or the colonial economy were more likely to see the possibilities of acquiring land titles of their own but also the risks that secularization presented to their livelihood in that economy.

The debate culminated in the Secularization Act, which passed the Mexican Congress on August 17, 1833. Governor Figueroa issued his own rules for the execution of the Secularization Act in which he promised that "the Missionary Priests will be exonerated from the administration of temporalities, and will only exercise the functions of their ministry in matters appertaining to the spiritual administration."[21] Thus, the territorial government assumed control over all mission property, and the missionaries now became parish priests. The missions changed from institutions of religious, social, and cultural indoctrination with large communal landholdings to regular Catholic parishes supported by a network of independent landholders.[22] The reformers planned a gradual process with paternalistic oversight over land distribution that would prevent the chaos that some had feared would result from Indian emancipation.

Ostensibly, the Secularization Act divided mission lands among the Indian inhabitants for whom the missionaries had built the institutions, but, in practice, most of the mission lands eventually fell under the ownership of Californio rancheros. Figueroa's rules called for each mission Indian head of household to receive a small "lot of land," and created a commons for each new pueblo of "sufficient quantity . . . for watering their cattle."[23] The rules distributed half of the missions' "self-moving property (cattle) . . . in a proportionable and equitable manner, at the discretion of the Governor," while giving the other half and all remaining land "to the care and responsibility of the Mayordomos."[24] While Figueroa's rules "emancipated" the mission Indians, they also declared that Indians were still "obliged to assist at . . . indispensable common labor."[25] Despite the liberal ideologies that motivated them, the rules also placed limitations on what the new Indian landholders could do with their property. Figueroa proclaimed that the beneficiaries of distributed mission lands "cannot sell, burden, or alienate, under any pretext, the lands which may be given them; neither can they sell their cattle."[26] Thus, secularization, as envisioned by Figueroa, represented a paternally guided transition of California Indians from laboring wards of the missions to independent landowners with no latitude to sell land or cattle.

This transition, compromised as it was, generally did not occur, as secularization impoverished the missions and left rancheros with large landholdings as the dominant economic and social power in California. Secularization fell out of favor as power shifted in Mexico City in 1835, and the Californios were able to assert control over the process.[27] While the missions retained some ranching lands and smaller herds, the missions also sold off most of their cattle. Angustias de la Guerra, the daughter of one of California's earlier and most prominent rancheros, remembered that "some people have stated that when the missionary Fathers sensed that the secularization of the missions was imminent, they decided to sell off as much of the cattle as they could."[28] The mission fathers may have slaughtered even more cattle for their hides. Although de la Guerra thought these rumors exaggerated, she noted that "thousands of cattle were killed and only the hides were used. The slaughter was so massive that the authorities feared the country would be left without any cattle if they did not put a stop to it. In fact, the *jefe politico* took steps to stop that destruction of animals."[29]

While some Californios claimed that the mission fathers plundered the missions before secularization, others claimed that rancheros plundered them afterward. The authorities in California appointed mayordomos to administer the mission lands and distribute them to the Indians. These mayordomos generally came from the politically connected ranchero class, and many of them managed to acquire much of the mission lands for themselves by purchasing them cheaply from the new Indian owners. It was in this context that Governor Alvarado asked rancher and former hide trader William Hartnell to audit the secularization process.

Hartnell sometimes defended the administradores against charges that they cheated or abused the Indians still under their care at the diminished missions of post-secularization California. He received a petition from the mission Indians at San Juan Capistrano about poor conditions under the mayordomo Don Santiago. After complaining that the petition was illegible, Hartnell explained to the Indians that "people have been allotted by the Father's own hands all he possibly could in proportion to the income."[30] He blamed the general poverty of the mission following secularization for the Indians' poor condition rather than Don Santiago. At other missions, however, Hartnell did side with the Indians. When he visited Mission Santa Inés in July 1839, Hartnell noted that the Indian vaqueros did not even receive adequate supplies to do their job. He explained that "the vaqueros are sorely in need of knapsacks and shoes because all the tanned hides are used for saddles, etc for the Government and white people."[31] Among the other Indians, Hartnell noted that "in spite of there being much grain, they are not given rations."[32] The Indians had plans to engage in the Pacific cattle economy in order to alleviate some of the financial burden on the land they inhabited; Hartnell related that "they want to kill bulls for hides to pay the mission debts."[33] As we have seen, debt was a hallmark of the hide and tallow trade. Secularization transferred that debt to some Indian landowners without transferring all the assets of the missions, and thus it became another obstacle to Indian entrance into the new liberal economy in the region. Hartnell supported the Indians against the mayordomo at Santa Inés in their request for supplies and their attempts to manage the mission debt with a matanza, but there is little indication that their condition improved after his visit.

Hartnell also learned that the administrator of Mission San Fernando had given away choice mission ranch lands to a ranchero. Hartnell explained that "the only complaint made by the Indian community here was that the place of San Francisco had been taken from them and given to Don Antonio del Valle. . . . I am convinced that if they are not heeded in this request, they will be extremely disgusted and the very least they do, many of them, is to flee the mission."[34] These various complaints from Indians on former mission lands suggest widespread abuse by administrators. Hartnell worried that the Indians would leave the mission lands, but disputes over secularization also led to violence. Pío Pico, the future governor of California, served as the administrator of San Luis Rey in the early 1840s. In a memoir, he claimed that as many as a thousand Indians under a literate Indian named Pablito planned to rise up against him, "protesting that I had disposed of the skins and tallow of the mission."[35] Pico managed to satisfy the Indians, but he admitted that he had sent hides and tallow to San Diego for sale.

In his decisions as visitador, Hartnell also advanced the liberal ideology of private property that had motivated the partition of the missions. In late May 1839, Hartnell visited the pueblo of Las Flores, formerly a ranch for Mission San Luís Rey. Noting that the current livestock on the ranch valued 876 reales but that the value was diminishing, Hartnell proposed what he termed "a final experiment . . . apportioning to each one privately what was due him from the communal property." He warned the Indians that he would revoke their property if they failed to manage it properly, and noted that they seemed "very content" with the arrangement.[36] Hartnell resigned his position long before he finished his visits to all of the missions, feeling powerless to stop ranchero abuse of the new socioeconomic order.

The Secularization Act heralded a transition to a more liberal, capitalistic system of land tenure. Hartnell's visits suggest some of the reasons that the manner of this transition came to exclude most Indians from participation in the new economy of Alta California. Indians had the skills to work the cattle, but paternalistic management by mission fathers had given them little education in running a commercial ranch or the navigation of the Mexican legal and economic systems, and they also had little capital. Furthermore, while both proponents and opponents of secularization argued that the land really belonged to the Indians, neither rancheros nor padres were particularly interested in seeing Indians as

successful individual ranchers; the former saw them as potential com-
petitors for land and stock, while the latter feared the loss of power that
would come with loss of control of mission lands, stock, and neophyte
labor. Indian landownership remained low by the late 1840s, suggesting
that administradores failed to distribute sufficient land, embezzled or
fraudulently distributed land to Californios, and that mission Indians
had abandoned or sold most of their holdings despite the prohibition in
Figueroa's rules. Duflot de Mofras observed that Figueroa "made a pretense of distributing land and a few cattle among the Indians. The latter,
however, soon lost, gambled or sold what was given them."[37] Mofras's use
of "pretense" suggests that the efforts to include Indians in land liberalization were often halfhearted. Californios' desire for the aggrandizement
of their own estates clearly played a role in the failures of secularization.
María Inocenta Pico, the wife of a prominent rancher (and Pío Pico's
cousin), remembered visiting a mission cannibalized by its administrador.
She stated that Don Vicente Cané, the administrador of Mission San Luis
Obispo, "took goods and other possessions from the mission to establish
his own rancho. Cané was the one who tore down the mission buildings.
He took everything that could be salvaged, such as beams, roof tiles, fur-
nishings, and even droves of oxen, to his rancho."[38] The American naval
officer Walter Colton also recounted an incident in which a "Spaniard"
took possession of a mission. Colton stated that he "extended his claims
over the grounds and the building, and was appropriating the whole to
his private purposes." When asked to show "evidence of his right and title
to the establishment . . . he had no document to exhibit" only the "vague
permission" of the government.[39]

Richard Henry Dana recorded his negative impression of secularization in *Two Years before the Mast*. He noted that the act had declared
"all the Indians free and independent Rancheros. The change in the condition of the Indians was, as may be supposed, only nominal: they are
virtually slaves, as much as they ever were."[40] Dana explained that "the
great possessions of the missions are given over to be preyed upon by
the harpies of the civil power, who are sent there in the capacity of *administradores*, to settle up the concerns; and who usually end, in a few
years, by making themselves fortunes, and leaving their stewardships
worse than they found them."[41] Like many others, he blamed corruption
for the program's failure. Dana concluded that secularization had a negative impact on the hide and tallow trade, and he lamented that "the
change had been made but a few years before our arrival upon the coast,

yet, in that short time, the trade was much diminished, credit impaired, and the venerable missions going rapidly to decay."[42]

On March 29, 1842, Governor Manuel Micheltorena, a staunch supporter of secularization, issued a proclamation to deal with some of the failings of the program. In this proclamation, he blamed both the Indians and the administrators for the poverty of the former missions. According to Micheltorena, Indians' racially inherent failings deprived newly secular California of an adequate labor force while thwarting liberal efforts to transfer land to the Indians. He explained that "the Indians, naturally lazy, from additional labor, scarcity of nourishment, and in a state of nudity, having no fixed employment or appointed Mission, prefer to keep out of the way and die in desert woods."[43] The governor did admit, however, that "in the administration of the Missions, there have been committed some frauds and notorious extravagance, which every inhabitant of California laments."[44]

The Secularization Act encouraged the governors of California to accelerate the distribution of private land grants, and they issued five hundred large land grants for cattle ranches between the passage of the Secularization Act in 1833 and the American conquest in 1846.[45] The total land distributed in grants during the Mexican period amounted to 10 million acres, 10 percent of California's surface area.[46] Between 1836 and 1842, Governor Juan Bautista Alvarado made several new land grants, many of which drew on former mission lands. These grants followed the pattern of earlier grants in that they tended to be very large. The extensive ranching needed to supply the hide and tallow trade encouraged these massive ranchos, and they easily outcompeted—and consumed—the smaller ranches created by the division of mission lands. The nature of California's maritime economy encouraged the economic and political domination of a few dozen major rancheros. Petitioners for land grants drew up a diseño. California did not contain enough surveyors to demarcate the boundaries of the ranchos with any exactitude, and land seemed so plentiful and the grants so large that such endeavors would have been impractical. Instead, a pair of vaqueros, measuring with a fifty vara reata (about 139 feet), usually determined the lengths and locations of the boundaries of their employer's ranch.[47] Increasingly, foreigners like John Sutter and William Leidesdorff obtained grants for their own operations. Sutter's grant for New Helvetia in the Central Valley covered nearly 50,000 acres, and he increased these holdings by purchasing Fort Ross from the Russians. Leidesdorff obtained a neighboring grant of about 35,000 acres in 1844.[48]

After secularization, the rancho rapidly supplanted the mission as the central economic and social institution of California, and ranching dons like the Picos and Vallejos became the dominant political figures in the region. All of this land served a clear purpose as pasturage, and cattle remained the dominant force in California's economy for the rest of the Mexican period. In 1842, the British explorer George Simpson noted that, in California, "the income of every farmer may be pretty accurately ascertained from the number of his cattle."[49] Considering each slaughtered animal's monetary value in hides and tallow and the fact that "the fourth part of the herd may generally be killed off every year without any improvidence," Simpson put the value of a herd at "a dollar and a quarter a head."[50] He then added examples, stating, "Thus, General Vallego [*sic*], who is said to possess 8,000 cattle, must derive about 10,000 dollars a year from this source alone and the next largest holders, an old man of the name of Sanches and his sons, must draw rather more than half of that amount from their stock of 4,500 animals."[51]

The largest ranchos were comparable in size to the enormous mission landholdings. Rancheros recruited Indian vaqueros from the missions, who now conducted rodeos and matanzas of rancho cattle rather than mission cattle to feed the Pacific hide and tallow market. Secularization may have had the goal of furthering the California Indians' transformation into economically independent gente de razón participating in a liberal, capitalistic economy, but it had the effect of dispossessing the mission Indians and transferring California's cattle economy into the hands of the ranchero class. Participation in the hide and tallow trade, made possible by the thriving herds established by the missionaries and their Indian laborers, had led to economic expansion in Alta California. Proponents of secularization hoped to liberalize and rationalize the economic exploitation of cattle by distributing the animals and land owned by the missions. The Secularization Act succeeded in privatizing California's bountiful pasturage, but most of the land went to large ranchos. Mission Indians, freed from a system that had exposed them to disease and death, corporal punishment, social control, and unfree labor did not always have an easy time finding a place in this liberalized California. Many had to seek work at low wages; many others moved back beyond colonial reach in the interior.

The Great Māhele and Hawaiian Ranching

In the mid-nineteenth century, the Hawaiians maintained a semblance of independence despite various European and American threats to their sovereignty. Nonetheless, Western ideas and economic systems also increased in influence among the islands' rulers. As discussed, until 1849, the Hawaiian royal family owned all the land, although much of it was still under the direct control of the Hawaiian nobility, who administered strips from the central mountains of each island to the sea called ahupua'a, which allowed each ali'i access to diverse resources. The maka'āinana, or commoners, held usufruct rights to farm certain portions of these lands, which they worked under the supervision of konohiki, land managers answerable to the ali'i. Unlike feudal serfs, maka'āinana could migrate freely, and they could also pass their land rights to descendants from generation to generation. Still, the ali'i retained ultimate control and could dispossess a commoner of their land rights at will, and maka'āinana could not buy or sell land.[52] Considering these limitations as disincentives to work and further development of the land, Western missionaries in the islands increasingly agitated for the right of commoners to buy land.

European and American immigrants and business interests, including those managing herds on the islands, also desired private ownership of land. From European contact, Hawai'i's native population had been steadily declining, due mainly to increased exposure to diseases.[53] This decline created vacancies, which haole businessmen saw as opportunities. In 1849, the royal family relented and instituted a land reform called the Great Māhele.[54] Hawai'i's minister of the interior, Gerritt Judd, an American missionary who had taken a position in Hawai'i's constitutional government, pushed for the measure, which effectively transformed the high chiefs' land into alienable private property.[55] Most land, except for reserved "Crown lands," passed from the royal family to the chiefs, who had now to survey their possessions. As one legal historian explained, "Indigenous oral property systems based on command over individual resources were converted into European written property systems based on command over zones of land."[56]

A variety of motivations, justifications, and interests prompted the reforms, including Western agrarian ideals and the missionary desire for independent commoners instead of tenants, chiefs who wished to increase their ability to profit from the land as Hawai'i increasingly engaged in international market economies, and the haole land speculators who eventually profited the most from the changes. Historian Lilikalā Kame'eleihiwa explains that "the publicly stated purpose of the Māhele was to create a body of landed commoners who would excel and prosper by means of small farms," but other interests often prevailed in the reform's execution.[57] Following policies that originated in colonial New England's "praying towns" and extended to the 1887 Dawes Act and beyond, American thinkers in the mid-nineteenth century held to an agrarian ideal in their attempts to "civilize" native peoples.[58] As in those cases, this ideal worked against the indigenous people it was meant to help.

English and American interests especially lobbied for such land reform, and clearly delineated land claims were central to Anglo-American concepts of colonial space. As historian Patricia Seed noted in her comparative study of colonialism, "Fixing the boundaries of plots carried far greater symbolic and cultural weight for settlers in the English colonies."[59] Discussions of borderlands often focus on the transition to bordered lands; contingent worlds of possibilities were reduced to a world of clear boundaries governed by identified and agreed-upon nation-states that were thus better able to exert their colonial will on conquered peoples. In the Anglo-American world, the important boundaries were not just between colonial powers but *within* colonial spaces. Clearly delineated titles made land legible and allowed greater power to the transnational force of capital. Officials transformed Hawai'i into a landscape of parceled fee simple land under the auspices of protecting royal Hawaiian sovereignty, and the imposition of national borders helped reify that sovereignty. But it also made Hawaiian land more vulnerable to the power of abundant foreign capital.

Cattle had begun this process, serving as vessels of property unleashed on the Hawaiian landscape and transforming that landscape, already portioned out for Hawaiian systems of agriculture, into a colonial commons. The landscape was then fenced in, or enclosed, in a manner that replicated European notions of landownership.[60] Richard Charlton's violent punishment of the Hawaiian who shot his cow demonstrates how Europeans could rewrite colonial conceptions of property by simply ignoring indigenous ideas of ownership. Kapu land, because it did not fit his concept of individual property ownership, became commons for his chattel animals. Because Charlton had the backing of an imperial power, his reading of the landscape could prevail over local customs. A comprehensive land reform was the next step in this process of shifting ideas about property.

Commoners could not legally fence in certain areas by orders of the ali'i, and the people who depended on such lands paid a price, which further drove home the lesson that fenced and bounded property would rule in Hawai'i. In some regions, the dryland or kula areas that ali'i and konohiki had allowed maka'āinana to use as commons had remained as commons. But, with cattle, those commons became open range. This is apparent in the northwestern portions of the Big Island, which included the Waimea Plains. With the increase of cattle on kula lands, agriculture began to diminish. On December 5, 1845, Lorenzo Lyons noted in his journal that "people are driven to the mountains to cultivate secure from cattle."[61] Some commoners could graze their own livestock on kula lands, but they increasingly found themselves competing with larger herds owned by foreigners and ali'i.[62] A letter in the August 26, 1848, edition of the *Polynesian* called the area "one great cattle pen."[63]

While ideology shaped the desire for land reform, the desire for personal profit motivated individuals to advance this colonial agenda. Many foreigners explicitly argued for land reform so that they could enter Hawaiian land markets. Hawaiian kings had granted foreigners land rights since the beginning of the nineteenth century. As we have seen, Francisco de Paula Marin and William French had acquired such grants, on Oahu and the Big Island, respectively, to run their own cattle. Other foreigners had similar grants for ranching and farming, and in 1844, a government official reported 125 usufruct land grants to foreigners.[64] However, their rights differed little from those of Hawaiians; they could not sell their land or increase their holdings through purchase, and they could lose their grants at the king's whim. Thus, land reform was of particular concern to these foreign land interests, but the British failed to acquire permanent land rights for British residents by treaty in the 1830s, and a similar American treaty effort failed in the early 1840s. The Hawaiian Privy Council actively resisted efforts to open Hawaiian land to foreign speculation throughout the 1830s and for most of the 1840s.[65]

Richard Charlton raised property issues with the attack on the Hawaiian who shot his cow, but he was at the center of an even larger international conflict over land. In 1826, the Hawaiian government had granted Charlton the plot of land in Honolulu on which he ran his herd of cattle. In 1840, Charlton produced another lease from 1826, signed by the deceased Governor Boki of Oahu, for an adjoining piece of land inhabited by Hawaiian commoners. The Hawaiian government refused to recognize the lease, and Charlton protested with the British government. British naval officers Alexander Simpson and Lord George Paulet used the consul's grievance as a pretext to annex the islands to the United Kingdom on February 25, 1843. After protests from the United States and resistance from the Hawaiian government, Paulet restored Hawaiian independence on July 31, 1843.[66] Imperial rivalries saved Hawaiian sovereignty, but issues of property, like the problem of debt, continually threatened the islands' continued independence. If not for Anglo-American rivalry, the Hawaiians may have lost sovereignty in 1843 over property issues.

Foreigners in Hawai'i had a significant voice in the islands' politics by the 1840s. While many Hawaiian commoners protested this influence and feared the consequences, most ali'i welcomed foreign expertise and the economic and political power that they gained through it.[67] In 1840, Hawai'i drafted its first written constitution, which established a constitutional monarchy following the British model. The constitution differentiated between the king's property and that of the government, though the king retained much authority over the government's property.[68] Several foreigners, largely from Great Britain and the United States, served in the Privy Council, advising the king. A New England missionary and physician named Gerritt P. Judd became one of the most powerful men in the Hawaiian government, and he served in a sequence of key cabinet positions beginning with his reform of the Treasury in 1842. Judd helped lead calls for land tenure reform.

The kingdom of Hawai'i's Scottish-born foreign minister Robert C. Wyllie was a strong proponent of ranching on the islands, and his views on the islands' cattle informed his influential advocacy of land reform. Wyllie wrote for the Royal Hawaiian Agricultural Society that with "God's promise to Abraham, Isaac, and Jacob . . . the pasturage of cattle, thus became and continues to be the chief occupations of God's chosen people."[69] Wyllie tied the march of Christian civilization to a pastoral economy, but he also took more pragmatic note of the islands' resources. He related to the French consul that "it is difficult to estimate exactly the number of Horned Cattle that there are on the Islands. But, if I put them down at 25 thousand wild and 10,000 tame on all the islands, I believe I would not over rate it."[70] Considering his observations of the opportunities presented by these animal resources, and the ideological imperative to exploit them, it is not surprising that ranching interests shaped Wyllie's advice to King Kamehameha III on the subject of land reform. He explained that "foreigners will never bring capital to your islands unless they can make a good profit from that capital. . . . If your islands produce Sugar, Coffee, Cotton, Indigo, Hides, Wool, the Foreigners will bring goods . . . or money."[71] Wyllie then stated that to fuel the productivity needed to generate these products "the native subjects must have land . . . and they must be sure that what they work for and what they produce will not be taken from them."[72] He then concluded that the king must grant "lands in the most liberal manner to all your subjects—of extending cultivation, or grazing, over your whole islands."[73] Wyllie linked capitalist production with a liberal land policy, and, highlighting the importance of ranching to Hawai'i's economy in the mid-nineteenth century, he noted the value of hides as a product and specifically pointed to grazing as a valid use of the land alongside cultivation.

The aliʻi shared much of Wyllie's philosophy. In his ethnographic work on the Hawaiian kingdom, Marshall Sahlins argued that the hide and tallow trade, along with the growing market for sugar, "had given values to Hawaiian lands which the chiefs could not capitalize on, except by trading off their proprietary rights."[74] In order to gain the profits from the land that cattle ranching made possible, aliʻi desired land reform to increase their rights to their holdings. Depopulation caused by disease had certainly cut the amount of ʻauhau, or tribute, that the land managers received from Hawaiʻi's peasant classes. This depopulation also probably added a moral component to the aliʻi's support of land reform; as historian Noenoe Silva argues, "The aliʻi . . . took the advice of the new kāhuna— missionaries and business advisors from England and America—that such a transformation of land management would act to restore the population, would inspire the makaʻāinana to work hard for material rewards in the capitalist economy being put into place, and would ease commercial treaty making with other members of the family of nations."[75] Just as many aliʻi saw the profits of cattle as a means to protect autonomy as well as for enrichment, they hoped to achieve the same ends by enacting land reform. They thought they could undo the disadvantages under which they labored in their contact with the West. However, by dissolving the reciprocal bonds of the feudal state so quickly, they left Hawaiian land vulnerable to foreign takeover.[76]

Legislation in December of 1845 formed the Board of Commissioners to Quiet Land Titles, or the Land Commission, to verify and record all land grants to aliʻi and foreigners. Written documents replaced customary recognition as part of the transition to a Western form of property. The original board's makeup further evidenced the influence of foreigners in the Hawaiian government. The commission had five members: two Americans, William Richards and John Ricord (the kingdom's attorney general); two Hawaiians educated by New England missionaries, Zorabella Kaauwai and John Ii; and James Young Kaneohoa, the half-Hawaiian son of John Young, Kamehameha I's British adviser.[77] William L. Lee, a lawyer from New York who became a justice in Hawaiʻi's Supreme Court, replaced William Richards in 1847 and served a long tenure on the Commission. The Commission had far-ranging powers and set the scene for broader reforms, and it acted as a court to adjudicate land claims for the next ten years. In 1848, King Kamehameha III formally divided land into royal holdings, government holdings, and chiefly holdings.

Native Hawaiians continued to fear the growing influence of foreigners in the government, and some protested the developing land reforms. Hawaiian petitioners from the Big Island wrote to the king that "We have heard the expressions made by Judd, to sell the lands to the foreigners. . . . The chiefs must not sell the lands to the whitemen nor the foreigners. . . . The selling of lands to outsiders is not a wise course, the lands being a source of benefit to the government, the throne, and the Hawaiian people."[78] In actuality, though Gerritt Judd favored land reform, he opposed legalizing the sale of land to foreigners in the short term, as he also feared that such an act would lead to a loss of Hawaiian sovereignty. However, in 1850, after Judd embarked on a diplomatic mission to Europe with members of the royal family, William L. Lee prompted the Hawaiian legislature to allow foreigners to buy land.[79] Maka'āinana petitioned the government to rescind this last law, realizing that many chiefs would readily sell their land to foreigners, which would deprive the commoners of their traditional farm lands. The House of Nobles firmly supported the law, suggesting that the commoners were correct in their assessment of the chiefs' desire to profit from land sales. The lower House initially opposed the law, but eventually relented.[80] While larger landowners stood to profit from lands sales and intensified commercial agriculture, evidence suggests that the king and other members of the government wanted to establish clear title to landholdings in case of annexation by a foreign power.[81]

In August of 1850, the legislature passed the Kuleana or "Rights" Act, which granted the commoners ownership of any land that they "occupy and improve."[82] In the culmination of a decade of land reform efforts, the maka'āinana now had access to fee simple ownership of land, but they could also sell that land to foreigners. The Land Commission continued to function, now verifying the claims of chiefs, commoners, and foreigners alike. Out of the approximately 72,000 commoners living in the islands by 1850, 12,000 (or one in six) filed for land claims. The Land Commission certified 9,300 land claims in all, most of them to commoners: 1.5 million acres went to the government, the king received 1 million acres, the ali'i possessed 1.6 million acres at an average of 1,532 each, and the commoners registered only 29,000 acres total, averaging 2.7 acres per claim. Illiteracy and remoteness, along with intimidation from konohiki, apparently prevented the vast majority of the maka'āinana from registering with the land commission, if they even realized the importance of doing so or the nature of the land reform.[83] G. M. Robertson, a young Scotsman appointed to the Land Commission in 1850, complained that the kuleana lands were too large, and he successfully worked to table legislation in the Hawaiian legislature to redress the unequal distribution of lands in the 1850s, leaving more land available to foreigners.[84] The lower Council House did resolve in August 1850 that "the Government and the chiefs should withhold the sale of lands to foreigners until after the people have had sufficient time to acquire what they want. Money should not be considered as of more importance, but that the common people be given ample opportunity to possess lands. Sales should be made to the people."[85]

The Council also declared that "the Government and landlords should not lease the lands in such a way as to cause the common people to be in want. Certain things of the mountains should not be tabooed such as grass, grass for thatching houses, and feed for stock to the common people of that land. Such things should be free for their benefit, for sale of for feeding their stock."[86] The Council worried that distribution of lands could tie up vital resources. The Council demonstrated its interest in an equal distribution of lands and the protection of native livelihoods, but its request held little power, and the Land Commission, governors, and ali'i often failed to comply. The comment implies that many commoners had access to livestock, perhaps cattle, that required pasturage, but it also demonstrates an astute awareness of the distinctions between the commons of the mixed ahupua'a and the parcels of the Western system. Some commoners had cultivated specific tracts of kula, the dryland agricultural areas, for generations, but the Land Commission granted very few pieces of kula to commoner claimants.[87] Government agents instead enforced the new property laws by excluding Hawaiians from traditional uses of former commons. Isaac Davis, an agent of the Department of the Interior on the Big Island (and the part-Hawaiian grandson of King Kamehameha's British adviser of the same name), noted with concern "the great number of people [kanaka] going up the mountain to chase wild pigs, and I have many times warned them about this matter."[88] Davis wrote to inquire how to deal with this infraction and "put more strength to the peace of the Government," suggesting, perhaps, the use of force to protect what was now clearly the Hawaiian government's property. He noted that "what I am sure about is this, that the wild pigs belong to the Government, and that the people have no right there."

In the Pacific economy of the mid-nineteenth century, the main methods to profit from Hawaiian land would be ranching and cash crop agriculture. Foreigners purchased large tracts of land for these purposes. Some Europeans and Americans had plans to establish sugar plantations; however, the acute shortage of labor in the disease-depleted islands made ranching the most profitable operation in the short term. Foreign-run sugar concerns would eventually dominate Hawai'i and become major suppliers to the United States, especially after a rapid increase in demand during the Civil War. However, ranchers made many of the initial land purchases in the first two decades. The kuleana tracts were generally too small and scattered to be of use as either ranch or plantation land. Ali'i sold some lands to foreigners, but the government's extensive landholdings, which the legislature made available for purchase at a dollar an acre in 1850, remained the most attractive. Ranchers purchased hundreds of acres of land from the government with approval from the Land Commission.[89] Europeans and Americans with herds of cattle soon established large ranches on several of the islands, including the vast Parker Ranch on the Big Island. When the United States annexed the Hawaiian Islands in 1898, whites owned four times as much land as native Hawaiians did.[90]

A Massachusetts man named John Palmer Parker founded what became Hawai'i's largest ranch. Parker was born in 1790, and he became a sailor at the age of eighteen. In 1815, Parker deserted his ship, the *Lelia Bird*, to take up residence in Hawai'i, and he eventually worked as a bullock hunter while maintaining a close relationship with the islands' monarchs. He claimed to have killed 1,200 cattle as a bullock hunter.[91] In the late 1810s, he married Kipikane, the daughter of an ali'i.[92] For his labors and presumably with the help of his aristocratic connections, he received a land grant in the Kohala district of the Big Island, and, in 1835, he built a house at Waimea and moved his family there.[93]

Bullock hunters tamed few of the wild cattle until horses from California became widely available in the 1820s, and tame cattle remained rare until the vaqueros arrived in 1832. William French, a Honolulu sandalwood trader, was "the first person that got a good private herd at Hawaii."[94] He moved to Waimea in the 1830s and gathered a tamed herd on a land grant from the government (probably from the governor of the island, "John Adams" Kuakini). The decline of the sandalwood trade and the rise of hides and tallow as valuable trade items had encouraged the merchant to change his focus. French hired experienced bullock hunters to manage his operation, including Parker and an Irish cowboy named W. W. "Harry" Purdy (Ikua Purdy's grandfather, more commonly known as Jack Purdy). While overseeing the successful growth of French's hide- and tallow-producing ranch, Parker also began to accumulate his own herd, and in the early 1840s, he ran his animals on government land on the slopes of Mauna Kea that he and French leased together.[95]

French and Parker both received land grants in fee simple from the Land Commission in 1846 and 1847, as well as continuing grazing rights on government lands in Waimea. On January 8, 1847, the Land Commission granted Parker two acres on the Waimea plains as a site for a new home; this grant would grow into the largest ranch in Hawaiʻi.[96] When French became embroiled in the bankruptcy of his firm, French & Greenway, he abandoned his cattle-ranching operation. Parker's remaining rival was George Beckley, the man appointed to watch the government cattle.[97] Beckley had several paniolo and an extensive range on which to pasture his animals. However, private ranchers like Parker and Purdy benefited a great deal from the law allowing foreigners to purchase government lands; the Land Commission allowed Purdy to purchase 500 acres.[98] Parker bought a series of parcels around his Waimea land grant. In 1850, Parker purchased 640 acres around his 2-acre home lot, on January 29, 1851, he acquired another 1,000 acres at seventy-five cents an acre, and he received a further grant from the king in 1852.[99] Parker, with active support from the Land Commission and the king, rapidly acquired a sizable ranch under the new fee simple land regime. He continued to purchase tracts through the 1850s as they became available, and by his death on March 20, 1868, Parker's ranch extended for almost 94,000 acres.[100] Parker's half-Hawaiian sons maintained the operation, which eventually grew to more than 150,000 acres, more than three times larger than all the grants to commoners on the islands combined, and remained an independent ranch in the hands of the Parker family until 1992.

The establishment of ranches did end the pressures on the cattle population that had prompted the second kapu in 1844. Levi Haʻalelea remembered the Māhele as a bookend to the kapu, and he related that it lasted "until the grants were issued."[101] The issuance of the grants that created Hawaiʻi's first private ranches served as an epochal marker in the islands' development. The new order of land tenure replaced previously informal arrangements. A member of the Ministry of Interior wrote to George Heue Davis, their agent in Waimea, to demand that a man named Farani (probably a partial Hawaiianization of French, as in William French) "compensate the Government for the use of the land by means of cattle. Because he has raised cattle on this land previously, without paying the Government for the use of the land for a number of years past, acting as if he really owns the land there."[102] Other applicants failed in their objectives to acquire newly scarce grazing lands. A clerk for the Department of the Interior wrote to a "Mr Kaoo" in 1850 to inform him that the government had refused his request because "the land applied for is now being put to use by the Government as grazing land for the cattle owned by the Government. Therefore your application has been denied."[103] On the Big Island, Western ranching began to spread. In 1848, Waimea had been "one great cattle pen." By 1864, cattle were spreading to the neighboring, rockier, Kohala district. That year, the missionary Reverend Elias Bond recorded that "the entire tract of country is gradually filling with cattle and sheep belonging to foreigners, and the natives, as a matter of necessity, are rapidly leaving the district, chiefly for Oahu."[104] With Land Commission decisions eschewing traditional rights to commons, Hawaiians had no choice but to abandon those commons in the face of ranging foreign cattle, which certainly made it easier for foreigners to gain even more land. They went to Oahu, probably to do wage work, perhaps on the growing plantations.

As the Western notion of alienable property in land took hold, the issue of the disposition of the feral cattle remained. While the king had always claimed a right to the wild animals scattered throughout the islands, since the advent of the paniolo, budding ranchers had used them as a common resource from which to build a herd, in a process parallel to the "mavericking" of unbranded cattle in Texas at the height of the cattle boom.[105] Before the Māhele proper had even begun, agents of the government, like William Beckley and George Heue Davis, began to brand the feral cattle on government lands on the Big Island.[106] Gerritt Judd hired a vaquero named Miguel (or "Miele") to brand and manage the feral cattle in the Wailua region of Kaua'i, and his contract stipulated that "Miguel will keep a record of the number of cattle."[107] The new approach to property in Hawai'i demanded a clearer dispensation of all of the cattle on the islands. John Young Kanehoa acknowledged the government's role in distributing cattle when he petitioned for his own herd in April 1850. John Young Kanehoa claimed that the king had granted his father, John Young, several cattle, which had become mixed in with the cattle now claimed by the Hawaiian government. As a result, he requested that Kamehameha III "give instructions that some of these cattle be given to me, and my younger brother and my sisters, the heirs of John Young, the close companion of your father."[108] John Young Kanehoa utilized family to navigate the new system of ownership and receive a dispensation of government resources. Word of such efforts to assert and consolidate control over bovine property on the islands must have spread. In November, a cowboy named Huana Paniolo (likely a vaquero named Juan), after explaining that "I am not employed by any person at the present nor am I very well in circumstances," wrote to John Young and claimed that "I can Get All you Bullock."[109]

In 1859, Hawai'i's minister of the interior leased some of the royal lands on Mauna Kea to the English merchants Robert Janion and William Green. The lease agreement gave these Englishmen the right to all the wild cattle on the leased lands. In early 1860, George Davis, who owned lands adjoining the royal lands on Mauna Kea leased by Janion and Green, took twenty-nine hides from unbranded cattle on his own lands only to have them confiscated by William Green. Davis sued in the Hawaiian courts, claiming that the unbranded cattle were *ferae naturae*, or wild animals held in common until someone asserted property rights to them by taking the energy to tame them. The case went all the way to the Hawaiian Supreme Court, where on March 28, 1861, Justice George Robertson wrote an opinion finding for the defendant. It seems that the "mountain cattle of the King and Government," despite their wild state, had always been the alienable property of the king.[110]

The overall effect of this decision was to assert again Western property rights in both the land and the animals themselves. Both sides of the case, with their European surnames (George Davis was the mixed-descent son of Isaac Davis, the first permanent American resident of the islands, and his Hawaiian wife), argued in terms of Western legal traditions of property. Davis evoked the principle of *ferae naturae* and disavowed the animals' domestic origin and long history of utilization. The animals had long been treated as part of the commons, but the leasing of the land and exclusive rights to the animals thereon specifically to Janion and Green signaled a change in the royal government's relationship to property. Earlier it had paid two dollars per hide to any bullock hunter willing to brave the feral longhorns; now the government, which no longer possessed the ultimate deed to all the land in the islands, was asserting a more direct control over the lands and resources that remained under its purview. Chief Justice Robertson fully endorsed this new relationship with the land, and Janion's right to the feral cows even as they wandered onto Green's land. British Consul Richard Charlton had enforced the property rights inherent in his cow with a violent attack; now the Hawaiian courts upheld the same idea.[111]

John Palmer Parker also became involved in the case, as he had a large ranch adjoining government lands and occasionally laid claim to unbranded cattle around Waimea. Parker also disputed the government's claim to all unbranded cattle, though he crafted an argument more in line with the post-Māhele construction of property rights in Hawai'i. Parker claimed that cattle in the Ohia forest on his lands presented a distinct case and that "the cattle running in the district I speak of are, and have always been considered as totally distinct from the so-called Mountain Cattle, inasmuch as they are the progeny of private herds, and generally speaking, of a totally different breed."[112] Parker argued that these particular cattle had escaped from the tame herds that he had assembled with William French and Harry Purdy in the late 1830s. He explained, "From the nature of the county to the windward of our private lands (a dense forest and almost impenetrable undergrowth covering nearly the whole of it), as the herds increased it became an impossibility to prevent cattle from time to time getting beyond the reach or our control, and gradually they have filled this land with their offspring." He concluded that these escaped cattle and their descendants "have not been generally branded, though their private origin and ownership is notorious and cannot be disputed."[113] Parker made his claim to unbranded cattle by reaffirming the government's claim that branding merely signified ownership but did not create it. The cattle had an inherent status as his "fixed property," even if he had not yet claimed them. The Department of the Interior responded with a compromise. They explained that "all unbranded cattle or horses of a certain age are considered to be the property of the government, but . . . [the minister of the interior] has never granted to anyone the privilege of taking wild cattle on private lands."[114] Thus, while the government still claimed the feral cattle, they would not disturb them on Parker's land.

Robertson's final decision recognized the government's right to lease the wild cattle while also reaffirming the sanctity of the private ranch, a growing concern by the 1860s. Robertson explained that "we wish it therefore to be distinctly understood that while we hold that neither the plaintiff, nor others, have a right to take and convert those cattle, because found upon their lands, Mr. Janion or his agents have no right to enter upon those lands, for the purposes of capturing cattle under his grant from the King and Government, without the consent of the owners of the lands, nor to take and convert the cattle of private owners, because found *unbranded* upon the lands leased by him."[115] The king's (and thus Janion's) rights to the feral cattle of Mauna Kea were sacrosanct, but so were Davis's land rights. Davis could not kill the king's cattle on his land, nor could Janion go onto Davis's land to do so. After more than three generations of Vancouver's introduction running feral on Hawai'i, land and animals, even wild ones, had become property with specific owners who held the rights to them.

Native Ranches

The sweeping land reforms in California and Hawai'i in the 1830s and 1840s cemented the control of European and American ranching and agricultural interests in both regions and led to the dispossession of native peoples. Both regions in the late 1840s and early 1850s fell under the economic domination of large ranch owners, who controlled native labor to produce hides and tallow for the Pacific market. Some Indian vaqueros used their newfound freedom to compete in an open labor market, moving to higher-paying ranches and relocating for work in urban centers.[116] Many more found themselves constrained in systems of debt peonage. Rarest of all were Indian-controlled ranches, as both land and animals increasingly fell into the orbit of large ranches. However, vestiges of native control over introduced livestock remained in the 1850s within this new capitalistic system of increasingly privatized pastoral economies. These native ranches reveal the contingencies of the shifting world of Pacific livestock economies in the mid-nineteenth century.

Many Indians did receive secularized mission lands as intended. While the largest rancheros came to dominate California's political life, most landholders, both white and Indian, owned small plots. Because of the nature of economic life in pre–gold rush California, even these small landholders often owned and managed a few cattle. A hundred Juaneño Indians from San Juan Capistrano received small plots of land from 1.8 to 10.8 acres, and, even as they worked as laborers on larger ranches, many used the skills they had gained to manage their own cattle grazing on the town commons created by Figueroa's secularization orders.[117] A third of San Carlos Borromeo's Indian population, or about a hundred, settled on small land grants around Carmel following secularization. Steven Hackel has observed that a select few "Indians who were acculturated and connected to Franciscan and Mexican officials" generally received the largest and most lasting ranch lands "of hundreds, perhaps thousands, of acres."[118] Most mission Indians, however, received small plots and no official recognition of title. The hide trade supercargo Faxon Dean Atherton recounted a typical encounter with these small Indian ranches. While traveling near San Francisco in 1836, he "stopped at a Rancho of some Indians, [and] had some dried beef broiled on the coals."[119] The lack of names and details suggest a landholding (and a people) of little importance to the hide trader.

Thirty-two families of Indians from Mission San Luis Rey obtained a twenty-square-mile block of land that they used communally to raise sheep and cattle and to grow other crops like wine grapes and corn. Their village was called Pueblito de las Flores.[120] By 1843, the influential Pico family had purchased this land. In 1834, Cristina Salgado, a widowed Esselen transplanted to San Carlos from San Luis Obispo, received recognition of her 2,200-acre rancho in the Salinas Valley. She emphasized the improvements she had made to develop the rancho.[121] Over the next decade, she operated a successful ranch that engaged in the Pacific hide and tallow trade. In 1844, she sold the property to a Californio named Rafael Estrada.[122] Cristina Salgado's ten years as the owner of her own rancho was rare for Indian rancho owners, who had difficulty acquiring large tracts of land and were prey to the deprivations of Californio landowners who challenged their land rights. The administrator of San Carlos after secularization, José Antonio Romero, created his own significant ranch by sequestering mission resources, rustling Indian cattle and moving on Indian lands.[123]

The two largest and most significant Indian ranchos in California developed near Mariano Guadalupe Vallejo's massive ranching operations on the northern edge of Californio settlement. The Miwok village of Olompali in the valley of the Petaluma River developed into a successful ranching operation under indigenous leadership. The village headman, Camillo Ynitia, maintained a friendly relationship with Vallejo, who had established the vast Rancho Petaluma nearby in 1836 while administering the secularization of Mission San Francisco de Solano in the Sonoma Valley. Vallejo distributed mission lands to the local Indians, but he failed to file for formal titles for any of these lands, and he confiscated these smaller grants in 1839 under the pretense that the Indians had not made use of their new property.[124] While many Indians in the region lost their land, Ynitia obtained his own cattle, five or six hundred head, and utilized his relationship with Vallejo to petition Governor Micheltorena successfully for official title to 8,000 acres around Olompali.[125] Though the Franciscans at Mission San Rafael had baptized many Indians from Olompali in the 1820s, the village had continued to operate as an independent ranchería and a successful ranch.[126] The second-generation Pacific trader and California resident William Heath Davis Jr. described Ynitia as a "fine, intelligent and shrewd man" who "owned 600 cattle, numerous horses and sheep, and was quite a noted breeder."[127] According to Davis, Ynitia had mastered a series of Western-style management skills for his participation in California's economy. Davis noted, "He was punctual in meeting his obligations, and, owing to this and to his affability and intelligence, was highly esteemed by us all. He could read and write and keep accounts, having been educated by the old missionaries."[128] In 1852, concerned that the U.S. Land Commission in California would not certify his title (though they eventually did), Camillo Ynitia sold his disputed Olompali lands to James Black for $5,200, well under market value.[129] Though he was by all accounts very successful, even Ynitia's ranching operation was short-lived.

The Patwin Indian Sem-Yeto, also known as Chief Solano, also exploited an alliance with Vallejo to establish an Indian rancho in Sonoma. Born in 1800, Sem-Yeto became a powerful leader of the Suisun band with regional influence among several other bands.[130] As Francisco Solano, he allied with the Vallejos in conflicts with the Indians around their Northern California landholdings. Mariano Vallejo knew that an alliance with the Suisun was crucial to solidifying his power in the north, and he won Sem-Yeto over during a negotiation in 1834. To secure peace, Vallejo offered a gift of horses with fine silver tack.[131]

Solano joined Vallejo in a military conflict against the Yolotoi band of Patwin, and he also recaptured horses stolen by the Mokelumnes.[132] In return for this alliance, Mariano Vallejo intervened to acquire a significant land grant for Solano. On January 16, 1837, Solano submitted a written request for the grant, in which he stated that "Francisco Solano, principle chief of the unconverted Indians and born Captain of the Suisuns submits that . . . being a free man, and owner of a sufficient number of horses and cattle to establish a rancho, asks that you grant him the land of Suisun."[133] The land that he received when the governor finally approved this grant extended more than four square leagues, or more than 30,000 acres. Solano successfully argued that his ownership and management of livestock validated his claim over the Suisun grant. Solano managed Suisun well for the next few years, but Vallejo eventually purchased the rancho, leading some to speculate that Vallejo had conspired with Solano for the Indian to receive title to the land before transferring it.[134] Vallejo did take control of native herds following depopulation due to malaria in 1835, as the Suisun population fell dramatically from perhaps 4,000 to 200. Rather than simply seizing the profits from this windfall, Vallejo took care to track the Indian titles of these animals.[135] These examples demonstrate successful indigenous adaptation to the opportunities presented by cattle and active participation in trans-Pacific cattle markets, but these Indians' ranches still depended on the support of the influential Californio leader Vallejo.

Cattle did not displace the Indians, but the exploitation of cattle resources by Spanish, Mexican, Californio, and American settlers did. The power of these groups precluded California's Indians from developing their own ranching operations without the umbrella of protection of influential, nonindigenous patrons. Charles Wilkes, discussing secularization, noted that "the claims of the Indians are entirely overlooked, and in the event of their taking the cattle that in truth belong to them, they are severely punished."[136] Despite short-lived legitimate ranching opportunities in the 1830s and 1840s, California Indian adaptation to old-world domestic animals remained for the most part confined to thievery on the fringes of Euro-American settlement in California. Most Californios and foreign settlers operated under the assumption that Indians with livestock had stolen the animals. This assumption led to violence and a near invasion on Sutter's ranch lands in 1845. A group of Walla Walla Indians from the Pacific Northwest traveled south to trade with Sutter, and they brought several horses and a herd of cattle. A California rancher named Grove Cook claimed that the Indians had stolen his mule, and he killed their leader's son in a fit of violence. The Indians fled, and rumors of a massive Walla Walla invasion circulated throughout California for the following months, as the Indians demanded the return of their livestock and retribution for the murder that Cook committed.[137] The invasion never materialized, and the Walla Walla eventually made peace with Sutter and joined one of his Indian brigades.

IN HAWAI'I, EVEN AS Western property values came to dominate the ranching economy and American-owned ranches grew, natives also continued to profit from cattle. An 1853 official registry of brands for the Big Island contained thirteen names of cattle owners, along with their brands. Two are identifiable as Western names ("Mr. H. Reed" and "Daniel Ely"), and one other seems unlikely to be Hawaiian ("P. Basenaba"); the rest seem to be Hawaiian, or at least Hawaiianized names ("Moke," "Aa," "Kahoonka," "Kaina," "Polili," "Kapunoho," "Olu," "Honoiwa," "Kapuahi," "Papu").[138] This snapshot of brand registration demonstrates that native Hawaiians persisted in the cattle industry even through the transition to ranching. At the same time, and in contrast to the agrarian values espoused by the proponents of the Māhele, most cattle remained in the hands of the former chiefly landlords of the ahupua'a, while cattle continued to threaten commoners' crops. Furthermore, enforcement of the Māhele actually made it difficult for the maka'āinana who ran a few cattle to keep their livestock. They had used kula lands, the portions of the ahupua'a reserved for dryland agriculture, as a commonage to run cattle. The Māhele ended this practice. To add insult to injury, aliʻi and haole cattle would trample boundary lines of the commoners' kuleana grants, making them harder to defend before the land commission.[139] As Marshall Sahlins explains, "Cattle was a business for chiefs and Haole," and archaeologists have found few remains of cattle in digs of commoners' landholdings.[140] Within a few decades of the Māhele, even the native elite's landholdings dwindled in the face of American advances in the islands' economy. Americans like Parker now owned most of the ranches and were able to gather up most of the feral cattle into permanent privately held herds.

Some Hawaiian commoners left out of the land and ranching order resisted in forms that echoed the actions of California Indians. In the 1850s, native cattle rustlers preyed on the large herds of Parker Ranch. A "huge, bearded Hawaiian" named Kamaka stole many animals from Big Island ranchers and confused trackers by shoeing his horses backward. Another Hawaiian rustler named Ioane kept a herd of stolen cattle hidden on the slopes of Mauna Kea and rode a specially trained horse.[141] In 1861, a circuit judge sentenced two other Hawaiians, Moo and Kahololio, to four years in prison "for two separate larcenies of Bullocks, the property of O. H. Gulick" on Molokai.[142] In 1849, a group of ranchers on Oahu named James Robinson, Robert Lawrence, R. W. Holt, and Joseph Booth complained of natives attacking their cattle, and they claimed that one of their animals was "beaten with stones and other missiles, until in plunging about the animal fell and broke its neck."[143] Hawaiians, like California Indians, continued to find ways to take advantage of livestock even after Western ideas about property closed avenues of legal exploitation.

Conclusion

Westerners proposed land reforms in the mid-nineteenth-century Pacific with the justification that it would lead to native control over land and domestic animal resources. Whether reformers were sincere or not, and there is ample evidence—like the makeup of the Hawaiian Land Commission—to suggest that they were not, land liberalization clearly led to further dispossession of native peoples. Mission Indians traded the limited security of the missions for the limited liberty of free labor. Indian vaqueros went from managing herds that were ostensibly theirs but paternalistically controlled by mission fathers to managing herds owned by rancheros for wages that were undercut by mounting debts. Native

Hawaiian paniolo traded peonage to native elites for poverty or debt peonage to haole. These transitions did nothing to avert ongoing demographic, cultural, and economic disasters for these peoples.

However, land reform did offer the promise of independence and self-sufficiency through domestic animals. Environmental historians have often depicted introduced livestock as organic technologies to dispossess native people of their land; however, in this moment, if native peoples had received title to land and animals, those animals could have served as a resource to allow native people to compete in the global markets into which they were being inexorably pulled. The roots of failure lie not in the very introduction of the animals or the mere proposal of land reform; rather, both represented opportunities, however risky. Paternalism, racism, and greed destroyed those opportunities. Land commissioners, ali'i, property speculators, and rancheros actively worked to keep native peoples uninformed of their rights as they seized property throughout the Pacific. Domestic animals were tools, and the flourishing of a few native ranches, big and small, show that they could have been tools for indigenous people. But colonial powers, both individuals and institutions, stacked the deck against them, and most native ranches did not survive for a decade because of colonizers' interventions. In the end, cattle were tools of Western colonization, and Western ranches came to dominate these Pacific landscapes by the 1850s. But it was the power of the colonizers, and not that of the cattle, that created this colonial world.

Conclusion

After 1850, the eastern Pacific economy shifted as hides and tallow became less profitable in the second half of the nineteenth century. In 1846, Thomas Larkin reported that annual hide exports had fallen to 85,000 and added that Californians exported 60,000 arrobas (1.5 million pounds) of tallow.[1] The trade from places like Hawai'i and especially California had glutted the market in Europe, while increased stability in Brazil, Chile, and Argentina had further increased supply. John Coffin Jones lamented price decreases for hides in 1846 and again in 1848.[2] The gold rush in California demanded importation of goods from around the world, and this new demand for beef temporarily kept Hawaiian ranchers' profit margins high as they now shipped salted beef back across the Pacific to the birthplace of the first Hawaiian longhorns and the vaqueros who had trained the paniolo. But this boom was short-lived. In 1848, producers could not keep up; by 1849, Hawaiian newspapers complained of a depression.[3] In subsequent decades, foreign landholders would focus Hawaiian lands on the production of sugar.

The gold rush created internal markets for beef within California, as well, which helped to replace the hide and tallow trade. Ranchos thrived through the 1850s, but they overstocked rangelands, especially in the southern half of the state. A succession of devastating floods and droughts in the early 1860s dealt a death blow to the traditional rancho operations.[4] While ranching of beef and dairy cattle remained a major industry in California, gold and then wheat quickly replaced ranching as economic foci. American visitors had always envisioned a California moving beyond its pastoral stage to an agricultural or even industrial economy, and American pioneers saw themselves as transforming wilderness into "beautiful, productive fields and farms."[5] Ranching was just a stop along the path to civilization in these visions, and Californians would come to see it as a romantic but lost part of California's past.

In the second half of the nineteenth century, the scale and efficiency of ranches in both regions expanded dramatically as industrial techniques and machinery came to dominate beef and dairy operations. In California, Miller & Lux built an integrated ranching monopoly that dominated the state.[6] In Hawai'i, the Parker Ranch continued to control much of the rangelands of Waimea. In 1899 the Parker family appointed Alfred Wellington Carter as manager of the ranch. Carter ran the ranch until 1937, and he introduced his own industrial accounting methods and labor systems.[7] The Hawaiian-born son of an American whaler who attended Yale, Carter increased the efficiency of many ranching operations and oversaw the improvement of breeding stock among ranch animals. These changes signaled the end of the ranching frontier and the advent of modern Western ranching economies.

While cattle diminished in economic importance, they had played their part in resolving the imperial contests of the Pacific. The United States had been one of the last entrants into these imperial rivalries, but as American merchants became more active throughout the region and as expansionism in the form of Manifest Destiny briefly dominated American politics, it rose to become the dominant force in the region. The United States conquered Alta California during the U.S.-Mexican War in 1846, and Mexico formally ceded the region to the United States in the Treaty of Guadalupe-Hidalgo in January 1848, the same month in which workers constructing a mill for John Sutter discovered gold. The Treaty of Guadalupe-Hidalgo and negotiations with Britain over the Oregon Territory reified and solidified the borders of North America's Pacific coast, and the possibilities of the eastern Pacific borderlands became constrained by the force of American law and the power of American capital both backed by the potential of American military force. Hide and tallow traders had played a key role in this transition, reporting to Washington, D.C., in the 1830s and 1840s, supporting American agents like John Charles Frémont, and gaining allies among the Californio elite through marriage alliances and promises of economic benefits.[8]

In 1851, while the Land Commission still operated in Hawai'i, a different Land Commission began its work in California. Rapid immigration to the gold fields, which included many Hawaiians, resulted in California statehood in 1850, before residents had time to resolve property conflicts resulting from the transition from Mexican rule. Because diseños did not match the standards of American surveying, extended and expensive legal battles tied up many of the Californios' ranchos. Legal fees and squatters drove many Californios' lands into American ownership.[9] Walter Colton, in his role as the first American alcalde of Monterey, often had to adjudicate property disputes. He recounted an incident in which "a farmer in Santa Cruz had extended his improvements over the lands of another, which lay contiguous to his own, and it became necessary to go and define the boundaries by the original titles."[10] He told another story of a ranchero who "not liking his own land, had lifted his boundary line, and projected it some six miles over that of his neighbor." When Colton asked the ranchero to produce a land grant to compare with the grant on file, he found that they were very different, and "the fact was, the man had two grants," and both were "signed, sealed and delivered with all the formalities of the law."[11] For many Californios, land reform was a double-edged sword. Rancheros could claim what they saw as common lands from missions and Indians, but American officials, in turn, created legal apparatuses that could make those claims difficult and costly to defend.

While further changes in California's land tenure dispossessed many of the Californios, these changes were even more disastrous for California Indians. They had failed to reap the benefits of secularization, and under U.S. rule, California Indians lost more land to prospectors and farmers, continued to fall victim to disease epidemics, and faced an escalation of violence from white settlers.[12] American ranches built on the transformation of Indian labor begun by the Spanish; they still used systems of debt peonage, and they reaped the benefits of the proletarianization of California Indians, though they complained that the vaqueros had become too independent following secularization.[13] In 1850, California passed "an Act for the Government and Protection of Indians," which codified the use of convict labor, child slavery, and added vagrancy laws to contain and coerce Indian labor. The Spanish and Mexican era cattle industries had prepared many Indians to serve as a cheap force of wage laborers, especially in California agriculture. Eventually, American policy toward Indians outside these systems of labor concentrated on gathering the Indians in reservations throughout the state.[14] California Indians again did their best to adapt to this new order and to subsist on the limited opportunities this new wage economy provided.[15] Indians who strayed from this system faced Anglo-American violence or legalized exploitation. For instance, the Modoc in northeastern California worked for low wages as ranch hands but also attempted to retain traditional lands and ran afoul of white Californians as a result. This conflict led to the Modoc War of 1872–73. Historian Andrew Isenberg has noted that the

Modoc readily adjusted to colonial economic transformations. They served as brokers for the Great Basin horse trade, herded sheep, and finally labored on cattle ranches. As Isenberg notes, "The Modocs resorted to violence in 1872 not to preserve their precontact traditions but to protect the adaptations they had made to the Anglo ranching economy."[16]

Although the kingdom of Hawai'i retained nominal sovereignty for most of the rest of the nineteenth century, the dispossession of commoners and haole control of most Hawaiian land created a powerful colonial force within Hawaiian society and the Hawaiian government. Foreign ranches profited from these changes for a few decades, but foreign-owned plantations began to dominate by the 1860s. Planters had made attempts to grow sugar in the islands before; the New England–born businessmen of Ladd & Co. founded a small sugar operation called Koloa Plantation on the island of Kaua'i in 1835. Even sugar depended somewhat on cattle in the 1830s. While inspecting Koloa Plantation, one American businessman observed that "the Lands . . . would be much improved by cattle dung, either from the pen, or cattle staking upon the land and that assisted by the plough would cause the land to give good return. . . . Were two or three hundred head of *tame* cattle introduced, they would add much to the value of the property by their dung alone."[17] The plantation struggled with Hawaiian laborers who resisted a harsh work regimen and protested for higher wages in 1841, and the plantation shut down in 1844.[18] Before the Māhele, Hawaiians were able to control, to some extent, the price and terms of their labor, even in the wage economy that Ladd & Co. sought to create at Koloa.

After the land reform, foreigners again attempted to found sugar plantations, and the industry grew rapidly during the American Civil War, which interrupted sugar production in the American South. Plantation owners no longer had to worry as much about the labor supply; native Hawaiians had fewer choices than at Koloa, and immigration from Asia added to the workforce. In 1875, two haole special commissioners negotiated a reciprocity treaty with the United States on behalf of the kingdom of Hawai'i that exempted much of Hawaiian sugar from U.S. tariffs. The treaty made little economic sense for the United States, but it did give the United States special status in Hawaiian trade and guaranteed that Hawai'i would not grant the same status, or yield its sovereignty, to any other imperial power.[19] The United States began to assert its control over Hawaiian affairs, and the American-allied sugar planters became a powerful interest against the reassertion of native Hawaiian rights. In 1887, a group of American businessmen oversaw the creation of a new Hawaiian constitution, the "Bayonet Constitution," which limited the elected king's power, denied the vote to Asians, and set property limits on voting that disenfranchised many Hawaiian commoners and gave naturalized Americans and Europeans disproportional power. On January 13, 1893, after Queen Lili'uokalani announced plans to rescind the 1887 constitution, a "Committee of Public Safety," made up of mostly American businessmen and professionals with ties to sugar plantations, seized power.[20] The new government petitioned for admission to the United States, and President William McKinley annexed the islands after the Spanish-American War in 1898. Plantation owners played the key role in these final assertions of American power in Hawai'i, but they, in turn, owed their presence and preeminence in no small part to the changes wrought by foreign cattle interests—the land reform and the proletarianization of Hawaiian workers at midcentury.

While native Hawaiians had lost most of their land, many white ranchers married native Hawaiians, and their mixed descendants inherited ranch lands and herds. Ikua Purdy, the aforementioned winner of a national rodeo championship in 1908, was one of bullock hunter Harry Purdy's part-Hawaiian descendants. During annexation, the part-Hawaiian descendants of John Palmer Parker and Harry Purdy remained loyalists; however, ranch manager Alfred Wellington Carter had previously served as the lawyer of Lorrin Thurston, the American ringleader of the Bayonet Constitution and the annexationist coup.[21] While the creation of large Hawaiian ranches depended on land reform, ranchers did not necessarily push for annexation as much as stockholders in sugar plantations, which U.S. tariffs impacted severely. The divided loyalties of the Parker ranch's owners and manager represent the changing identities within the Hawaiian ranching community during the late nineteenth and early twentieth centuries as well as conflicts over the annexation of Hawai'i within the islands.

WHILE A POTENTIAL WORLD of native ranch owners collapsed following mid-nineteenth-century land reforms, native cattle cultures still flourished. Immigrants filled the cowboy ranks, as well, and California Indian vaqueros competed with white, Mexican, and African American labor while Japanese, Filipinos, haole, and others became paniolo. Indigenous cowboys continued to know the animals and the land through their labor, and they were frontline witnesses of the changes wrought by cattle. Cattle and cowboys reshaped the land as the land shaped and influenced them. Indian vaqueros, and Indian labor in general, faded somewhat from the romanticized version of California's Spanish and Mexican past that emerged around the turn of the twentieth century, though some writers worked to keep the historical memory of their work alive, and many Indians continued to work on ranches.[22] On the other hand, paniolo became and have remained a celebrated part of Hawaiian culture. Ikua Purdy's victory at the Frontier Days' World Steer Roping Championship in 1908 embodied paniolo culture as well as trans-Pacific biological and cultural exchanges. Slack key guitar playing, designs for saddles, and the use of the lei all represent unique Hawaiian cowboy traditions.[23] In 1987, the Honolulu Academy of the Arts organized a traveling exhibition of paniolo folk arts called *Nā Paniolo o Hawai'i*. The exhibition collected examples of the cultural connections between Hawaiian paniolo and Californian vaqueros, as well as the unique cultural adaptations made by Hawaiian cowboys. These indigenous cattle cultures, although forged in the context of imperial advance and ecological devastation, embody notions of cultural survival through adaptation. That said, they are meager consolation for a tragic history of dispossession. And outside Hawai'i and the Indian communities of California, few heard their stories. Performers of memory like Buffalo Bill's Wild West show whitewashed cowboy history. Owen Wister's honorable and civilized, but not *too* civilized, Anglo cowboy in *The Virginian* became the prototype for cowboy heroes as the Western genre conquered print fiction and film in the twentieth century. Thus, Ikua Purdy and his fellow paniolo from the Parker Ranch were not "real cowboys" in 1908 Wyoming.

The island biogeographies of Hawai'i and California were overwhelmed, and the two regions' relative isolation disappeared in the few decades between the Spanish colonization of Alta California in 1769 and the Māhele and Treaty of Guadalupe-Hidalgo in 1848. They found themselves colonial prizes in well-trafficked seas between clamoring imperial powers. Over the course of just two generations, the indigenous inhabitants saw seismic shifts all around them. Cattle were at the heart of these transformations. Cook, Vancouver, Serra, Anza, and others all saw cattle as the key to remaking the indigenous peoples they encountered, and this did occur over the following decades, though perhaps not as they imagined. The cattle ate native grasses, outcompeted native grazers, encouraged invasive species, and changed Pacific landscapes in the process. They also enabled the permanent establishment of European influence and colonists, and they created interlinked economies that furthered conquest. The vast herds of California existed to feed the extensive tallow-rendering and hide-tanning operations. Beef was also an important resource to feed the crews of European and Euro-American ships, which increased their Pacific traffic throughout the nineteenth century as a result of the exploitation of oceanic resources like whales, shipping routes to Asian markets, and the settlement of Europeans and Euro-Americans in Pacific regions. Their common roles in livestock-related commerce and the movement of native laborers and European traders between California and Hawai'i served to link the two regions. Thus, capitalists in Honolulu, Monterey, Lima, and Boston influenced the development of California's central pre–gold rush resource and helped shape the ranching frontiers of the Southwest in the context of a broader Pacific. Flows of goods and capital shaped the course of eastern Pacific colonial contests.

Still, California Indians and native Hawaiians made adaptations that allowed them to harvest the opportunities for wealth and flexibility these biological resources presented. The works of Alfred Crosby and Elinor Melville have established an important background for historical understandings of the roles played by biological invasions in the history of places like Hawai'i, and their declensionist ecological narratives are probably correct to a great extent. Still, the history of indigenous adaptation complicates the conclusions reached through their broad and mechanistic approaches. The processes that helped integrate Hawai'i into a broader Pacific World and the American West via California illustrate the complicated relationships that Europeans (including European Americans) and native peoples had with respect to the introduction of domestic animals. Cattle aided European settlement and profit, and thus abetted the conquest of the eastern Pacific. But the mere introduction of bovine species did not make that conquest a fait accompli. The framework of colonial power that served as the context for the introduction of these animals is the truer culprit. Cattle came into a Pacific World alongside conquest, disease, and expanding capitalism.

In Hawai'i, once the Pandora's box of trade with Europeans opened and debts mounted, the last, best hope for autonomy was to offer the most valuable goods at the shrewdest prices. In the markets of the mid-nineteenth century, cattle products were the likeliest goods to achieve those ends. Under the feudal system, most of the feral cattle belonged to the royal family, and thus, to the state. And it was the royal family that began to market the animals. Almost as soon as the kapu ended, Hawaiian rulers rapidly began to harvest the population for profit in Pacific markets increasingly interconnected through maritime trade. The sale of cattle products allowed Hawaiian leaders to service mounting debts for decades, and thus helped to forestall an annexation crisis that might have spelled the end of Hawaiian sovereignty. A sort of stalemate between imperial rivals over Hawai'i also played a role, but considering the role that insolvency played in imperial annexations, this economic explanation cannot be wholly discounted.

In the shifting landscapes of California after 1769, Indians could choose to go into the missions or stay outside their reach. Within the paternalistic world within the missions, gathering cattle offered the most independence and mobility of any work, and neophytes had to work hard to convince the padres that they should be trained to ride a horse and rope livestock. Outside the missions, cattle allowed Indians like Solano an avenue to make alliances with the conquerors, and the raiding cultures of the Tulares turned introduced livestock into a new source of subsistence. At the same time that westerners used cattle to underwrite their expansion, native peoples, as with the horse on the Great Plains, made real attempts to protect or gain greater independence through the animals and the opportunities that they represented. Thus, the native cattle cultures that developed in California and Hawai'i represent the contingencies of ecological imperialism.

The rise of British capital, and then an even greater rise of American capital, closed off avenues of opportunity. The imposition of Western ideas of property, and the power dynamics that played into the enforcement of those ideas, not only closed off cattle as a source of mobility and revenue for many native peoples seeking to protect their sovereignty; it also handed native lands to foreign interests as colonial ranchers bounded cattle on new private ranches. Dispossession of native lands combined with the experience of cattle labor to proletarianize the indigenous peoples of the eastern Pacific. Those that survived the diseases and violence of conquest found themselves in wage work, often first experienced as cattle work in California and Hawai'i. And that wage work was further circumscribed by racist laws under colonial regimes. Introduced animals offered new mobility to indigenous people, but the colonial systems they underwrote and helped succeed took that mobility away through military, economic, and legal conquest.

These are important stories to keep in mind in this age of globalization as issues of introduced species and the rights of disenfranchised and dispossessed people are of paramount importance. Many more introductions have followed, some unintentional, but many in the same hope of "improving" landscapes. Such introduction are often freighted with ideas and hopes of progress as Vancouver had with the cattle he left in Hawai'i.[24] It is easy to view globalization as the expansion of a hegemonic monoculture—one that destroys ecological biodiversity while erasing unique cultural traditions and exploiting the labor of those with less power to resist—and sometimes it seems that the only reasonable answer to these seemingly intractable issues is isolation. What if cattle had never come to California or Hawai'i? Could the Europeans have gained an imperial foothold? However, even if isolation were possible, it would be a paternalistic answer that would take away the agency of billions of people. And since it is not possible, it is important to recognize the structures and practices that led to dispossession. Animals were only tools for the colonizers, and they could work as tools to the colonized as well. And they did, until those avenues were closed off by elite rancheros, haole in the Hawaiian government, and, eventually, the policies of the United States as it came to incorporate California and Hawai'i. While it is important to understand the essential roles that nonhumans played in the European conquest of the globe, it is far too convenient to see nonhumans as the prime movers.

Notes

ABBREVIATIONS

BML   Bishop Museum Library
ECPP   Early California Population Project Database, the Huntington Library
HHS   Hawaiian Historical Society
HL   Huntington Library
HMCS   Hawaiian Mission Children's Society
HSA   Hawai'i State Archives

INTRODUCTION

1. Cowan-Smith and Stone, *Aloha Cowboy*, 33.

2. "Ten Thousand Coming for Last Frontier Days." "Kanaka" is a Hawaiian word designating a Native Hawaiian.

3. The role of rodeos in the creation of a mythic West in American popular culture appears in Butler, "Selling the Myth," 781–83. See also Lawrence, *Rodeo*.

4. Monroy, *Thrown among Strangers*, 264–68; Deverell, *Whitewashed Adobe*.

5. Vallejo, "Ranch and Mission Days in Alta California," 190.

6. Rojas, *Vaqueros and Buckaroos*, 136.

7. Mora, *Trail Dust and Saddle Leather*; Mora, *Californios*.

8. Warren, *Buffalo Bill's America*, 51.

9. Ibid., 400.

10. Matsuda, *Pacific Worlds*, 3.

11. This work focuses on the region David Igler has dubbed the eastern Pacific. He defines the region in Igler, *Great Ocean*.

12. Crosby, *Columbian Exchange*; Crosby, *Ecological Imperialism*; Diamond, *Guns, Germs, and Steel*; Melville, *Plague of Sheep*.

13. For a concise definition and discussion of borderlands as a historical concept, see Adelman and Aron, "From Borderlands to Borders."

14. The rich borderlands literature that has helped to shape the arguments of this book includes Duval, *Native Ground*; Whaley, *Oregon and the Collapse of Illahee*; and White, *Middle Ground*. For discussions on how the borderlands shaped conflict, see Delay, *War of a Thousand Deserts*; Hämäläinen, *Comanche Empire*. For discussions on shifting ethnicity in borderlands, see D. Gutiérrez, *Walls and Mirrors*; Meeks, *Border Citizens*. For discussions on how borderlands shape constructions of gender, see Barr, *Peace Came in the Form of a Woman*; R. Gutiérrez, *When Jesus Came, the Corn Mothers Went Away*. For discussion on how borderlands affect labor and capital, see Foley, *White Scourge*; Truett, *Fugitive Landscapes*. For discussions on how borderlands

affect land tenure, see Hinderaker, *Elusive Empires*; Taylor, *Divided Ground*. For discussion on trade in borderlands, see Reséndez, *Changing National Identities at the Frontier*; Usner Jr., *Indians, Settlers & Slaves in a Frontier Exchange Economy*.

15. Adelman and Aron, "From Borderlands to Borders," 840.

16. For more on cultural exchange in the context of Pacific Islands, see Dening, *Islands and Beaches*; Matsuda, *Pacific Worlds*.

17. G. C. Anderson, *Indian Southwest*; V. D. Anderson, *Creatures of Empire*; Brooks, *Captives & Cousins*; Cronon, *Changes in the Land*; Flores, "Bison Ecology and Bison Diplomacy"; Isenberg, *Destruction of the Bison*; Iverson, *When Indians Became Cowboys*; Merrell, *Indians' New World*; Weisiger, *Dreaming of Sheep in Navajo Country*; White, *Roots of Dependency*. Andrew Isenberg criticizes the "cultural and temporal linearity" of Crosby's works as it assumes clear differences between settlers and Indians and a clear domination of the landscape by settlers in Isenberg, "Between Mexico and the United States," 86.

18. Works that have challenged the trend to exclude the Pacific from histories of the American West include Igler, *Great Ocean*; Whaley, *Oregon and the Collapse of Illahee*; and Whitehead, "Hawai'i: The First and Last Far West?"

CHAPTER ONE

1. Font, *Font's Complete Diary*, 22.

2. Cook, *Voyage of the* Resolution *and the* Discovery, 1:3.

3. Dodge, *Islands and Empires*, 46. For more on Omai's journey, see McCormick, *Omai*; McCormick, *Cook & Omai*; Chappell, *Double Ghosts*, 32–34.

4. For an extended debate concerning the manner of and reasons for Cook's demise, see Sahlins, *How "Natives" Think*; Obeyeskere, *Apotheosis of Captain Cook*.

5. Igler, *Great Ocean*, 5.

6. New Spain was an agent of expansion for "capitalist globalization" in the region, as areas "from San Antonio through Santa Fe to San Francisco were tied into a colonial order generating mining wealth while sustained by irrigated cultivation and commercial grazing" (Tutino, "Capitalist Foundations," 37).

7. Crosby, *Columbian Exchange*, 76.

8. Seed notes that Captain Cook, in particular, released domestic animals to fulfill his orders "to distribute among the Inhabitants such Things as will remain as Traces and Testimonies of your having been there" (Seed, *Ceremonies of Possession*, 35–39).

9. Ibid., 86–87.

10. Weber, *Bárbaros*, 94–95.

11. Crosby, *Columbian Exchange*, 64. In Crosby's *Ecological Imperialism*, he identifies the "portmanteau biota," a group of coevolved species, including the Europeans themselves, that traveled together and benefited from each other as they spread across the globe. He argues that "its members did not function alone, but as a team." Europeans, diseases, domestic animals, and domestic plants, all functioned together to change world environments to serve European markets. Crosby's conclusions, however, are severely limited by his methodologies, which focus on large movements

and phenomena to the detriment of human agency and cultural contingencies (Crosby, *Ecological Imperialism*, 287).

12. Rigby, "Politics and Pragmatics of Seaborne Plant Transportation," 82.

13. Ritvo, *Animal Estate*, 15.

14. Ibid., 16.

15. V. D. Anderson, *Creatures of Empire*.

16. Ibid., 8.

17. Ibid., 11.

18. McCoy, *Elusive Republic*; Meek, *Social Science and the Ignoble Savage*.

19. Dodge, *Our Wild Indians*, 584.

20. White, "Animals and Enterprise," 238.

21. Smith, *Southwest Expedition*, 93.

22. Mapp, *Elusive West*.

23. Steven Hackel observes that the Manila galleon trade probably led to further contacts between the Spanish and California Indians before the expeditions of the late eighteenth century (Hackel, *Children of Coyote*, 36). There is also evidence that Spanish explorers in the Pacific made contact with Hawai'i as early 1527, long before Captain Cook. Shinseki, "El Pueblo Mexicano de Hawai'i."

24. Andrews, *Trade, Plunder and Settlement*, 145–58.

25. The site of Drake's landing is one of the oldest debates in California history. The most detailed account of Drake's voyage was published by his nephew almost fifty years after the fact. For an attempt to locate the site of Drake's landing using linguistic evidence of the Indians he encountered, see Heizer, *Francis Drake and the California Indians*. For an overview of the debate, see Hanna, *Lost Harbor*. One author has claimed that Drake did not land in California at all; see Kelsey, "Did Francis Drake Really Visit California?"

26. Cook, *Voyage of the* Resolution *and the* Discovery, 1:4.

27. McCormick, *Omai*.

28. Cook to Sandwich, November 26, 1776, reprinted in Cook, *Voyage of the* Resolution *and the* Discovery, 2:1520.

29. Ibid.

30. As Gananath Obeyeskere explained it, "When Cook lands in a new land, he not only takes over for the crown in a series of ceremonial acts but wherever he goes he plants English gardens. The act is primarily symbolic, supplanting the disorderly ways of savage peoples with ordered landscapes on the English model. Pairs of domestic animals are carefully set loose, away from the depredations of unthinking savages, to *domesticate* a savage land" (Obeyeskere, *Apotheosis of Captain Cook*, 12).

31. Cook, *Voyage of the* Resolution *and the* Discovery, 1:24.

32. Ibid., 1:23. The adjective "stone" that Cook applied to the horses meant that they were not castrated, an important prerequisite if they were to establish a local population on seeded islands.

33. Ibid., 1:53.

34. Ritvo, *Animal Estate*, 21.

35. Ryan, *Aboriginal Tasmanians*.

36. Cook, *Voyage of the* Resolution *and the* Discovery, 1:211.

37. Ibid., 1:133.

38. McCormick, *Omai*, 284. Chappell discusses Omai's final years in Chappell, *Double Ghosts*, 145–48.

39. Cook, *Voyage of the* Resolution *and the* Discovery, 1:276.

40. Ibid., 1:273.

41. Tomich, *Mammals in Hawai'i*, 120.

42. Cook, *Voyage of the* Resolution *and the* Discovery, 1:265.

43. Ibid., 1:474.

44. Ibid., 1:498.

45. Ibid.

46. Bushnell, *Gifts of Civilization*; Crosby, *Germs, Seeds, and Animals*.

47. Cook, *Voyage of the* Resolution *and the* Discovery, 1:578.

48. Sahlins, *Historical Metaphors and Mythical Realities*.

49. Font, *Font's Complete Diary*, 23.

50. Weber, *Spanish Frontier in North America*, 236–41.

51. Companys, *Gaspar de Portolá*, 137–38. Fray Fermín Francisco de Lasuén protested the removal of these cattle from his mission in Baja California; as he explained, "I regard the cattle of this mission as its most prized possession." Fermín Francisco de Lasuén to Don José de Gálvez, December 20, 1768, in Lasuén, *Writings of Fermín Francisco de Lasuén*, 1:20.

52. Jean Comaroff and John Comaroff have noted that in South Africa, missionaries similarly utilized agricultural instruction. They note that "it was not mere necessity that persuaded them to make their agricultural labors into an exercise in moral instruction, their gestures into metonyms of a mode of production. What they were sowing was a new hegemony." They further explain that "the savage would, by careful tending, be elevated into something like the late British yeomanry. . . . The countryside, in other words, would be tilled and planted anew—cultivating the heathen workers as they cultivated the soil. . . . But the African garden was to be a part of the imperial marketplace. After all, commerce, like money, was an integral—even sanctified—aspect of civilization" (Comaroff and Comaroff, *Of Revelation and Revolution*, 36, 80).

53. Bishko, "Peninsular Background," 493–94.

54. Jordan, *North American Cattle Ranching Frontiers*, 18–42.

55. Bishko, "Peninsular Background," 497–98.

56. Chevalier, *Land and Society in Colonial Mexico*, 85.

57. Ibid., 86.

58. Ibid., 93. D. K. Abbass has argued using estimates based on a variety of constraints that contemporary accounts of large domestic animal multiplication were highly exaggerated. While Abbass's reasoning is sound, I think he overemphasizes mortality rates and fails to properly account for the unique circumstances of the New World. While it is likely that there is some hyperbole in firsthand accounts of herd growth, the ubiquity of such statements, and the occasional existence of numerical data to support the accounts, suggest that exaggeration or not, people were reacting to some sort of phenomenon of rapid herd growth (Abbass, "Herd Development").

59. For descriptions of the evolution of Iberian cattle culture in the New World, see Jordan, *North American Cattle Ranching Frontiers*; Slatta, *Cowboys of the Americas*; Slatta, *Comparing Cowboys and Frontiers*.

60. Serra, *Writings*, 1:59.

61. Though the words were used interchangeably, *zacate* may have implied the presence of forbs, nongrasses that provided good fodder like chia (*Salvia columbariae*). Richard Minnich has closely analyzed Spanish explorers' language in *California's Fading Wildflowers*, 26.

62. Serra, *Writings*, 1:71.

63. Companys, *Gaspar de Portolá*, 371.

64. Serra, *Writings*, 1:119.

65. Ibid., 1:123.

66. Junípero Serra to Juan Andres, July 3, 1769, reprinted in ibid., 1:137.

67. Ensminger, *Beef Cattle Science*, 370.

68. Ibid., 272–73.

69. Ibid.

70. Junípero Serra to Antonio María de Bucareli y Ursúa, March 13, 1773, reprinted in Serra, *Writings*, 1:311.

71. Ibid.

72. Font, *Font's Complete Diary*, 24.

73. Ibid., 61.

74. Ibid., 125.

75. Ibid., 149.

76. Ibid., 209. For a fuller account of Anza's role in investigating the uprising, see Bolton, *Outpost of Empire*, 226–31.

77. Font, *Font's Complete Diary*, 332.

78. Ibid., 333.

79. George Vancouver to Phillip Stephens, November 8, 1794, reprinted in Vancouver, *Voyage of Discovery*, 4:704.

80. Ibid.

81. Ibid.

82. Spate, *Paradise Found and Lost*, 175–80.

83. Vancouver, *Voyage of Discovery*, 3:1133.

84. Vancouver claims in his notes to have taken on board "four cows, four ewes, two bulls, and two rams," though later references seem to indicate that there were seven cows and four rams (ibid., 3:787).

85. Ibid., 3:828.

86. Ibid., 3:801.

87. Ibid., 3:806.

88. George Vancouver to Phillip Stephens, November 8, 1794, reprinted in ibid., 4:1596.

89. Vancouver, *Voyage of Discovery*, 3:1180. Italics from the original text. The more appropriate Hawaiian term would be *kapu*.

90. Ibid.

91. White, "Animals and Enterprise," 238.

92. Shaler, *Journal of a Voyage*, 87.

93. Cleveland, *Narrative of Voyages and Commercial Enterprises*, 223–25.

94. Ibid., 230.

95. Ibid.

96. For more on Young and early Europeans in Hawai'i, see Kuykendall, *Foundation and Transformation*, 27.

97. Cleveland, *Narrative of Voyages and Commercial Enterprises*, 229.

98. Historian Thomas R. Dunlap has discussed the affinity of Anglo settlers for certain European plants and animals and their tendency to import such biota (see Dunlap, *Nature and the English Diaspora*).

99. Cleveland, *Narrative of Voyages and Commercial Enterprises*, 229.

100. Ibid., 230.

101. Ibid., 231.

102. Bernard Smith has examined the racial constructions of Hawaiians through the images produced by the Cook expedition as varyingly peaceful or violent. Condescension and chauvinism were par for the course (B. Smith, "Constructing 'Pacific' Peoples").

103. White, *Roots of Dependency*, 179–83.

CHAPTER TWO

1. Wilkes, *Narrative of the United States Exploring Expedition*, 4:201. Ranunculus is a family of flowering plants that includes buttercups. Some species are native to Hawai'i. Most species are poisonous to livestock.

2. Ibid., 5:153.

3. Culliney, *Islands in a Far Sea*, 3–6.

4. Hubbell, "Biology of Islands," 25–26.

5. Armstrong, *Atlas of Hawaii*, 12.

6. Bakker, *Island Called California*, viii.

7. California Native Plant Society, *Inventory of Rare and Endangered Plants*, 4.

8. Wilkes, *Narrative of the United States Exploring Expedition*, 5:154.

9. Frémont, *Life of Colonel John C. Fremont*, 417.

10. Ibid., 382.

11. Wilkes, *Narrative of the United States Exploring Expedition*, 5:193.

12. Robinson, *Life in California*, 61.

13. Burcham, *California Range Land*, 60.

14. Simmons, "Indian Peoples of California," 56.

15. Gamble, *Chumash World at European Contact*, 280.

16. Farris, "Quality Food."

17. La Pérouse, *Journal*, 1:173.

18. Raab, "Political Ecology of Prehistoric Los Angeles," 31–33.

19. Roquefeuil, *Voyage Round the World*, 105.

20. Lewis, "Patterns of Indian Burning." One study has shown a deer population of ninety-eight per square mile after a prescribed burning versus just thirty per square mile in the control area. Biswell, "Use of Fire in Wildland Management in California."

21. La Pérouse, *Journal*, 1:169.

22. Junípero Serra to Franciso Pangua, July 18, 1774, reprinted in Serra, *Writings*, 2:115.

23. M. K. Anderson, *Tending the Wild*, 59.

24. For an analogous system in eastern North America, see V. D. Anderson, *Creatures of Empire*, 30.

25. McEvoy, *Fisherman's Problem*, 31; M. K. Anderson, *Tending the Wild*, 133–34.

26. Goldschmidt, Foster, and Essene, "War Stories from Two Enemy Tribes," 151–52.

27. M. K. Anderson, *Tending the Wild*, 51–53.

28. The most famous such conflict is the debate between Sherburne Cook and Francis Guest. Cook contended that disease, malnutrition, and Catholic indoctrination at the missions were together responsible for the precipitous decline in native populations, and that, consequently, conversion was often forced through raids on native communities necessitated by the need for labor (see Cook, *Conflict between the California Indians and White Civilization*). Guest responded that such forced conversions would have been against Catholic doctrine and against Spanish (or Mexican) policy (see Guest, "Examination of the Thesis of S. F. Cook"). While it seems unlikely that the missions could have sustained themselves if all the converts were there unwillingly, it does seem clear that some Indians were brought to or held at the missions by force of arms, as Cook contended. At the very least, the Spanish forced runaway neophytes to return to the missions against their wills. The more interesting question for today's scholars, however, is why did the vast preponderance of neophytes come to and stay at the missions despite the high mortality therein?

29. Melville, *Plague of Sheep*, 39–40.

30. Burcham, *California Range Land*, 12.

31. F. J. Weber, *Mission in the Sierras*, 8–9.

32. Serra wrote to Fray Pangua noting that he had received sixty cattle with four bulls from Baja California on October 7, 1776, reprinted in Serra, *Writings*, 3:55.

33. Colton, *Three Years in California*, 40.

34. Hackel, *Children of Coyote*, 77. Hackel's argument draws from Milliken, *Time of Little Choice*.

35. Hackel, *Children of Coyote*, 79.

36. M. K. Anderson, *Tending the Wild*, 85.

37. Fray Joseph Antonio Murguía and Fray Thomás de la Peña to Fray Junípero Serra, November 2, 1782, reprinted in Serra, *Writings*, 4:400.

38. Ibid.

39. Ibid.

40. M. K. Anderson, *Tending the Wild*, 286.

41. Barbour, Pavlik, Drysdale, and Lindstrom, *California's Changing Landscapes*, 88.

42. For a detailed discussion of the proliferation of wild oats in California, see Wyatt, *Five Fires*, 12–19.

43. Barbour, Pavlik, Drysdale, and Lindstrom, *California's Changing Landscapes*, 77. Others have argued that contemporary accounts indicate that flowering annuals

dominated California's landscape before Spanish colonization. See, for instance, Hamilton, "Changing Perceptions of Pre-European Grasslands in California." Proponents of this view contend that old-world plants' superior adaptations to a Mediterranean climate played a larger role than California plants' poor adaptations to heavy grazing. Richard Minnich has used a detailed analysis of Spanish explorers' accounts to make a compelling argument against the perennial bunchgrass theory, though he still sees introduced grazers, especially cattle, as players in changing California's grasslands near Spanish settlements (see Minnich, *California's Fading Wildflowers*, 67).

44. Mack, "Temperate Grasslands Vulnerable to Plant Invasion."

45. Clark, "Impact of Exotic Invasion," 750; Minnich, *California's Fading Wildflowers*, 107–15.

46. Dasmann, "Environmental Changes before and after the Gold Rush," 106; Hendry, "Adobe Brick as a Historical Source," 115, 125; West, "Early Historic Vegetation Change in Alta California," 335–44.

47. Longinos Martínez, *Journal*, 31.

48. Barbour, Pavlik, Drysdale, and Lindstrom, *California's Changing Landscapes*, 167.

49. Graham, "Re-Creative Power of Plant Communities," 684.

50. Beck and Peek, "Diet Composition, Forage Selection."

51. Barbour, Pavlik, Drysdale, and Lindstrom, *California's Changing Landscapes*, 79.

52. See, for instance, Morris, "Elk and Livestock Competition."

53. Anderson and Scherzinger, "Improving Quality of Winter Forage"; Burritt and Banner, "Elk and Cattle Grazing Can Be Complementary."

54. Minnich, *California's Fading Wildflowers*, 104.

55. Simpson, *Narrative of a Journey*, 1:300.

56. Phillips, *Indians and Intruders*, 47.

57. Beechey, *Account of a Visit to California*, 37.

58. Dasmann, "Environmental Changes before and after the Gold Rush," 109.

59. Cook, *Conflict between the California Indian and White Civilization*; Jackson and Castillo, *Indians, Franciscans and Spanish Colonization*.

60. Lasuén suggests that the Indians would still desire to return to their "mountains and beaches" even if the missions provided an overabundance of food, but the existence of the practice reveals that they often provided little enough to cause hunger among the neophytes, Lasuén, *Writings*, 2:204.

61. Beechey, *Account of a Visit to California*, 30.

62. Jackson, *Missions and the Frontiers of Spanish America*, 298.

63. Lasuén to Fray José Gasol, July 21, 1802, reprinted in Lasuén, *Writings*, 2:210.

64. Geiger, *As the Padres Saw Them*, 74.

65. Valle, "Prevention of Smallpox in Alta California." Elizabeth Fenn's discussion of smallpox in Alta California in 1782 is inaccurate (see Fenn, *Pox Americana*, 154–55).

66. Boyd, *Coming of the Spirit of Pestilence*, 98.

67. Kelton, *Epidemics and Enslavement*, 16, 79.

68. La Pérouse, *Journal*, 186.

69. For an example of the "peaceful" view, see Margolin, *Ohlone Way*, 113.

70. Kroeber, *Handbook of the Indians of California*, 49.

71. LeBlanc and Register, *Constant Battles*, 137, 154.

72. Longinos Martínez, *Journal*, 117.

73. Lambert, "Osteological Evidence for Indigenous Warfare in America," 204. Lambert notes that the incidence of violence in California seems to have peaked before about A.D. 1380, though evidence of violence continues after this period.

74. La Pérouse, *Journal*, 180.

75. Geiger, *As the Padres Saw Them*, 140.

76. "Seven Indian tribes live at this mission. They are the Excelen, the Egeac, Rumsen, Sargenta Ruc, Sarconeños, Guachiron and Calenda Ruc. The first two are from the interior and have the same language or speech which is totally different from the other five. The latter also speak the same language. At the beginning of the conquest the missionaries experienced great difficulty in getting them to assemble for religious services, for agricultural pursuits or for any duty whatever. Today they have succeeded in making them associate. This exclusiveness and meager fraternal spirit resulted from the fact that in their pagan state they ordinarily lived in a state of war. The troops tried to counteract this condition from the beginning. Since all have been Christianized they recognize the advantages of the peace in which they live" (ibid., 13).

77. Beechey, *Account of a Visit to California*, 63–64.

78. Ibid., 23.

79. For a parallel example, see Ned Blackhawk's excellent history of the Utes after Spanish contact, which emphasizes that the violence of Spanish colonial power was "redirected" toward other communities, creating cycles of violence in the Great Basin (Blackhawk, *Violence over the Land*).

80. Johnson, "Ethnohistoric Descriptions," 87–89. Johnson notes a lack of physical evidence to back up reports of scalping in California.

81. Lasuén, *Writings*, 2:18. Johnson, "Ethnohistoric Descriptions," 90.

82. Johnson, "Ethnohistoric Descriptions," 105.

83. Kroeber, *Handbook of the Indians of California*, 647, 752.

84. Whaley, *Oregon and the Collapse of* Illahee, 211–12.

85. Work, *Fur Brigade to the Bonaventura*, 18.

86. Osio, *History of Alta California*, 92.

87. Duggan, "Market and Church," 35, 46. Parallel uses of gifts to form Indian alliances and the resulting shifts in Indian polities are discussed at length in White, *Middle Ground*.

88. Duggan, "Market and Church," 76.

89. Gamble, *Chumash World at European Contact*, 270–74.

90. Larson, Johnson, and Michaelsen, "Missionization among the Coastal Chumash," 264.

91. Haas, *Saints and Citizens*, 28.

92. Brown and Fernandez, "Tribe and State in a Frontier Mosaic," 193.

93. Merrell, *Indians' New World*.

94. For more anthropological research on how colonial intrusion can increase indigenous conflict, see Ferguson and Whitehead, *War in the Tribal Zone*.

95. Culliney, *Islands in a Far Sea*, 313.

96. Kirch, "Impact of the Prehistoric Polynesians on the Hawaiian Ecosystem."

97. Culliney, *Islands in a Far Sea*, 314. The extent to which this was a system of reciprocal exchange as opposed to a system of feudal labor exploitation is a matter of some scholarly debate; however, it is clear that chiefs and managers could assert a great deal of control over commoner labor (see Kameʻeleihiwa, *Native Land and Foreign Desires*, 26–31).

98. Handy and Handy, *Native Planters in Old Hawaii*, 76.

99. Culliney, *Islands in a Far Sea*, 318.

100. Linnekin, *Sacred Queens*, 90–91.

101. Newman, "Hawaii Island Agricultural Zones," 341–42; Kirch, "Regional Variation and Local Style."

102. Handy and Handy, *Native Planters in Old Hawaii*, 89.

103. Tuggle, "Hawaii," 175.

104. Valeri, *Kingship and Sacrifice*, 10–14. For the controversy concerning James Cook's potential perceived manifestation as the god Lono, see Sahlins, *Historical Metaphors*; Sahlins, *How "Natives" Think*; and Obeyeskere, *Apotheosis of Captain Cook*.

105. Valeri, *Kingship and Sacrifice*, 29.

106. Ibid., 46; Tomich, *Mammals of Hawaii*, 230.

107. Campbell, *Voyage Round the World*, 118.

108. Valeri, *Kingship and Sacrifice*, 58–63.

109. Rappaport, *Pigs for the Ancestors*, 3.

110. Dening, *Islands and Beaches*, 53–55.

111. Valeri, *Kingship and Sacrifice*, 112–13.

112. Ibid., 115.

113. Ibid., 121.

114. Kirch, "Regional Variation," 48; Linnekin, *Sacred Queens*, 38–40.

115. Linnekin, *Sacred Queens*, 5, 13.

116. Ibid., 35

117. Ibid., 67–68.

118. Delano, *Narrative of Voyages*, 390.

119. Schmitt, *Historical Statistics of Hawaii*, 337–40.

120. Vancouver, *Voyage of Discovery*, 2:477.

121. Ibid.

122. Daws, *Shoal of Time*, 29.

123. Ibid., 32.

124. Archibald Menzies, the naturalist who accompanied Vancouver's expedition, claimed that the British chose to believe that Kamehameha was not involved in the taking of the *Fair American*, even though he did reap the rewards. He stated that "we naturally infer that he took no part in this horrid transaction; on the contrary, much disapproved of it" (Menzies, *Hawaii Nei*, 65).

125. Daws, *Shoal of Time*, 35.

126. Ibid., 43.

127. Bushnell, *Gifts of Civilization*, 198.

128. Linnekin, *Sacred Queens*, 129, 158.

129. Ibid., 165–67.

130. Hubbell, "Biology of Islands," 22–32. Hubbell uses Hawai'i as his case study and notes that the islands are especially isolated. Robert H. MacArthur and Edward O. Wilson describe these processes of evolution on islands in their classic work, *Theory of Island Biogeography*. C. S. Elton also deals with the devastating effects of biological invasions on isolated islands, and specifically Hawai'i, in *Ecology of Invasions by Animals and Plants* (81–89).

131. Lever, *Naturalized Animals*, 44.

132. Ibid., 45.

133. Koebele, "Hawaii's Forest Foes," 96.

134. Roots, *Animal Invaders*, 34.

135. Precontact Hawaiian agriculture is described in great detail in Handy and Handy, *Native Planters in Old Hawaii*.

136. Delano, *Narrative of Voyages*, 389.

137. Hussey, *Voyage of the Racoon*, 34.

138. *George Davis v. Wm Green for RC Janion*, July 14, 1860, HSA.

139. Maly and Wilcox, "Short History of Cattle and Range Management in Hawai'i," 21. Patrick V. Kirch describes some of these walls at archaeological sites in the Anahulu valley of Oahu in *Archaeology of History* (70).

140. Campbell, *Voyage Round the World*, 118.

141. L. Lyons, *Makua Laiana*, 48.

142. "Influence of the Cattle on the Climate of Waimea," 46. Though anonymous, similarities with material in *Makua Laiana* suggest that this is also the work of the Reverend Lorenzo Lyons.

143. Ibid., 46.

144. *George Davis v. Wm Green for RC Janion*, July 14, 1860, HSA.

145. Ibid.

146. L. Lyons, *Makua Laiana*, 49.

147. Ibid. It is difficult to explain how deforestation could have lessened the mumuku, though the removal of natural windbreaks and/or more exposure of soil to direct heat from the sun may have altered wind patterns.

148. "Influence of the Cattle on the Climate of Waimea," 46.

149. Wilkes, *Narrative of the United States Exploring Expedition*, 3:392.

150. Ibid.

151. Varigny, *Fourteen Years in the Sandwich Islands*, 94. Wild indigo (*Baptisia spp.*) is native to North America and is another plant unpalatable to livestock, which again suggests that heavy grazing had eliminated more palatable plants.

CHAPTER THREE

1. Hackel, *Children of Coyote*, 46.

2. Companys, *Gaspar de Portolá*, 297.

3. Ibid.

4. San Luis Obispo Death 01170, May 21, 1806, ECPP.

5. San Luis Obispo Baptism 01263, November 8, 1794, ECPP.

6. For example: Hilarion, San Diego Death 01871, July 7, 1809, ECPP; Rumualdo, San Fernando Death 02981, July 27, 1811, ECPP; Nazaro, "a bull killed him on the beach," San Luis Obispo Death 01719, December 3, 1816, ECPP; Rosendo, "killed suddenly by a bull," San Gabriel Death 04020, June 19, 1818, ECPP.

7. San Jose Death 04084, June 11, 1828, ECPP.

8. Delano, *Narrative of Voyages*, 389.

9. Lisianski, *Voyage Round the World*, 135.

10. V. D. Anderson, *Creatures of Empire*, 38.

11. Palóu, *Historical Memoirs*, 2:84.

12. Serra, *Writings*, 2:87.

13. Reid, *Indians of Los Angeles County*, 64.

14. Ibid., 68.

15. Carrico, "Sociopolitical Aspects of the 1775 Revolt at Mission San Diego."

16. Junípero Serra to Francisco Fermín de Lasuén, January 12, 1780, reprinted in Serra, *Writings*, 3:421.

17. Ibid.

18. For similar Indian strategies targeting domestic animals in colonial New England, see V. D. Anderson, *Creatures of Empire*, 183, 226.

19. Mission Fathers of La Purísima to Don Diego, December 1800, reprinted in Englehardt, *Mission La Concepcion Purísima*, 16.

20. Ibid.

21. Palóu, *Historical Memoirs*, 4:199–203.

22. Ibid., 4:202.

23. Haas, *Saints and Citizens*, 19.

24. Haas, "Raise Your Sword and I Will Eat You," 94.

25. Street, *Beasts of the Field*, 48–49.

26. Governor Felipe de Neve, "Regulation and Instruction for the Presidios of the Peninsula of the California," June 1, 1779, reprinted in Jones, *Land Titles in California*, 52–53.

27. Jordan, *North American Cattle-Ranching Frontiers*, 93–96; Slatta, *Cowboys of the Americas*, 68–74, 85–87.

28. Petition, July 10, 1770, reprinted in Lasuén, *Writings*, 1:111–12.

29. V. D. Anderson, *Creatures of Empire*, 70. Douglas Monroy argues that "the mass production of animals for food and as trade items, such as occurred with the huge mission cattle herds, further alienated people from an interconnected and companionate relationship to animals" (Monroy, *Thrown among Strangers*, 55).

30. Iverson, *When Indians Became Cowboys*, 19; Weisiger, *Dreaming of Sheep in Navajo Country*.

31. James Downs noted that the Navajo accomplished this feat by clearly marking their sheep as owned by humans (Downs, *Animal Husbandry in Navajo Society*, 90).

32. Palóu, *Historical Memoirs*, 4:118–19.

33. Geiger, *As the Padres Saw Them*, 131.

34. Beebe and Senkewicz, *Testimonios*, 108.

35. Ibid., 104.

36. Ibid.

37. Ibid.

38. Geiger, *As the Padres Saw Them*, 151.

39. Street, *Beasts of the Field*, 25.

40. Lasuén, *Writings*, 1:150.

41. Lightfoot, *Indians, Missionaries, and Merchants*, 105.

42. San Buenaventura Baptism 01372, August 14, 1801, ECPP.

43. San Buenaventura Marriage 00291, February 17, 1802, ECPP.

44. San Buenaventura Death 00807, April 17, 1804, ECPP.

45. San Buenaventura Baptism 00116, May 29, 1785, ECPP.

46. San Buenaventura Marriage 00077, May 10, 1790, ECPP.

47. San Jose Baptism 05278, May 29, 1829, ECPP.

48. Their five-year-old daughter at the time also took the name Dioscora. San Jose Baptism 01917, April 1, 1811; San Jose Baptism 01957, April 16, 1811; and San Jose Baptism 01958, April 16, 1811, ECPP.

49. San Jose Baptism 00328, August 22, 1800, ECPP.

50. Haas, *Saints and Citizens*, 45.

51. Ibid., 51.

52. Phillips, *Indians and Intruders*, 60.

53. Ibid., 100–101.

54. Colton, *Three Years in California*, 37–38.

55. Duhaut-Cilly, *Voyage to California*, 160.

56. Ibid.

57. Ibid., 168.

58. Haas, *Saints and Citizens*, 127–28.

59. Langsdorff, *Langsdorff's Narrative*, 64–65.

60. Duhaut-Cilly, *Voyage to California*, 74.

61. Geiger, *As the Padres Saw Them*, 85–86.

62. Ibid., 85–87.

63. Ibid., 87.

64. Hoover, "Archaeology of Spanish Colonial Sites in California," 100.

65. Lightfoot, *Indians, Missionaries, and Merchants*, 168.

66. Powers, *Tribes of California*, 271.

67. Shipek, "California Indian Reactions to the Franciscans," 490.

68. Junípero Serra to Antonio María de Bucareli y Ursua, March 9, 1773, reprinted in Serra, *Writings*, 3:41.

69. Palóu, *Historical Memoirs*, 4:161.

70. Manby, *Journal of Vancouver's Voyage*, 126.

71. Ibid., 124.

72. Martin, *Nā Paniolo o Hawai'i*, 18. In his linguistic analysis of the post-conquest survival of native culture in central Mexico, James Lockhart explores similar native naming practices in the Americas, in which animals like horses were designated by the Nahuatl word for "deer." Lockhart states that "the Nahuas used primarily the resources of their own language to deal with the phenomena the newcomers introduced" (Lockhart, *Nahuas after the Conquest*, 264, 280).

73. Menzies, *Hawaii Nei*, 145.

74. Ibid.

75. Ibid.

76. Cox, *Adventures on the Columbia River*, 62–64.

77. Ibid., 64.

78. Delano, *Narrative of Voyages*, 389.

79. Linnekin, *Sacred Queens*, 90.

80. Petition from 'Ewa to Keoni Ana, Honolulu, June 2, 1847, Interior Department Documents—Miscellaneous Box 141, HSA.

81. Ibid.

82. Cox, *Adventures on the Columbia River*, 64.

83. Malo, *Hawaiian Antiquities*, 41.

84. *George Davis v. Wm Green for RC Janion*, July 14, 1860, HSA.

85. Ibid.

86. Von Kotzebue, *New Voyage Round the World*, 219–20.

87. Ruschenberger, *Voyage around the World*, 455.

88. Wilkes, *Narrative of the United States Exploring Expedition*, 4:52.

89. Colvocorresses, *Four Years in a Government Exploring Expedition*, 185.

90. Ibid.

CHAPTER FOUR

1. W. H. Davis, *Sixty Years in California*, 301.

2. Ibid.

3. Ibid.

4. Ibid., 300.

5. Igler, *Great Ocean*, 64–65.

6. Farnham, *Travels in the Californias*, 57; Starr, *Americans and the California Dream*, 19–20.

7. W. H. Davis, *Sixty Years in California*, 188.

8. Ibid., 382.

9. Thomas O. Larkin to James Buchanan, October 17, 1845, in Larkin, *Larkin Papers*, 4:37.

10. Olmsted, *Incidents in a Whaling Voyage*, 209.

11. Mills, "*Neo* in Oceania."

12. Thomas O. Larkin to M[oses] Y[ale] Beach, May 31, 1845, reprinted in Larkin, *Larkin Papers*, 3:219.

13. Gibson, *Otter Skins, Boston Ships, and China Goods*, 85.

14. Irving, *Astoria*, 199–200.

15. Igler, *Great Ocean*, 29.

16. Matsuda, *Pacific Worlds*, 184.

17. Turnbull, *Voyage Round the World*, 199.

18. Ibid., 223–24.

19. Ibid., 235.

20. Iselin, *Journal of a Trading Voyage*, 69.

21. Ibid.

22. Franchère, *Journal*, 61.

23. Kuykendall, *Foundation and Transformation*, 57–58.

24. Thompson, *Russian Settlement at Fort Ross*, 13.

25. Pritchard, "Joint Tenants of the Frontier," 87.

26. Mariano Payéras report, May 2, 1817, reprinted in Payéras, *Writings*, 121.

27. Ibid.

28. Archibald, *Economic Aspects of the California Missions*, 55.

29. Jackson, *Missions and the Frontiers of Spanish America*, 125; Hackel, "Land, Labor, and Production," 118.

30. Mariano Payéras to Josef Guilez, Oct 1810, reprinted in Payéras, *Writings*, 55. Botas are the bags that were often used as the main measurement in the tallow trade.

31. Ibid.

32. Historians have argued that the fur trade created new economic opportunities for Indians of which they readily took advantage. However, participation in the fur trade encouraged dependency on European manufactures; see Ray, *Indians in the Fur Trade*. Competition for furs may have exacerbated the conflicts discussed in chapter 2, as occurred in many other regions of North America, though there is little direct evidence of this.

33. Ogden, *California Sea Otter Trade*, 15–16.

34. Ibid., 32–33.

35. Lasuén to the Royal Governing Audiencia, September 24, 1787, reprinted in Lasuén, *Writings*, 1:157.

36. Ibid., 1:156.

37. Lasuén to Revered Father Guardian, undated, Lasuén, *Writings*, 1:215.

38. For more on frontier exchange economies, see Usner, *Indians, Settlers, and Slaves*.

39. Shineberg, *They Came for Sandalwood*, 7–9.

40. Kuykendall, *Foundation and Transformation*, 86.

41. Kamehameha's purchase of the *Albatross* is discussed in Bradley, *American Frontier in Hawaii*, 56; Gabriel Franchère reported on the *Lilly Bird* as a Hawaiian ship in Franchère, *Journal*, 70; Mills, "*Neo* in Oceania."

42. Tinker, "Ka Moolelo Hawaii," 2:227.

43. Tucker, *Insatiable Appetite*, 74–76.

44. In December 1829, the *Kamehameha* with 300 men and the *Becket* with 179 men left Honolulu for the islands upon hearing news of Sandalwood there. Australian naturalist George Bennett said, "The whole endeavors of the Sandwich Islanders seem to have been to carry on war against the aborigines—not to conciliate them: thus putting in practice their original intention of taking permanent possession of the island, and exterminating the original possessors," quoted in Shineberg, *They Came for Sandalwood*, 20–21. The invasion ended with the loss at sea of one ship, carrying Boki, the governor of Oahu, and to an outbreak of disease among the others. See Matsuda, *Pacific Worlds*, 188.

45. Chappell, *Double Ghosts*, 28.

46. Franchère, *Journal*, 70.

47. Ibid.

48. Turnbull, *Voyage Round the World*, 229.

49. Chappell, *Double Ghosts*, 58.

50. Cox, *Adventures on the Columbia River*, 65.

51. Ibid.

52. Chappell, *Double Ghosts*, 161.

53. Corney, *Early Voyages in the North Pacific*, 201.

54. Franchère, *Journal*, 65.

55. Turnbull, *Voyage Round the World*, 199.

56. Von Kotzebue, *New Voyage Round the World*, 1:61.

57. Ibid., 1:61–62.

58. Mariano Payéras to Baldomero López, May 25, 1820, reprinted in Payéras, *Writings*, 256.

59. W. H. Davis, *Seventy-Five Years in California*, 154.

60. The younger Davis also reports that these otter skins sold for eight to a hundred dollars each in China (ibid., 154–55).

61. Miller, *Yankee Smuggler*, 1.

62. Peggy, also known as Maria Stewart, married a Californian named Secondino Olivera and remained in Santa Barbara until her death in 1871 (ibid., 31).

63. Testimony quoted in Richman, *California under Spain and Mexico*, 206.

64. Miller, *Yankee Smuggler*, 31.

65. Ibid., 46. Eayrs battled the legal system of New Spain for his ship and his freedom until Mexican independence in 1821.

66. Uhrowczik, *Burning of Monterey*, 116. Buying Western ships represented an adoption and cultural transformation that parallels that use of cattle. For a discussion of these changes, see Mills, "*Neo* in Oceania."

67. Uhrowczik *Burning of Monterey*, 57–58.

68. Ibid., 115.

69. Historians have contrasted the often strict discipline on privateers with the more egalitarian mode of pirate crews; see Linebaugh and Rediker, *Many-Headed Hydra*, 161. For more on privateers, see Ritchie, *Captain Kidd*, 11–13.

70. Corney, *Early Voyages in the North Pacific*, 217. For a discussion of similar diverse crews operating in the American Revolution, see Linebaugh and Rediker, *Many-Headed Hydra*, 241.

71. Mariano Payéras to Don José de la Guerra, October 12, 1818, reprinted in Payéras, *Writings*, 157.

72. Corney, *Early Voyages in the North Pacific*, 218.

73. Ibid., 220.

74. Mariano Payéras to Don José de la Guerra, October 11, 1818, reprinted in Payéras, *Writings*, 157.

75. Payéras made it clear that José Andrés was an Indian when he explained that he believed Andrés's report "because he knows Spanish very well." He adds as further verification, "And he is so brave that he has matched strength with bears, using no other weapons than his bare hands" (Mariano Payéras to Román de Ulibarri, December 4, 1818, reprinted in Payéras, *Writings*, 162–63).

76. Ibid.

77. Corney, *Early Voyages in the North Pacific*, 219.

78. Mariano Payéras to Román de Ulibarri, December 4, 1818, reprinted in Payéras, *Writings*, 162.

79. Blaufarb, "Western Question," 743.

80. Osio, *History of Alta California*, 26.

81. Archibald, *Economic Aspects of the California Missions*, 122.

82. Ibid., 129.

83. Ibid., 125.

84. Geiger, *As the Padres Saw Them*, 86. For more on the missions' changing priorities, see Hornbeck, "Economic Growth and Change at the Missions of Alta California."

85. Ibid.

86. Osio, *History of Alta California*, 69.

87. Ibid.

88. Mariano Payéras to Don José de la Guerra, October 12, 1818, reprinted in Payéras, *Writings*, 157.

89. Osio, *History of Alta California*, 70.

90. Igler, *Great Ocean*, 25.

91. Ibid., 26.

92. Dakin, *Lives of William Hartnell*, 29.

93. Ibid., 30.

94. Ogden, *California Sea Otter Trade*, 91.

95. Dakin, *Lives of William Hartnell*, 31.

96. Ogden, "Hides and Tallow," 255.

97. Mariano Payéras to Ministers of Our Missions, June 17, 1822, reprinted in Dakin, *Lives of William Hartnell*, 35.

98. Mariano Payéras to José Gasol, July 30, 1822, reprinted in Payéras, *Writings*, 325.

99. Ibid.

100. Mariano Payéras to José Gasol, July 27, 1822, reprinted in Payéras, *Writings*, 322.

101. William Hartnell, July 1822 note, reprinted in Ogden, "Hides and Tallow," 256.

102. Ogden, "Hides and Tallow," 260; Mofras, *Travels on the Pacific Coast*, 1:257.

103. Duhaut-Cilly, *Voyage to California*, 173.

104. W. H. Davis, *Seventy-Five Years in California*, 117.

105. Duhaut-Cilly, *Voyage to California*, 173.

106. Mofras, *Travels on the Pacific Coast*, 1:257.

107. W. P. Hartnell to John Begg & Co., September 18, 1822, reprinted in Dakin, *Many Lives of William Hartnell*, 42–43.

108. Osio, *History of Alta California*, 70.

109. Gibson, *Otter Skins, Boston Ships, and China Goods*, 260.

110. Ogden, "Boston Hide Droughers along California Shores," 290.

111. Osio, *History of Alta California*, 70.

112. Ogden, *California Sea Otter Trade*, 90.

113. Beechey, *Account of a Visit to California*, 12–13.

114. Ibid., 31.

115. Ogden, "Boston Hide Droughers along California Shores," 294.

116. W. H. Davis, *Seventy-Five Years in California*, 197; Mofras, *Travels on the Pacific Coast*, 1:255.

117. Hackel, "Land, Labor, and Production," 132.

118. Mofras, *Travels on the Pacific Coast*, 1:276.

119. Ibid., 1:265; Dana, *Two Years before the Mast*, 68.

120. Ogden, "Hides and Tallow," 258.

121. Duhaut-Cilly, *Voyage to California*, 173.

122. Osio, *History of Alta California*, 119–20, 287.

123. Hornbeck, "Economic Growth and Change at the Missions of Alta California," 426–29. Robert Jackson argues that the decline in agricultural production had more to do with climate in "Changing Economic Structure of Alta California."

124. Duhaut-Cilly, *Voyage to California*, 173.

125. San Gabriel's herd officially peaked in 1828 at 26,300, though Osio believed that it controlled more than 100,000 at its peak (see Osio, *History of Alta California*, 119, 287).

126. Dana, *Two Years before the Mast*, 53.

127. Simpson, *Narrative of a Journey*, 1:289.

128. Atherton, *California Diary*, 62.

129. John Girdler to John Low, December 7, 1844, Manuscripts, HL.

130. Dana, *Two Years before the Mast*, 86.

131. Simpson, *Narrative of a Journey*, 1:289–90.

132. Dana, *Two Years before the Mast*, 72.

133. Ibid.

134. Mofras, *Travels on the Pacific Coast*, 1:259.

135. Fritzsche, "On Liberal Terms," 481.

136. John Girdler to John Low, December 7, 1844, Manuscripts, HL.

137. Dana, *Two Years before the Mast*, 72.

138. Duhaut-Cilly, *Voyage to California*, 59.

139. Ibid.

140. Ibid.

141. Wilkes, *Narrative of the United States Exploring Expedition*, 5:209.

142. Ibid.

143. Ibid.

144. Dana, *Two Years before the Mast*, 75.

145. Ogden, "Boston Hide Droughers along California Shores," 302.

146. John Girdler to John Low, December 7, 1844, Manuscripts, HL.

147. For an overview on the cultural and economic histories of credit and risk in the early republic, see Matson, "Ambiguities of Risk in the Early Republic."

148. Thomas Larkin to Joseph Carter, November 18, 1842, reprinted in Larkin, *Larkin Papers*, 1:323.

149. Isenberg, *Mining California*, 109.

150. Nathan Spears to Thomas Oliver Larkin, December 7, 1841, reprinted in Larkin, *Larkin Papers*, 1:140.

151. W. Mark West to Henry Delano Fitch, August 20, 1841, reprinted in Larkin, *Larkin Papers*, 1:112.

152. Mofras, *Travels on the Pacific Coast*, 1:261.

153. Ibid., 1:262.

154. Marzagalli, "Establishing Transatlantic Trade Networks in Times of War," 812.

155. Nunis, "Alta California's Trojan Horse," 306.

156. Hurtado, *John Sutter*, 60.

157. Reséndez, *Changing National Identities*.

158. Ethan Estabrook to Thomas Oliver Larkin, January 29, 1841, reprinted in Larkin, *Larkin Papers*, 1:77.

159. Rich, *History of the Hudson's Bay Company*, 2:716.

160. Sánchez, *Telling Identities*, 166.

161. Dana, *Two Years before the Mast*, 114–15.

162. Ibid., 143.

163. Ibid., 84, 243.

164. Osio, *History of Alta California*, 26.

165. Ibid.

166. John Forster to Abel Stearns, November 2, 1840, Abel Stearns papers, HL.

167. Ogden, "Hides and Tallow," 261.

168. Lightfoot, *Indians, Missionaries, and Merchants*, 103.

169. Sánchez, *Telling Identities*, 168.

170. Dana, *Two Years before the Mast*, 212.

171. Osio, *History of Alta California*, 195.

172. August 22, 1846, contract with William A. Leidesdorff, William A. Leidesdorff papers, Box 2, HL.

173. December 1848 contract with William A. Leidesdorff, William A. Leidesdorff papers, Box 5, HL.

174. Dana, *Two Years before the Mast*, 56–57.

175. Ibid., 144.

176. Ibid., 133.

177. Ibid.

178. Ogden, "Boston Hide Droughers along California Shores," 299.

179. Tinker, "Ka Moolelo Hawaii," 2:227.

180. Bradley, *American Frontier in Hawaii*, 59–61.

181. Andrews, "On the Decrease of Population on the Hawaiian Islands," 125–26.

182. "Reign of Liholiho."

183. G. A. Smith, *Thomas ap Catesby Jones*, 62.

184. Gibson and Whitehead, *Yankees in Paradise*, 323. Jones later mistakenly seized California for the United States in 1842. After returning California to Mexico, he sailed to Hawai'i, where he picked up a young deserter from the U.S. Navy named Herman Melville.

185. Ibid., 143.

186. Igler, *Great Ocean*, 118.

187. William French to Theo Cordua[?], February 17, 1846, William French Letterbook, HSA.

188. *George Davis v. Wm Green for RC Janion*, July 14, 1860, HSA.

189. Don Francisco de Paula Marin's diary reports on June 16, 1821, "This day Cajumanu [Ka'ahumanu] killed a cow & divided it among the captains" (Marin, *Letters and Journal*, 251–52).

190. "Communications—Waimea."

191. Colvocorresses, *Four Years in a Government Exploring Expedition*, 188.

192. Belcher, *Narrative of a Voyage Round the World*, 1:61–67.

193. Byron, *Voyage of HMS* Blonde *to the Sandwich Islands*, 41–42.

194. Boelen, *Merchant's Perspective*, 61.

195. Mathison, *Narrative of a Visit*, 411, 425.

196. Ibid., 425.

197. Gast, *Don Francisco de Paula Marin*, 37.

198. Marin, *Letters and Journal*, 290.

199. Vaqueros would tie a wild cow or bull to the especially tame cabestro with strips of leather tied through holes drilled into the animals' horns (Osio, *History of Alta California*, 30).

200. Anthony Allen to Doctor Dougal, October 11, 1822, reprinted in Scruggs, "Anthony D. Allen," 92.

201. Tyerman and Bennet, *Journal of Voyages and Travels*, 2:50.

202. Stewart, *Journal of a Residence in the Sandwich Islands*, 157.

203. Daws, *Shoal of Time*, 47.

204. Davis, *Sixty Years in California*, 385.

205. The timing of this change, shortly before the Great Māhele (chapter 6), certainly cost many Hawaiian women access to newly privatized lands; see Linnekin, *Sacred Queens*, 191.

206. Cowan-Smith and Stone, *Aloha Cowboy*, 8–10.

207. Wilkes, *Narrative of the United States Exploring Expedition*, 4:205.

208. Paalua to John Adams Kuakini, June 24, 1823, Foreign Office and Executive Documents, Series 402, Box 2, folder 12, HSA.

209. *George Davis v. Wm Green for RC Janion*, July 14, 1860, HSA.

210. Wellmon, "Frontier Traders and Pioneer Cattlemen," 48.

211. Bates, *Sandwich Island Notes*, 367.

212. Knapp, Journal #2, October 4, 1837, manuscript, HMCS.

213. Ibid.

214. Hill, *Travels in the Sandwich and Society Islands*, 156–57.

215. Wilkes, *Narrative of the United States Exploring Expedition*, 4:204.

216. Greenwell, "Kaluakauka Revisited," 151.

217. Ibid., 155.

218. Ibid., 160.

219. Mills, "Keanakolu," 100.

220. Van Kirk, *Many Tender Ties*.

221. Bates, *Sandwich Island Notes*, 276.

222. William French to John P. Parker, November 19, 1844, William French Letter-book, HSA.

223. Kehunaoa, *In Admiralty.*

224. L. Lyons, *Makua Laiana,* 64.

225. Ibid.

226. Linnekin, *Sacred Queens,* 183.

227. Bates, *Sandwich Island Notes,* 276.

228. Mofras, *Travels in the Pacific,* 1:276.

229. Igler, "Alta California, the Pacific, and International Commerce," 120.

230. Igler, "Diseased Goods," 714.

231. Mofras, *Travels on the Pacific Coast,* 1:260.

232. Green, *Journey of a Tour in 1829,* 92.

233. Osio, *History of Alta California,* 198.

234. Larkin, *Larkin Papers,* 4:306.

235. Corney, *Early Voyages in the North Pacific,* 88.

236. Mills, "*Neo* in Oceania," 66.

237. Henry A. Peirce to James Hunnewell, August 8, 1834, HMCS.

238. John D. McLoughlin to Captain William Ryan, October 19, 1831, reprinted in McLoughlin, *Letters,* 233.

239. Henry Peirce to Thomas Larkin, January 12, 1842, reprinted in Larkin, *Larkin Papers,* 1:151.

240. Thomas Larkin to John Coffin Jones, March 12, 1842, reprinted in ibid., 1:173.

241. Balleisen, *Navigating Failure,* 31.

242. Two studies that examine finance in colonial provinces as they changed possession (as California would in the 1840s) are Reséndez, *Changing National Identities*; and Breen, *Marketplace of Revolution.*

243. Kirch, *Archaeology of History,* 44, 167.

244. Chace, "Archaeology of 'Cienaga,'" 48, 52.

CHAPTER FIVE

1. Santa Cruz Death 02177, December 19, 1850, ECPP.

2. San Diego Baptism 03446, February 28, 1808, ECPP.

3. Ralph Kuykendall to Leon Rowland, April 23, 1940, Biographical File U171, HSA; and Leon Rowland to R. S. Kuykendall, May 1, 1940, Biographical File U171, HSA.

4. I follow Terry Jordan and other historians of different herding regimes in referring to "cattle culture" as the particular practices (from tools to music to dress) that pastoral laborers in different regions developed (see Jordan, *North American Cattle-Ranching Frontiers*).

5. Isenberg, "Between Mexico and the United States."

6. Slatta, *Cowboys of the Americas,* 21.

7. Osio, *History of Alta California,* 32–33.

8. Mora, *Californios,* 17.

9. Ibid.

10. Ibid., 107.

11. Ibid., 110.

12. Ibid., 99.

13. Robinson, *Life in California*, 85.

14. Osio, *History of Alta California*, 30.

15. Ibid., 31.

16. Mora, *Californios*, 157–58.

17. Ibid., 161.

18. Sánchez, *Telling Identities*, 168.

19. Hackel, "Land, Labor, and Production," 123.

20. Osio, *History of Alta California*, 31.

21. Vallejo, "Ranch and Mission Days in California," 191.

22. Ibid.

23. Osio, *History of Alta California*, 28.

24. Ibid.

25. Street, *Beasts of the Field*, 101.

26. Mofras, *Travels on the Pacific Coast*, 1:261–62.

27. Osio, *History of Alta California*, 28.

28. Mora, *Californios*, 90.

29. J. Smith, *Southwest Expedition*, 97.

30. Ibid., 97–98.

31. Robinson, *Life in California*, 86.

32. Mora, *Californios*, 70.

33. Atherton, *California Diary*, 65.

34. San Jose Death 03159, July 4, 1824, ECPP.

35. San Jose Death 05554, July 13, 1836, ECPP.

36. San Francisco Solano Death 00365a, September 9, 1830, ECPP.

37. Edwards, *California in 1837*, 17.

38. J. Smith, *Southwest Expedition*, 97–98.

39. Osio, *History of Alta California*, 27.

40. Ibid.

41. Ibid.

42. Robinson, *Life in California*, 220.

43. Isenberg, *Mining California*, 107.

44. For more on the ecological effects of this commodity harvesting, see Tucker, *Insatiable Appetite*.

45. James A. Forbes to Larkin, November 4, 1844, reprinted in Larkin, *Larkin Papers*, 3:277.

46. Salvatore, "Modes of Labor Control in Cattle-Ranching Economies," 445.

47. Hackel, "Land, Labor, and Production," 125.

48. Clyman, *Frontiersman*, 175.

49. Wilkes, *Narrative of the United States Exploring Expedition*, 5:176.

50. Ibid., 5:198.

51. Robinson, *Life in California*, 25.

52. Dana, *Two Years before the Mast*, 84.

53. Atherton, *California Diary*, 10.

54. Hackel, "Land, Labor, and Production," 127.

55. For more on the implications for Indian identity, see Monroy, *Thrown among Strangers*, 78.

56. Osio, *History of Alta California*, 44.

57. Hurtado, *Indian Survival*, 55.

58. "Cuenta de los sirvientes pos la mes de abril 1843," Box 73, Abel Stearns papers, HL.

59. Details of Dalton's operation in Callao can be found in Henry Dalton papers, Box 1, HL. He discussed his decision to establish himself in California on the producing end in a letter, Henry Dalton to Mess. B. Y. Pain, June 2, 1843, Box 1, Henry Dalton papers, HL.

60. 1845 Datebook "Occurrences at Azusa," vol. 1, Henry Dalton papers, HL; Memo Book, Henry Dalton papers, HL.

61. Martín Duarte is a clear example of a laborer who had to work to pay off a thirty-three-peso debt laid out in Gutierrez, "Bell Towers, Crucifixes, and Canones Violentos," 310.

62. Dalton's wage rates were not consistent, but entries such as "4 indians 2 day on brick 6.0" and "12 indians 3 days pulling up stakes 27.0" suggest that each Indian earned about 6 reales or three-fourths of a peso a day. Memo Book, Henry Dalton papers, HL.

63. For example, May 1, 1863 entry in "Occurrences at Azusa," vol. 4, Henry Dalton papers, HL.

64. 1845 Datebook "Occurrences at Azusa," vol. 1, Henry Dalton papers, HL.

65. Hurtado, *John Sutter*, 63–65.

66. Wilkes, *Narrative of the United States Exploring Expedition*, 5:179.

67. Okihiro, *Island World*, 150.

68. Hurtado, *John Sutter*, 68, 74.

69. Beebe and Senkewicz, *Testimonios*, 12.

70. Ibid.

71. Hurtado, *Indian Survival*, 59.

72. Wilkes, *Narrative of the United States Exploring Expedition*, 5:179.

73. J. A. Sutter to William Leidesdorff, October 14, 1846, William Leidesdorff papers, Box 2, HL.

74. Undated receipt, William Leidesdorff papers, Box 1, HL.

75. Palmer, *History of Napa and Lake Counties*, 49.

76. Ibid.

77. Ibid.

78. Wilkes, *Narrative of the United States Exploring Expedition*, 5:198.

79. Palmer, *History of Napa and Lake Counties*, 50.

80. Ibid.

81. Ibid., 56; see also Hurtado, *Indian Survival*, 106.

82. Melville, *Omoo*, 536–37.

83. Ibid., 537–38.

84. Ibid., 538.

85. Ibid.

86. The date 1832 appears in several works on paniolo, though Joaquin Armas (about whom more below) claims to have been hired in May 1831.

87. As archaeologist Peter Mills has noted, Dana said that some of his Hawaiian coworkers played with horses and lassoes while he worked there in the late 1830s (Mills, "Keanakolu," 21). There is no direct evidence of Hawaiians returning with vaquero skills and training others, and the hiring of vaqueros suggests that this was not a major factor in the transfer of cattle culture.

88. Brennan, *Parker Ranch of Hawai'i*, 45. Contemporary records of these three vaqueros are lacking; their names come to Brennan through oral tradition and are sometimes attributed to stories told by the famous paniolo Eben "Rawhide Ben" Low.

89. Ibid.

90. Shinseki, "El Pueblo Mexicano de Hawai'i," 4.

91. Kossuth is a Hungarian name shared with a democratic activist named Lajos "Louis" Kossuth. Louis Kossuth was famous through the English-speaking world (a county in Iowa is named for him), but he was not well known before the revolutions of 1848, so the origin of Hawai'i's Kossuth's name remains unclear. He may have been Hungarian or of Hungarian descent, he could be an Indian with a coincidentally Hungarian-sounding name, or folk traditions may have misremembered his name. I have found no contemporary records of a Kossuth to clear up the matter.

92. April 27, 1833, "Stephen Reynolds Journal 1823–1842, 1855," HHS.

93. Armas is discussed at length in Frost and Frost, "King's Bullock Catcher." Kyle Ko Francisco Shinseki discusses Armas, as well as the lasting influence of other Mexican vaqueros in Hawai'i in Shinseki, "El Pueblo Mexicano de Hawai'i."

94. October 2, 1848, Foreign Office and Executive Documents, Passport no. 160, HSA.

95. Joaquin Armas to Alexander Simpson, February 13, 1843, Interior Department Documents, HSA.

96. Ibid.

97. Ibid.

98. Ibid.

99. Ibid.

100. In one letter from 1833, he noted, "I have sent on board the Brig Dolla 30 bullocks according to you letter and likewise 12 to trade for Article rec'd from Capt. Mart. I Remain Your Majesty's Obed't Servant, Hoakini" (Hoakini to King Kamehameha III, December 5, 1833, Interior Department Documents, HSA).

101. "Wokine" Armas to Kamehameha III, August 22, 1838, Interior Department Documents, HSA.

102. Joaquin Armas to Alexander Simpson, February 13, 1843, Interior Department Documents, HSA.

103. Ibid.

104. Ibid.

105. C.J. Lyons, "Traces of Spanish Influence," 26.

106. Ibid., 25.

107. Ibid., 26.

108. Ibid.

109. Ibid.

110. Ibid.

111. Olmsted, *Incidents of a Whaling Voyage*, 230. Emphasis from original text.

112. Ibid., 232.

113. Ibid., 233.

114. Ibid., 235.

115. Ibid.

116. Colton, *Deck and Port*, 343.

117. Ibid.

118. Ibid.

119. E. B. Robinson to Robinsons, September 6, 1846, Dwight Baldwin letters, HMCS.

120. Ruschenberger, *Voyage around the World*, 455.

121. Martin, *Nā Paniolo o Hawaiʻi*, 36.

122. Bergin, *Loyal to the Land*, 129.

123. "Cattle Hunting on Hawaii," August 11, 1859.

124. Letter to the editor, signed "Gimel," May 26, 1849.

125. Cowan-Smith and Stone, *Aloha Cowboy*, 95–100. For masculinity in cowboy cultures, see Najera-Ramirez, "Engendering Nationalism," 9–10. For cowboys developing into a masculine ideal see Downs, "Cowboy and the Lady," 278–89. Further research also needs to be done on the native wives of married male European ranch proprietors and their relationship to the ranches.

126. Bergin, *Loyal to the Land*, 36.

127. *George Davis v. Wm Green for RC Janion*, July 14, 1860, HSA.

128. John A. Simmons to William Pitt, June 8, 1844, Interior Department Documents, HSA.

129. Ibid.

130. Bennett, *Narrative of a Whaling Voyage*, 248.

131. Ibid.

132. E. B. Robinson to Robinsons, September 6, 1846, Dwight Baldwin letters, HMCS.

133. "Law for protection of persons who wish to cultivate and persons who wish to raise livestock," undated, reign of Kamehameha III, Foreign Office and Executive Documents, Doc. 168, HSA.

134. Ibid.

135. Ibid.

136. "Statute Laws of His Majesty Kamehameha III, King of the Hawaiian Islands, Passed by the Houses of Nobles and Representatives during the Twenty-First Year of His Reign, and the Third and Fourth Years of His Public Recognition A.D. 1845 and 1846," Interior Department Documents, HSA.

137. Ibid.

138. *George Davis v. Wm Green for RC Janion*, July 14, 1860, HSA.

139. L. Lyons, "Report of Waimea Field Station." Though the context of New England settler colonialism differs significantly, David J. Silverman has made compelling arguments about the indigenous adoption of livestock and fences as a method to protect their autonomy (see Silverman, "We Chuse to Be Bounded").

140. For the role fences play in enclosing colonial commons, see Greer, "Commons and Enclosure." More on this in chapter 6.

141. *Kamaina v. Piena*—"*both native*," August 23, 1859, Third Circuit Court—Civil, HSA. The judge dismissed the case because of "disagreement of the witnesses."

142. Wilkes, *Narrative of the United States Exploring Expedition*, 4:203.

143. *George Davis v. Wm Green for RC Janion*, July 14, 1860, HSA.

144. "To the Editor of *The Polynesian*," September 4, 1841.

145. Wilkes, *Narrative of the United States Exploring Expedition*, 4:200.

146. *George Davis v. Wm Green for RC Janion*, July 14, 1860, HSA. Judd's advice would have been in 1840, not 1842 or 1843.

147. Wilkes, *Narrative of the United States Exploring Expedition*, 4:218.

148. Ibid.

149. Linnekin, *Sacred Queens*, 69–70.

150. Wilkes, *Narrative of the United States Exploring Expedition*, 4:200.

151. *H. King v. Naipualoha*, December 21, 1851, South Kona Appeals Court, HSA.

152. Iselin, *Journal of a Trading Voyage*, 47.

153. Haas, *Saints and Citizens*, 136.

154. Ibid., 141.

155. Ibid., 152.

156. Payéras, *Writings*, 184.

157. Mariano Payéras to Baldomero López, July 4, 1819, reprinted in Payéras, *Writings*, 197.

158. Phillips, *Indians and Intruders*, 98–100.

159. Minnich, *California's Fading Wildflowers*, 98.

160. Haas, *Saints and Citizens*, 61; Phillips, *Indians and Intruders*, 85–87.

161. Vallejo, "Ranch and Mission Days in Alta California," 190.

162. Hyde, *Empires, Nations, and Families*, 178.

163. T. O. Larkin to "Journal of Commerce," July 1845, reprinted in Larkin, *Larkin Papers*, 3:294.

164. Wilkes, *Narrative of the United States Exploring Expedition*, 5:174.

165. San Jose Death 03718, November 1826, ECPP.

166. San Jose Baptism 02390, March 23, 1812, ECPP.

167. Simpson, *Narrative of a Journey*, 1:398.

168. Ibid.

169. Petit-Thouars, *Voyage of the Venus*, 44–45.

170. Smith, *Southwest Expedition*, 83.

171. Simpson, *Narrative of a Journey*, 1:406.

172. Phillips, *Indians and Intruders*, 104.

173. Wilkes, *Narrative of the United States Exploring Expedition*, 5:174.

174. T. O. Larkin to M. Y. Beach, May 31, 1845, reprinted in Larkin, *Larkin Papers*, 3:219.

175. Osio, *History of Alta California*, 134.

176. Ruschenberger, *Voyage around the World*, 507.

177. Osio, *History of Alta California*, 134.

178. Phillips, *Indians and Intruders*, 102.

179. Colton, *Three Years in California*, 48.

180. See, for instance, Hämäläinen, *Comanche Empire*, 244.

181. Phillips, *Indians and Intruders*, 97.

182. Garner, *Letters from California*, 164.

183. Beebe and Senkewicz, *Testimonios*, 130.

184. Ibid., 131.

185. Mofras, *Travels on the Pacific Coast*, 1:179.

186. Cook, "Expeditions to the Interior of California," 190.

187. Wilkes, *Narrative of the United States Exploring Expedition*, 5:183.

188. T. O. Larkin to M. Y. Beach, May 31, 1845, reprinted in Larkin, *Larkin Papers*, 3:219.

189. Brooks, *Captives & Cousins*, 250.

190. Larkin, *Larkin Papers*, 4:306.

191. Mofras, *Travels on the Pacific Coast*, 1:253.

192. Belcher, *Narrative of a Voyage Round the World*, 1:116.

193. DeLay, *War of a Thousand Deserts*, 264–65.

CHAPTER SIX

1. An excellent description on native Hawaiian land practices can be found in Kameʻeleihiwa, *Native Lands and Foreign Desires*. Noenoe K. Silva discusses the moral economy of the ahupuaʻa in *Aloha Betrayed*, 39–40.

2. Daws, *Shoal of Time*, 85.

3. Hartnell, *Diary and Copybook*, 11.

4. Weaver, *Great Land Rush*, 11–13.

5. Banner, *Possessing the Pacific*, 316–18.

6. Cleland, *Cattle on a Thousand Hills*, 9.

7. Nieto's land grant amounted to 300,000 acres, though Mission San Gabriel eventually claimed half of it. Domínguez's grant encompassed 75,000 acres (ibid., 11–12).

8. Ibid., 26.

9. Hornbeck, "Land Tenure and Rancho Expansion," 374.

10. "General Rules and Regulations for the Colonization of Territories of the Republic," reprinted in Dwinelle, *Colonial History of San Francisco*, 25.

11. Hornbeck, "Land Tenure and Rancho Expansion," 376.

12. Geiger, *As the Padres Saw Them*, 110.

13. Hornbeck, "Land Tenure and Rancho Expansion," 379.

14. Hundley, *Great Thirst*, 49.

15. Beechey, *Account of a Visit to California*, 10.

16. Robinson, *Life in California*, 218.

17. Ibid., 219.

18. Hutchinson, *Frontier Settlement in Mexican California*, 129.

19. Phillips, "Indians and the Breakdown of the Spanish Mission System," 299.

20. Bancroft, *History of California*, 3:331. Lisbeth Haas presents a good analysis of some of those wishing to stay in the missions in *Saints and Citizens*, 154–55.

21. "Governor Figueroa's Provisional Rules for the Secularization of the Missions," reprinted in Dwinelle, *Colonial History of San Francisco*, 31.

22. Weber, *Mexican Frontier*, 46.

23. Dwinelle, *Colonial History of San Francisco*, 31.

24. Ibid.

25. Ibid., 32.

26. Ibid.

27. Weber, *Mexican Frontier*, 66.

28. Beebe and Senkewicz, *Testimonios*, 233.

29. Ibid.

30. Hartnell, *Diary and Copybook*, 33.

31. Ibid., 63.

32. Ibid.

33. Ibid.

34. Ibid., 46.

35. Pico, *Narrative*, 91–92.

36. Hartnell, *Diary and Copybook*, 29.

37. Mofras, *Travels on the Pacific Coast*, 1:151.

38. Beebe and Senkewicz, *Testimonios*, 314.

39. Colton, *Three Years in California*, 68.

40. Dana, *Two Years before the Mast*, 159.

41. Ibid.

42. Ibid.

43. "Governor Micheltorena's Proclamation Respecting the Missions, March 29, 1843," reprinted in Dwinelle, *Colonial History of San Francisco*, 83.

44. Ibid.

45. Cleland, *Cattle on a Thousand Hills*, 33.

46. Hackel, "Land, Labor, and Production," 133.

47. Cleland, *Cattle on a Thousand Hills*, 38.

48. Hurtado, *John Sutter*, 121.

49. Simpson, *Narrative of a Journey*, 1:199.

50. Ibid.

51. Ibid.

52. Banner, *Possessing the Pacific*, 132.

53. Crosby, *Germs, Seeds, and Animals*.

54. For a discussion on the increasing influence of Anglo-American legal traditions and the resulting changes in Hawaiian power dynamics, see Merry, *Colonizing Hawai'i*. Jon J. Chinen offers an overview of the Māhele in *They Cried for Help*. See also Silva, *Aloha Betrayed*, 41–42.

55. LaCroix and Roumasset, "Evolution of Private Property in Nineteenth-Century Hawaii."

56. Banner, *Possessing the Pacific*, 128.

57. Kameʻeleihiwa, *Native Lands and Foreign Desires*, 297.

58. Prucha, *Great Father*, 1:28–31; Wallace, *Jefferson and the Indians*, 168–69, 180–91; Sheehan, *Seeds of Extinction*, 121–47.

59. Seed, *Ceremonies of Possession*, 144.

60. Greer, "Commons and Enclosure in the Colonization of North America," 383–84.

61. L. Lyons, *Makua Laiana*, 139.

62. Linnekin, *Sacred Queens*, 200.

63. "Anonymous letter," August 26, 1848.

64. Banner, *Possessing the Pacific*, 134.

65. Ibid., 136.

66. Daws, *Shoal of Time*, 112–17.

67. Merry, *Colonizing Hawaiʻi*, 14.

68. Banner, *Possessing the Pacific*, 138–39.

69. Wyllie, "Address before Royal Hawaiian Agricultural Society," August 12, 1850, Wyllie Papers, BML.

70. Wyllie, "Answers to question put forth by M Dudoit Consul of France," April 22, 1846, Wyllie Papers, BML.

71. R. C. Wyllie to Kamehameha III, December 1, 1847, Foreign Office and Executive Documents 402, Box 21, Folder 452, HSA.

72. Ibid.

73. Ibid.

74. Sahlins, *Historical Ethnography*, 134–35.

75. Silva, *Aloha Betrayed*, 41–42.

76. Ibid., 43. For more on the problems of transforming a peasant society in a colonial context, see Scott, *Moral Economy of the Peasant*.

77. Chinen, *Great Mahele*, 9.

78. "Petition from citizens of Kona to His Majesty Kamehameha III," June 12, 1845, Interior Department Documents, HSA.

79. Chinen, *They Cried for Help*, 129.

80. Banner, *Possessing the Pacific*, 141–42.

81. Ibid., 154.

82. Ibid., 142.

83. Chinen, *They Cried for Help*, 72; Stauffer, *Kahana*. As Kameʻeleihiwa puts it, "claiming the ʻĀina [land] was a very foreign idea, generally outside the common Hawaiian's reality" (Kameʻeleihiwa, *Native Lands and Foreign Desires*, 296).

84. Chinen, *They Cried for Help*, 32.

85. *Journal of Legislature 1841-1850*, 158, HSA.

86. Ibid.

87. Linnekin, *Sacred Queens*, 205.

88. Isaac Y. Davis to Keoni Ana, May 15, 1851 (trans. E. H. Hart), Interior Department Documents, HSA.

89. Chinen, *They Cried for Help*, 138.

90. Daws, *Shoal of Time*, 128.

91. B. B. Wellmon, "Parker Ranch," 34.

92. Ibid., 22.

93. Brennan, *Parker Ranch*, 37, 65.

94. *George Davis v. Wm Green for RC Janion*, July 14, 1860, HSA.

95. B. B. Wellmon, "Parker Ranch," 59. An 1844 contract between French and Purdy (which also mentions Parker) read, "Leiliohoka [French] hereby give his consent in relations to the land which he had leased from the government viz Puaka [Parker] and which joins that of HW Podua [Purdy] that they will feed their cattle together. . . . Each shall take good care of the cattle of the other should they stray away or wander from their own herd, and both H W Podua and myself with faithfully protect our watch said land as specified in the lease. . . . We will kindly let our cattle run together, as tenants of our king. But if either of us should disregard the stipulation expressed in the lease, are and pasture the cattle of others on said land without paying for it, then that destroy this agreement and make it null" ("Agreement between H W Podua and Wm P. Leilohoka," August 23, 1844, Interior Department Documents, HSA). Although both parties were native English speakers, a copy of the document in Hawaiian suggests the government's oversight of these ranching activities.

96. B. B. Wellmon, "Parker Ranch," 72.

97. Ibid., 74.

98. Chinen, *They Cried for Help*, 138.

99. B. B. Wellmon, "Parker Ranch," 75.

100. Ibid., 126.

101. *George Davis v. Wm Green for RC Janion*, July 14, 1860, HSA.

102. [Unsigned] to W. P. Leleiohoku and G. D. Heue, undated [1849?], Interior Department Documents, Letterbook 2, HSA.

103. W. Goodale (clerk) to Mr. Kaoo, February 11, 1850, Interior Department Documents, Letterbook 2, HSA.

104. Bond, *Father Bond of Kohala*, 207.

105. Atherton, *Cattle Kings*, 161, 181.

106. In January 1847, William Beckley reported branding three hundred feral cattle, for which he charged the government $27.75. William Beckley to G. P. Judd, January 7, 1847, Interior Department Documents, Land Doc 185, HSA.

107. Agreement between G. P. Judd and Miele, August 1, 1848 (trans. E. H. Hart), Interior Department Documents, HSA.

108. John Young Kanehoa to Kamehameha III (in Privy Council), April 6, 1850, (trans. E. H. Hart), Interior Department Documents, HSA.

109. Huanu Paniolo to John Young, November 28, 1850, Interior Department Documents, HSA.

110. Davis, *Reports of a Portion of the Decisions of the Supreme Court*, 367–78.

111. This again illustrates the argument of Allan Greer in "Commons and Enclosure in the Colonization of North America." William Cronon notes that English colonists in New England maintained title to their livestock even when they wandered into

Indian lands. A "fixed property right inhered" in a colonists' hog or cow no matter where it wandered (Cronon, *Changes in the Land*, 129).

112. J. P. Parker to L. Kamehameha, April 11, 1859, Interior Department Documents, HSA.

113. Ibid.

114. S. Spencer to J. P. Parker, April 27, 1859, Interior Department Documents, HSA.

115. Davis, *Reports of a Portion of the Decisions of the Supreme Court*, 377.

116. Hackel, "Land, Labor, and Production," 134–35; Phillips, *Vineyards and Vaqueros*, 328.

117. Haas, *Conquests and Historical Identities in California*, 54–55.

118. Hackel, *Children of Coyote*, 390.

119. Atherton, *California Diary*, 10.

120. Street, *Beasts of the Field*, 92.

121. Hackel, *Children of Coyote*, 392.

122. Ibid., 394.

123. Ibid., 391–95. For another listing and discussion of Indian landholders, including their ranching activities, see Haas, *Saints and Citizens*, 167–72.

124. Carlson and Parkman, "Exceptional Adaptation," 244.

125. Ibid., 239.

126. Ibid., 241.

127. Davis, *Seventy-Five Years in California*, 103.

128. Ibid.

129. Carlson and Parkman, "Exceptional Adaptation," 246.

130. Peterson, "Career of Solano," 2, 22.

131. Hyde, *Empires, Nations, and Families*, 148.

132. Peterson, "Career of Solano," 25, 31.

133. Ibid., 41, 61.

134. Ibid., 77–78.

135. Hyde, *Empires, Nations, and Families*, 335.

136. Wilkes, *Narrative of the United States Exploring Expedition*, 5:172.

137. John Sutter to Thomas Larkin, July 21, 1845; Thomas Larkin to John Sutter, November 1, 1845, Leidesdorff Papers, Box 1, HL.

138. L. L. Austin to John Young, Interior Department Documents, October 16, 1853, HSA. These are the brands registered from April 1 through September 30, 1853.

139. Linnekin, *Sacred Queens*, 201, 206.

140. Sahlins, *Historical Ethnography*, 148; Kirch, *Archaeology of History*, 170.

141. B. B. Wellmon, "Parker Ranch," 117–18.

142. Hutchinson to L. Kamehameha, May 15, 1861, Interior Department Documents, HSA.

143. James Robinson, Robert Lawrence, R. W. Holt, Joseph Booth to John Young, November 14, 1849, Interior Department Documents, HSA. The ranchers believed that a missionary named John L. Emerson had incited the Hawaiians against their cattle, though it was unclear why.

1. Thomas O. Larkin, Consular Report to the United States State Department, April 20, 1846, reprinted in Larkin, *Larkin Papers*, 4:305.

2. John Coffin Jones to Larkin, September 26, 1846, reprinted in Larkin, *Larkin Papers*, 5:252; John Coffin Jones to Larkin, October 8, 1848, reprinted in Larking, *Larkin Papers*, 8:56.

3. Linnekin, *Sacred Queens*, 182.

4. Isenberg, *Mining California*, 123–29.

5. Fiege, *Irrigated Eden*, 171. "The Garden Myth" discussed by Fiege was coined in H. N. Smith, *Virgin Land*.

6. Igler, *Industrial Cowboys*.

7. Brennan, *Parker Ranch*. Carter represented the rationalization of U.S. extraction in the Pacific. For more, see Tucker, *Insatiable Appetite*, 315–16.

8. Nunis, "Alta California's Trojan Horse."

9. Pitt, *Decline of the Californios*.

10. Colton, *Three Years in California*, 146.

11. Ibid., 198.

12. Hurtado, *Indian Survival*.

13. Isenberg, *Mining California*, 120.

14. Phillips, *Indians and Indian Agents*.

15. Bauer, *"We Were All Like Migrant Workers Here."*

16. Isenberg, "Between Mexico and the United States," 100–101.

17. Alexander Pennie to G. P. Judd, April 4, 1845, Interior Department Documents, Letterbook 1, HSA. Emphasis is in the original.

18. Arthur, *Koloa Plantation*, 37.

19. Daws, *Shoal of Time*, 202–3.

20. Weigle, "Sugar and the Hawaiian Revolution," 58.

21. Najita, "History, Trauma, and the Discursive Construction of Race," 194.

22. Rojas, *Vaqueros and Buckaroos*; Mora, *Trail Dust and Saddle Leather*; Mora, *Californios*.

23. For more on the evolution of Hawaiian music and paniolo influences see Okihiro, *Island World*, 175–205.

24. For instance, see Tyrell, *True Gardens of the Gods*; Sackman, *Orange Empire*.

Bibliography

PRIMARY SOURCES

Andrews, L., trans. "On the Decrease of Population on the Hawaiian Islands." *Hawaiian Spectator* 2 (April 1839): 121–30.

"Anonymous letter." *Polynesian*, August 26, 1848.

Atherton, Faxon Dean. *The California Diary of Faxon Dean Atherton*. Edited by Doyce B. Nunis Jr. San Francisco: California Historical Society, 1964.

Baldwin, Dwight. Dwight Baldwin Letters. Albert J. Baldwin Collection. Hawaiian Mission Children's Society, Honolulu.

Bates, George Washington. *Sandwich Island Notes by a Haole*. New York: Harper and Brothers, 1854.

Beebe, Rose Marie, and Robert M. Senkewicz, trans. and ed. *Testimonios: Early California through the Eyes of Women, 1815–1848*. Berkeley: Heyday Books, 2006.

Beechey, William. *An Account of a Visit to California 1826–27: Reprinted from a Narrative of a Voyage to the Pacific and Bering's Strait Performed in His Majesty's Ship Blossom under the Command of Captain F. W. Beechey in 1825, '26, '27, '28*. San Francisco: Book Club of California, 1941.

Belcher, Edward. *Narrative of a Voyage Round the World, Performed in Her Majesty's Ship Sulphur during 1836–1842*. 2 vols. London: Henry Colburn, 1842.

Bennett, Frederick Debell. *Narrative of a Whaling Voyage Round the Globe from the Year 1833 to 1836*. London: Richard Bentley, 1840.

Boelen, Jacubus. *A Merchant's Perspective: Capt Jacubus Boelen's Narrative of a Visit to Hawai'i in 1828*. Translated by Frank J. A. Broeze. Honolulu: Hawaiian Historical Society, 1988.

Bond, Elias. *Father Bond of Kohala: A Chronicle of Pioneer Life in Hawaii*. Edited by Ethel M. Damon. Honolulu: The Friend, 1927.

Byron, Lord. *Voyage of HMS Blonde to the Sandwich Islands in the Years 1824–1825*. London: John Murray, 1826.

Campbell, Archibald. *A Voyage Round the World*. Honolulu: University of Hawai'i Press, 1967.

"Cattle Hunting on Hawaii." *Pacific Commercial Advertiser*, August 11, 1859.

Cleveland, Richard J. *A Narrative of Voyages and Commercial Enterprises*. Cambridge: John Owen, 1842.

Clyman, James. *Frontiersman: The Adventures of a Trapper and Covered-Wagon Emigrant as Told in His Own Reminiscences and Diaries*. Edited by Charles L. Camp. Portland, Ore.: Champoeg Press, 1960.

Colton, Walter. *Deck and Port: Incidents of a Cruise in the United States Frigate Congress to California*. New York: D. W. Evans & Co., 1860.

———. *Three Years in California*. New York: S. A. Rollo and Company, 1859.

Colvocorresses, George Musalas. *Four Years in a Government Exploring Expedition*. New York: Cornish Lamport and Co., 1852.

"Communications—Waimea." *Sandwich Island Gazette*, September 17, 1836.

Companys, F. Boneu. *Gaspar de Portolá, Explorer and Founder of California*. Translated by Alan K. Brown. Lerida: Instituto de Estudios Ilerdenses, 1983.

Cook, James. *The Voyage of the* Resolution *and the* Discovery, *1776–1780*. 2 parts. Vol. 3 of *The Journals of Captain James Cook on his Voyages of Discovery*. Edited by J. C. Beaglehole. London: Cambridge University Press, 1967.

Corney, Peter. *Early Voyages in the North Pacific 1813–1818*. Fairfield, Wash.: Ye Galleon Press, 1965.

Cox, Ross. *Adventures on the Columbia River*. London: Henry Colburn and Richard Bentley, 1831.

Dalton, Henry. Henry Dalton Papers. Huntington Library, San Marino, Calif., 1840–1883.

Dana Jr., Richard Henry. *Two Years before the Mast: A Personal Narrative of Life at Sea*. Boston: Estes and Lauriat, 1895.

Davis, Robert G. *Reports of a Portion of the Decisions of the Supreme Court of the Hawaiian Islands in Law, Equity, Admiralty and Probate, 1857–1865*. Honolulu: J. H. Black, 1866.

Davis Jr., William Heath. *Seventy-Five Years in California*. San Francisco: John Howell Books, 1967.

———. *Sixty Years in California*. San Francisco: A. J. Leary, 1889.

Delano, Amasa. *Narrative of Voyages and Travels in the Northern and Southern Hemispheres: Comprising Thee Voyages Round the World Together with a Voyage of Survey and Discovery in the Pacific and Oriental Islands*. Boston: E. G. House, 1817.

Dodge, Colonel Richard Irving. *Our Wild Indians: Thirty-Three Years' Personal Experience among the Red Men of the Great West*. Freeport, N.Y.: Books for Libraries Press, 1970.

Duhaut-Cilly, August. *A Voyage to California, the Sandwich Islands & Around the World*. Translated by August Frugé and Neal Harlow. San Francisco: Book Club of California, 1997.

Early California Population Project Database. The Huntington Library, 2006.

Edwards, Philip L. *California in 1837: Diary of Col Philip L. Edwards*. Sacramento: A. J. Johnston & Co, 1890.

Farnham, Thomas Jefferson. *Travels in the Californias, and Scenes from the Pacific Ocean*. New York: Saxton & Miles, 1844.

Font, Pedro. *Font's Complete Diary: A Chronicle of the Founding of San Francisco*. Edited by Herbert Eugene Bolton. Berkeley: University of California Press, 1931.

Forbes, Alexander. *California: A History of Upper and Lower California from Their First Discovery to the Present Time*. London: Smith, Elder and Co., Cornhill, 1839.

Foreign Office and Executive Documents. Hawai'i State Archives, Honolulu.

Franchère, Gabriel. *The Journal of Gabriel Franchère*. Toronto: Champlain Society, 1969.

Frémont, John C. *The Life of Colonel John C. Fremont and His Narrative of Explorations and Adventures in Kansas, Nebraska, Oregon, and California.* New York: Miller, Orton, and Mulligan, 1856.

French, William. William French Letterbook. Hawaiʻi State Archives, Honolulu.

Garner, William Robert. *Letters from California, 1846–1847.* Edited by Daniel Munro Craig. Berkeley: University of California Press, 1970.

Geiger, Maynard, ed. and trans. *As the Padres Saw Them: California Indians Life and Customs as Reported by the Franciscan Missionaries, 1813–1815.* Santa Barbara: Santa Barbara Mission Archive Library, 1976.

George Davis v. Wm Green for RC Janion. Case 219. Hawaiian First Circuit Court. Hawaiʻi State Archives, Honolulu.

Gimel. "Letter to the Editor." *Polynesian*, May 26, 1849.

Girdler, John. Letter to John Low, December 7, 1844. Manuscripts, Huntington Library, San Marino, Calif.

Green, Jonathan S. *Journey of a Tour in 1829: Containing a Description of a Part of Oregon, California, and the Northwest Coast and the Numbers, Manners and Customs of the Native Tribes.* New York: Charles Frederick Heartman, 1915.

Hartnell, William E. P. *The Diary and Copybook of William E. P. Hartnell: Visitador of the Missions of Alta California 1839–1840.* Edited by Glenn J. Farris. Glendale, Calif.: Arthur H. Clark Co., 2004.

Hill, Samuel S. *Travels in the Sandwich and Society Islands.* London: Chapman and Hall, 1856.

Hussey, John A., ed. *The Voyage of the* Racoon: *A "Secret" Journal of a Visit to Oregon, California and Hawaii, 1813–1814.* San Francisco: Book Club of California, 1958.

"Influence of the Cattle on the Climate of Waimea and Kawaihae, Hawaii." *Sandwich Island Monthly Magazine* 1 (February 1856): 44–47.

Interior Department Documents. Hawaiʻi State Archives, Honolulu.

Irving, Washington. *Astoria: or, The Antecedents of an Enterprise beyond the Rocky Mountains.* In *Three Western Narratives.* New York: Library of America, 2004.

Iselin, Isaac. *Journal of a Trading Voyage around the World, 1805–1808.* Fairfield, Wash.: Ye Galleon Press, 1999.

Jones, William Carey. *Land Titles in California.* Washington: Gideon and Co., 1850.

Journal of Legislature 1841–1850. Hawaiʻi State Archives, Honolulu.

Kehunaoa, M. *In Admiralty, Average Adjustment in the Case of American Brigantine Lafeyette.* Honolulu: Government Press, 1844. Hawaii Mission Children's Society, Honolulu.

Knapp, H. O. Journal #2, March 18–December 19, 1837. Hawaii Mission Children's Society, Honolulu.

Langsdorff, Georg Heinrich. *Langsdorff's Narrative of the Rezanov Voyage to Nueva California in 1806.* Translated by Thomas C. Russell. San Francisco: Private Press of Thomas C. Russell, 1927.

La Pérouse, Jean-François de Galaup. *The Journal of Jean-François de Galaup de LaPérouse 1785-1788*. 2 vols. Translated and edited by John Dunmore. London: Hakluyt Society, 1995.

Larkin, Thomas Oliver. *The Larkin Papers: The Personal, Business, and Official Correspondence of Thomas Oliver Larkin*. 10 vols. Edited by Everett Gordon Hager and Anna Marie Hager. Berkeley: University of California Press, 1951.

Lasuén, Fermín Francisco. *The Writings of Fermín Francisco de Lasuén*. 2 vols. Translated by Finbar Kenneally. Washington, D.C.: Academy of American Franciscan History, 1965.

Leidesdorff, William. William A. Leidesdorff Papers. Huntington Library, San Marino, Calif.

Lisianski, Urey. *A Voyage Round the World in the Years 1803, 4, 5, and 6 Performed by Order of His Imperial Majesty, Alexander the First, Emperor of Russia in the Ship Neva*. London: Booth, 1814.

Longinos Martínez, José. *Journal of José Longinos Martínez: Notes and Observations of the Botanical Expedition in Old and New California and the South Coast*. Translated and edited by Lesley Byrd Simpson. San Francisco: John Howell Books, 1961.

Lyons, Curtis J. "Traces of Spanish Influence in the Hawaiian Islands." In *Hawaiian Historical Society Papers of 1892*, 25–27. Honolulu: Bulletin Publishing Company, 1904.

Lyons, Lorenzo. *Makua Laiana: The Story of Lorenzo Lyons: Compiled from the Manuscript Journals, 1832-1886*. Edited by E. L. Doyle. Honolulu: Honolulu Star Bulletin, 1945.

———. "Report of Waimea Field Station," May 1837, Manuscript. Hawaiian Mission Children's Society, Honolulu.

Malo, David. *Hawaiian Antiquities: Moolelo Hawaii*. Translated by Nathaniel B. Emerson. Honolulu: Bishop Museum Press, 1951.

Manby, Thomas. *Journal of Vancouver's Voyage*. Typescript acquired 1928. Hawai'i State Archives, Honolulu.

Marin, Franciso de Paula. *The Letters and Journal of Francisco de Paula Marin*. Edited by Agnes C. Conrad. Honolulu: University Hawai'i Press, 1973.

Mathison, Gilbert Farquhar. *Narrative of a Visit to Brazil, Chile, Peru and the Sandwich Islands during the Years 1821 and 1822*. London: Charles Knight, Pall Mall East, 1825.

McLoughlin, John. *The Letters of Dr. John McLoughlin*. Edited by Burt Brown Barket. Portland, Ore.: Binford & Mort, 1948.

Melville, Herman. *Omoo*. In *Typee, Omoo, Mardi*. New York: Library of America, 1982.

Menzies, Archibald. *Hawaii Nei: 128 Years Ago*. Honolulu: n.p., 1920.

Miller, Robert Ryal. *A Yankee Smuggler on the Spanish California Coast: George Washington Eayrs and the Ship Mercury*. Santa Barbara: Santa Barbara Trust for Historic Preservation, 2001.

Mofras, Duflot de. *Duflot de Mofras' Travels on the Pacific Coast*. 2 vols. Translated and edited by Marguerite Webb Hodge. Santa Ana, Calif.: Fine Arts Press, 1937.

Mora, Jo. *Californios: The Saga of the Hard-Riding Vaqueros, America's First Cowboys*. Garden City, N.Y.: Doubleday, 1949.

——. *Trail Dust and Saddle Leather*. New York: Charles Scribner's Sons, 1946.

Olmsted, Francis Allyn. *Incidents of a Whaling Voyage*. Rutland, Vt.: Charles E. Tuttle Co., 1969.

Osio, Antonio María. *The History of Alta California: A Memoir of Mexican California*. Translated and edited by Rose Marie Beebe and Robert M. Senkewicz. Madison: University of Wisconsin Press, 1996.

Palóu, Francisco. *Historical Memoirs of New California*. 4 vols. Edited and translated by Herbert Eugene Bolton. Berkeley: University of California Press, 1926.

Payéras, Mariano. *Writings of Mariano Payéras*. Translated and edited by Donald W. Cutter. Santa Barbara: Bellerophon Press, 1995.

Petit-Thouars, Abel de. *Voyage of the Venus: Sojourn in California*. Translated by Charles N. Rukin. Los Angeles: Glen Dawson, 1956.

Pico, Pío. *Don Pío Pico's Narrative*. Translated by Arthur P. Botello. Glendale, Calif.: Arthur H. Clark Co., 1973.

Reid, Hugo. *The Indians of Los Angeles County: Hugo Reid's Letters of 1852*. Edited by Robert F. Heizer. Los Angeles: Southwest Museum, 1968.

"Reign of Liholiho." *Polynesian*, August 1, 1840.

Reynolds, Stephen. "Stephen Reynolds Journal 1823–1842, 1855." Typescript. Hawaiian Historical Society, Honolulu.

Robinson, Alfred. *Life in California during a Residence of Several Years in That Territory*. New York: Wiley and Putnam, 1846.

Rojas, Arnold R. *Vaqueros and Buckaroos*. Bakersfield: Hall Letter Shop, 1979.

Roquefeuil, Camille de. *A Voyage Round the World, between the Years 1816–1819*. London: Sir Richard Phillips and Co., 1823.

Ruschenberger, William Samuel Waithman. *A Voyage around the World Including an Embassy to Muscat and Siam in 1835, 1836, and 1837*. Philadelphia: Carey, Lea and Blanchard, 1838.

Serra, Junípero. *Writings of Junípero Serra*. 4 vols. Edited by Antonine Tibesar. Washington, D.C.: Academy of American Franciscan History, 1955.

Shaler, William. *Journal of a Voyage between China and the Northwestern Coast of America Made in 1804*. Claremont, Calif.: Saunders Studio Press, 1935.

Simpson, George. *Narrative of a Journey Round the World during the Years 1841 and 1842*. 2 vols. London: Henry Colburn, 1847.

Smith, Jedediah. *The Southwest Expedition of Jedediah S. Smith: His Personal Account of the Journey to California, 1827–1827*. Edited by Gerald R. Brooks. Glendale, Calif.: Arthur H. Clark Company, 1977.

South Kona Appeals Court. Hawai'i State Archives, Honolulu.

Stearns, Abel. Abel Stearns Papers. Huntington Library, San Marino, Calif., 1821–1935.

Stewart, C. S. *Journal of a Residence in the Sandwich Islands during the Years 1823, 1824, and 1825*. Honolulu: University of Hawai'i Press, 1970.

"Ten Thousand Coming for Last Frontier Days." *Cheyenne Daily Leader*, August 22, 1908.

Third Circuit Court—Civil. Hawai'i State Archives, Honolulu.

Tinker, Reuben, trans. "Ka Moolelo Hawaii." *Hawaiian Spectator* 2 (April 1839): 211–31.

"To the Editor of *The Polynesian*." *Polynesian*, September 4, 1841.

Turnbull, John. *Voyage Round the World in the Years 1800, 1801, 1802, 1803 and 1804*. Philadelphia: Benjamin and Thomas Kite, 1810.

Tyerman, Daniel, and George Bennet. *Journal of Voyages and Travels*. 3 vols. Boston: Crocker and Brewster, 1832.

Vallejo, Guadalupe. "Ranch and Mission Days in Alta California." *Century Magazine*, December 1890.

Vancouver, George. *A Voyage of Discovery to the North Pacific Ocean and Round the World, 1791–1795*. 5 vols. Edited by W. Kaye Lamb. London: Halkuyt Society, 1984.

Varigny, Charles Victor Crosnier de. *Fourteen Years in the Sandwich Islands*. Translated by Alfonso L. Korn. Honolulu: University of Hawai'i Press, 1991.

Von Kotzebue, Otto. *A New Voyage Round the World, Years 1823, 24, 25, and 26*. London: Henry Colburn and Richard Bentley, 1830.

Wilkes, Charles. *Narrative of the United States Exploring Expedition during the Years 1838, 1839, 1840, 1841, 1842*. 5 vols. Philadelphia: Lea and Blanchard, 1845.

Work, John. *Fur Brigade to the Bonaventura*. Edited by Alice Bay Maloney. San Francisco: California Historical Society, 1945.

Wyllie, Robert Crichton. Robert Wyllie Papers. Bishop Museum, Honolulu.

SECONDARY SOURCES

Abbass, D. K. "Herd Development in the New World Spanish Colonies: Conquistadors and Peasants." In *Themes in Rural History of the Western World*, edited by Richard Herr, 165–93. Ames: Iowa State University Press, 1993.

Adelman, Jeremy, and Stephen Aron. "From Borderlands to Borders: Empires, Nation-States, and the People in Between in North American History." *American Historical Review* 104 (June 1999): 814–41.

Anderson, E. W., and R. J. Scherzinger. "Improving Quality of Winter Forage for Elk by Cattle Grazing." *Journal of Range Management* 28 (1975): 120–25.

Anderson, Gary Clayton. *The Indian Southwest, 1580–1830: Ethnogenesis and Reinvention*. Norman: University of Oklahoma Press, 1999.

Anderson, M. Kat. *Tending the Wild: Native American Knowledge and the Management of California's Natural Resources*. Berkeley: University of California Press, 2006.

Anderson, Virginia DeJohn. *Creatures of Empire: How Domestic Animal Transformed Early America*. Oxford: Oxford University Press, 2004.

Andrews, Kenneth R. *Trade, Plunder and Settlement: Maritime Enterprise and the Genesis of the British Empire, 1480–1630*. Cambridge: Cambridge University Press, 1984.

Archibald, Robert. *Economic Aspects of the California Missions*. Washington, D.C.: Academy of American Franciscan History, 1978.

Armstrong, R. Warwick. *Atlas of Hawaii*. Honolulu: University of Hawai'i Press, 1973.

Arthur, Alexander. *Koloa Plantation, 1835–1935.* Honolulu: Honolulu Star-Bulletin, 1937.

Atherton, Lewis. *The Cattle Kings.* Bloomington: Indiana University Press, 1961.

Bakker, Elna. *An Island Called California: An Ecological Introduction to Its Natural Communities.* Berkeley: University of California Press, 1971.

Balleisen, Edward J. *Navigating Failure: Bankruptcy and Commercial Society in Antebellum America.* Chapel Hill: University of North Carolina Press, 2001.

Bancroft, Hubert Howe. *History of California.* 6 vols. San Francisco: History Company, 1886.

Banner, Stuart Banner. *Possessing the Pacific: Land, Settlers, and Indigenous People from Australia to Alaska.* Cambridge, Mass.: Harvard University Press, 2007.

Barbour, Michael, Bruce Pavlik, Frank Drysdale, and Susan Lindstrom. *California's Changing Landscapes: Diversity and Conservation of California Vegetation.* Sacramento: California Native Plant Society, 1993.

Barr, Juliana. *Peace Came in the Form of a Woman: Indians and Spaniards in the Texas Borderlands.* Chapel Hill: University of North Carolina Press, 2007.

Bauer Jr., William J. *"We Were All Like Migrant Workers Here": Work, Community and Memory on California's Round Valley Reservation, 1850–1941.* Chapel Hill: University of North Carolina Press, 2009.

Beck, Jeffrey L., and James M. Peek. "Diet Composition, Forage Selection, and Potential for Forage Competition among Elk, Deer, and Livestock on Aspen-Sagebrush Summer Range." *Rangeland Ecology & Management* 58 (March 2005): 135–47.

Bergin, Billy. *Loyal to the Land: The Legendary Parker Ranch, 750–1950.* Honolulu: University of Hawai'i Press, 2004.

Bishko, Charles Julian. "The Peninsular Background of Latin American Cattle Ranching." *Hispanic American Historical Review* 32 (November 1952): 491–515.

Biswell, H. H. "The Use of Fire in Wildland Management in California." In *Natural Resources: Quality and Quantity*, edited by S. V. Ciriacy-Wantrup and J. J. Parsons, 71–87. Berkeley: University of California Press, 1967.

Blackhawk, Ned. *Violence over the Land: Indians and Empires in the Early American West.* Cambridge, Mass.: Harvard University Press, 2006.

Blaufarb, Rafe. "The Western Question: The Geopolitics of Latin American Independence." *American Historical Review* 112 (June 2007): 742–63.

Bolton, Herbert Eugene. *Outpost of Empire: The Story of the Founding of San Francisco.* New York: Alfred A. Knopf, 1931.

Boyd, Robert. *The Coming of the Spirit of Pestilence: Introduced Infectious Diseases and Population Decline among Northwest Coast Indians, 1774–1875.* Seattle: University of Washington Press, 1999.

Bradley, Harold Whitman. *The American Frontier in Hawaii: The Pioneers 1789–1843.* Stanford, Calif.: Stanford University Press, 1942.

Breen, T. H. *The Marketplace of Revolution: How Consumer Politics Shaped the American Revolution.* Oxford: Oxford University Press, 2004.

Brennan, Joseph. *The Parker Ranch of Hawai'i: The Saga of a Ranch and a Dynasty.* New York: John Day Company, 1974.

Brooks, James F. *Captives & Cousins: Slavery, Kinship and Community in the Southwest Borderlands*. Chapel Hill: University of North Carolina Press, 2002.

Brown, Michael F., and Eduardo Fernandez. "Tribe and State in a Frontier Mosaic: The Asháninka of Eastern Peru." In *War in the Tribal Zone: Expanding States and Indigenous Warfare*, edited by R. Brian Ferguson and Neil L. Whitehead, 175–98. Santa Fe: School of American Research, 1992.

Burcham, L. T. *California Range Land: A Historico-Ecological Study of the Range Resource of California*. Sacramento: Department of Natural Resources, 1957.

Burritt, Beth, and Roger Banner. "Elk and Cattle Grazing Can Be Complementary: Elk Response to a 19-Year Exclusion of Cattle Grazing." *Rangelands* 35 (February 2013): 34–39.

Bushnell, O. A. *The Gifts of Civilization: Germs and Genocide in Hawai'i*. Honolulu: University of Hawai'i Press, 1993.

Butler, Anne M. "Selling the Popular Myth." In *The Oxford History of the American West*, edited by Clyde A. Milner II, Carol A. O'Connor, and Martha A. Sandweiss, 771–801. New York: Oxford University Press, 1994.

California Native Plant Society. *Inventory of Rare and Endangered Plants of California*. 6th ed. Sacramento: California Native Plant Society, 2001.

Carlson, Pamela McGuire, and F. Breck Parkman. "An Exceptional Adaptation: Camillo Ynitia, the Last Headman of the Olompalis." *California History* 65 (December 1986): 238–47.

Carrico, Richard L. "Sociopolitical Aspects of the 1775 Revolt at Mission San Diego de Alcala: An Ethnohistorical Approach." *Journal of San Diego History* 43 (Summer 1997): 142–57.

Chace, Paul G. "The Archaeology of 'Cienaga.'" *Pacific Coast Archaeology Society Quarterly* 5 (July 1969): 39–55.

Chappell, David A. *Double Ghosts: Oceanic Voyager on Euro-American Ships*. Armonk, N.Y.: M. E. Sharpe, 1997.

Chevalier, Francois. *Land and Society in Colonial Mexico: The Great Hacienda*. Translated by Alvin Eustis. Berkeley: University of California Press, 1963.

Chinen, Jon J. *The Great Mahele: Hawaii's Land Division of 1848*. Honolulu: University of Hawai'i Press, 1958.

———. *They Cried for Help: The Hawaiian Land Revolution of the 1840s & 1850s*. Xlibris Corporation, 2002.

Clark, Andrew H. "The Impact of Exotic Invasion on the Remaining New World Mid-Latitude Grasslands." In *Man's Role in Changing the Face of the Earth*, edited by William L. Thomas Jr., 737–62. Chicago: University of Chicago Press, 1956.

Cleland, Robert Glass. *The Cattle on a Thousand Hills*. San Marino, Calif.: Huntington Library, 1941.

Comaroff, Jean, and John Comaroff. *Of Revelation and Revolution: Christianity, Colonialism and Consciousness in South Africa*. Chicago: University of Chicago Press, 1991.

Cook, Sherburne F. *The Conflict between the California Indians and White Civilization*. Berkeley: University of California, 1943.

———. "Expeditions to the Interior of California: Central Valley, 1820–1840." *Anthropological Records* 20 (February 1962): 151–213.

Cowan-Smith, Virginia, and Bonnie Domrose Stone. *Aloha Cowboy*. Honolulu: University of Hawai'i Press, 1988.

Cronon, William. *Changes in the Land: Indians, Colonists, and the Ecology of New England*. New York: Hill and Wang, 1983.

Crosby, Alfred. *The Columbian Exchange: Biological and Cultural Consequences of 1492*. Westport, Conn.: Greenwood Press, 1972.

———. *Ecological Imperialism: The Biological Expansion of Europe, 900–1900*. Cambridge: Cambridge University Press, 1986.

———. *Germs, Seeds, and Animals: Studies in Ecological History*. Armonk, N.Y.: M. E. Sharpe, 1994.

Culliney, John L. *Islands in a Far Sea: The Fate of Nature in Hawai'i*. Honolulu: University of Hawai'i Press, 2006.

Dakin, Susanna Bryant. *The Lives of William Hartnell*. Stanford, Calif.: Stanford University Press, 1949.

Dasmann, Raymond F. "Environmental Changes before and after the Gold Rush." In *A Golden State: Mining and Economic Development in Gold Rush California*, edited by James J. Rawls and Richard J. Orsi, 105–22. Berkeley: University of California Press, 1998.

Daws, Gavan A. *Shoal of Time: A History of the Hawaiian Islands*. Honolulu: University of Hawai'i Press, 1968.

DeLay, Brian. *War of a Thousand Deserts: Indians Raids and the U.S.-Mexican War*. New Haven, Conn.: Yale University Press, 2008.

Dening, Greg. *Islands and Beaches: Discourse on a Silent Land, Marquesas 1774–1880*. Honolulu: University of Hawai'i Press, 1980.

Deverell, William. *Whitewashed Adobe: The Rise of Los Angeles and the Remaking of Its Mexican Past*. Berkeley: University of California Press, 2004.

Diamond, Jared. *Guns, Germs, and Steel: The Fates of Human Societies*. New York: W.W. Norton, 1998.

Dodge, Ernest R. *Islands and Empires: Western Impact on the Pacific and East Asia*. Minneapolis: University of Minnesota Press, 1976.

Downs, James F. *Animal Husbandry in Navajo Society and Culture*. Berkeley: University of California Press, 1964.

———. "The Cowboy and the Lady: Models as a Determinant of the Rate of Acculturation among the Piñon Navajo." In *Native Americans Today: Sociological Perspectives*, edited by Howard M. Bahr, Bruce A. Chadwick, and Robert C. Day, 275–90. New York: Harper & Row, 1972.

Duggan, Marie Christine. "Market and Church on the Mexican Frontier: Alta California, 1769–1832." Ph.D. diss., New School University, 2000.

Dunlap, Thomas R. *Nature and the English Diaspora: Environment and History in the United States, Canada, Australia, and New Zealand*. New York: Cambridge University Press, 1999.

Duval, Kathleen. *The Native Ground: Indians and Colonists in the Heart of the Continent*. Philadelphia: University of Pennsylvania Press, 2006.

Dwinelle, John W. *The Colonial History of San Francisco*. Kentfield, Calif.: Ross Valley Book Co., 1978.

Elton, C. S. *The Ecology of Invasions by Animals and Plants*. Chicago: University of Chicago Press, 1958.

Englehardt, Zephyrin. *Mission La Concepcion Purisma*. Santa Barbara: Mission Santa Barbara, 1932.

Ensminger, M. E. *Beef Cattle Science*. 6th ed. Danville, Ill.: Interstate Printers and Publishers, 1987.

Farris, Glenn. "Quality Food: The Quest for Pine Nuts in Northern California." In *Before the Wilderness: Environmental Management by Native Californians*, edited by Thomas C. Blackburn and Kat Anderson, 229–44. Menlo Park, Calif.: Ballena Press, 1993.

Fenn, Elizabeth A. *Pox Americana: The Great Smallpox Epidemic of 1775-1782*. New York: Hill and Wang, 2001.

Ferguson, Brian, and Neil L. Whitehead, eds. *War in the Tribal Zone: Expanding States and Indigenous Warfare*. Santa Fe, N.Mex.: School of American Research, 1992.

Fiege, Mark. *Irrigated Eden: The Myth of an Agricultural Landscape in the American West*. Seattle: University of Washington Press, 1999.

Flores, Dan. "Bison Ecology and Bison Diplomacy: The Southern Plains from 1800 to1850." *Journal of American History* 78 (September 1991): 465–85.

Foley, Neil. *The White Scourge: Mexicans, Blacks, and Poor Whites in Texas Cotton Culture*. Berkeley: University of California Press, 1997.

Fritzsche, Bruno. "'On Liberal Terms': The Boston Hide-Merchants in California." *Business History Review* 42 (Winter 1968): 467–81.

Frost, Rossie, and Locky Frost. "The King's Bullock Catcher." *Hawaiian Journal of History* 11 (1977): 175–87.

Gamble, Lynn H. *The Chumash World at European Contact: Power, Trade, and Feasting among Complex Hunter-Gatherers*. Berkeley: University of California Press, 2008.

Gast, Ross H. *Don Francisco de Paula Marin: A Biography*. Honolulu: University of Hawaiʻi Press, 1973.

Gibson, Arnell Morgan, and John S. Whitehead. *Yankees in Paradise: The Pacific Basin Frontier*. Albuquerque: University of New Mexico Press, 1993.

Gibson, James R. *Otter Skins, Boston Ships, and China Goods: The Maritime Fur Trade of the Northwest Coast, 1785-1841*. Seattle: University of Washington Press, 1992.

Goldschmidt, Walter, George Foster, and Frank Essene. "War Stories from Two Enemy Tribes." In *The California Indians: A Sourcebook*, edited by R. F. Heizer and M. A. Whipple, 141–54. Berkeley: University of California Press, 1960.

Graham, Edward H. "The Re-Creative Power of Plant Communities." In *Man's Role in Changing the Face of the Earth*, edited by William L. Thomas Jr., 677–91. Chicago: University of Chicago Press, 1956.

Greenwell, Jean. "Kaluakauka Revisited: The Death of David Douglas in Hawaiʻi." *Hawaiian Journal of History* 22 (1988): 147–69.

Greer, Allan. "Commons and Enclosure in the Colonization of North America." *American Historical Review* 117 (April 2012): 365–86.

Guest, Francis F. "An Examination of the Thesis of S. F. Cook on the Forced Conversions of Indians in the California Missions." *Southern California Quarterly* 61 (Spring 1979): 1–78.

Gutiérrez, Davis G. *Walls and Mirrors: Mexican Americans, Mexican Immigrants, and the Politics of Ethnicity.* Berkeley: University of California Press, 1995.

Gutierrez, Gabriel. "Bell Towers, Crucifixes, and Canones Violentos: State and Identity Formation in Pre-Industrial Alta California." Ph.D. diss., University of California, Santa Barbara, 1997.

Gutiérrez, Ramón. *When Jesus Came, the Corn Mothers Went Away: Marriage, Sexuality, and Power in New Mexico, 1500-1846.* Stanford, Calif.: Stanford University Press, 1991.

Haas, Lisbeth. *Conquests and Historical Identities in California, 1769-1936.* Berkeley: University of California Press, 1995.

———. "'Raise Your Sword and I Will Eat You': Luiseño Scholar Pablo Tac, ca. 1841." In *Alta California: Peoples in Motion, Identities in Formation, 1769-1850*, edited by Steven W. Hackel, 79–110. Berkeley: University of California Press, 2010.

———. *Saints and Citizens: Indigenous Histories of Colonial Missions and Mexican California.* Berkeley: University of California Press, 2013.

Hackel, Steven W. *Children of Coyote, Missionaries of St. Francis: Indian-Spanish Relations in Colonial California, 1769-1850.* Chapel Hill: University of North Carolina Press, 2005.

———. "Land, Labor, and Production: The Colonial Economy of Spanish and Mexican California." In *Contested Eden: California before the Gold Rush*, edited by Ramón A. Gutierrez and Richard J. Orsi, 111–46. Berkeley: University of California Press, 1998.

Hämäläinen, Pekka. *The Comanche Empire.* New Haven, Conn.: Yale University Press, 2008.

Hamilton, J. G. "Changing Perceptions of pre-European grasslands in California." *Madroño* 44 (1997): 11–33.

Handy, E. S. Craighill, and Elizabeth Green Handy. *Native Planters in Old Hawaii: Their Life, Lore, and Environment.* Honolulu: Bishop Museum Press, 1972.

Hanna, Warren. *Lost Harbor: The Controversy over Drake's California Anchorage.* Berkeley: University of California Press, 1979.

Heizer, Robert. *Francis Drake and the California Indians, 1579.* Berkeley: University of California Press, 1947.

Hendry, George W. "The Adobe Brick as a Historical Source." *Agricultural History* 5 (July 1931): 110–27.

Hinderaker, Eric. *Elusive Empires: Constructing Colonialism in the Ohio Valley, 1673-1800.* Cambridge: Cambridge University Press, 1997.

Hoover, Robert L. "The Archaeology of Spanish Colonial Sites in California." In *Comparative Studies in the Archaeology of Colonialism*, edited by Stephen L. Dyson, 93–114. Oxford: BAR, 1985.

Hornbeck, David. "Economic Growth and Change at the Missions of Alta California, 1769–1846." In *Archaeological and Historical Perspectives on the Spanish Borderlands West*. Vol. 1 of *Columbian Consequences*, edited by David Hurst Thomas, 423–33. Washington, D.C.: Smithsonian Institution Press, 1989.

———. "Land Tenure and Rancho Expansion in Alta California, 1784–1846." *Journal of Historical Geography* 4 (October 1978): 371–90.

Hubbell, Theodore H. "The Biology of Islands." *Proceedings of the National Academy of Sciences of the United States of America* 60 (May 1968): 22–32.

Hundley, Norris. *The Great Thirst, Californians and Water: A History*. Berkeley: University of California Press, 2001.

Hurtado, Albert. *Indian Survival on the California Frontier*. New Haven, Conn.: Yale University Press, 1988.

———. *John Sutter: A Life on the North America Frontier*. Norman: University of Oklahoma Press, 2006.

Hutchinson, C. Alan. *Frontier Settlement in Mexican California: The Híjar-Padrés Colony and Its Origins*. New Haven, Conn.: Yale University Press, 1969.

Hyde, Anne. *Empires, Nations, and Families*. Lincoln: University of Nebraska Press, 2011.

Igler, David. "Alta California, the Pacific, and International Commerce before the Gold Rush." In *A Companion to California History*, edited by William Deverell and David Igler, 116–26. Malden, Mass.: Wiley-Blackwell, 2008.

———. "Diseased Goods: Global Exchanges in the Eastern Pacific Basin, 1770–1850." *American Historical Review* 109 (June 2004): 693–719.

———. *The Great Ocean: Pacific Worlds from Captain Cook to the Gold Rush*. Oxford: Oxford University Press, 2013.

———. *Industrial Cowboys: Miller & Lux and the Transformation of the Far West, 1850–1920*. Berkeley: University of California Press, 2001.

Isenberg, Andrew C. "Between Mexico and the Unites States: From *Indios* to Vaqueros in the Pastoral Borderlands." In *Mexico and Mexicans in the Making of the United States*, edited by John Tutino, 83–109. Austin: University of Texas Press, 2012.

———. *The Destruction of the Bison*. Cambridge: Cambridge University Press, 2000.

———. *Mining California: An Ecological History*. New York: Hill and Wang, 2005.

Iverson, Peter. *When Indians Became Cowboys: Native Peoples and Cattle Ranching in the American West*. Norman: University of Oklahoma Press, 1994.

Jackson, Robert H. "The Changing Economic Structure of Alta California." *Pacific Historical Review* 61 (August 1992): 387–415.

———. *Missions and the Frontiers of Spanish America*. Scottsdale, Ariz.: Pentacle Press, 2005.

Jackson, Robert Howard, and Edward D. Castillo. *Indians, Franciscans and Spanish Colonization: The Impact of the Mission System on California Indians*. Albuquerque: University of New Mexico Press, 1995.

Johnson, John R. "Ethnohistoric Descriptions of Chumash Warfare." In *North American Indigenous Warfare and Ritual Violence*, edited by Richard J. Chacon and Rubén E. Mendoza, 74–113. Tucson: University of Arizona Press, 1997.

Jordan, Terry. *North American Cattle-Ranching Frontiers: Origins, Diffusion and Differentiation*. Albuquerque: University of New Mexico Press, 1993.

Kameʻeleihiwa, Lilikalā. *Native Lands and Foreign Desires*. Honolulu: Bishop Museum Press, 1992.

Kelsey, Harry. "Did Francis Drake Really Visit California?" *Western History Quarterly* 21 (November 1990): 444–62.

Kelton, Paul. *Epidemics and Enslavement: Biological Catastrophe in the Native Southeast, 1492–1715*. Lincoln: University of Nebraska Press, 2007.

Kirch, Patrick V. *The Archaeology of History*. Vol. 2 of *Anahulu, the Anthropology of History in the Kingdom of Hawaii*. Chicago: University of Chicago Press, 1992.

———. "The Impact of the Prehistoric Polynesians on the Hawaiian Ecosystem." *Pacific Science* 36 (1982): 1–14.

———. "Regional Variation and Local Style: A Neglected Dimension in Hawaiian Prehistory." *Pacific Studies* 13 (March 1990): 41–54.

Koebele, A. "Hawaii's Forest Foes." *Thrum's Hawaiian Almanac for 1900*: 90–97.

Kroeber, A. L. *Handbook of the Indians of California*. Washington, D.C.: Smithsonian, 1925.

Kuykendall, Ralph S. Biographical File. Hawaiʻi State Archives, Honolulu.

———. *Foundation and Transformation, 1778–1854*. Vol. 1 of *The Hawaiian Kingdom*. Honolulu: University of Hawaiʻi Press, 1957.

LaCroix, Sumner J., and James Roumasset. "The Evolution of Private Property in Nineteenth-Century Hawaii." *Journal of Economic History* 50 (December 1990): 829–52.

Lambert, Patricia M. "Osteological Evidence for Indigenous Warfare in America." In *North American Indigenous Warfare and Ritual Violence*, edited by Richard J. Chacon and Rubén E. Mendoza, 202–21. Tucson: University of Arizona Press, 1997.

Larson, Daniel O., John R. Johnson, and Joel C. Michaelsen. "Missionization among the Coastal Chumash of Central California: A Study of Risk Minimization Strategies." *American Anthropologist* 96 (June 1994): 263–99.

Lawrence, Elizabeth Atwood. *Rodeo: An Anthropologist Looks at the Wild and the Tame*. Knoxville: University of Tennessee Press, 1982.

LeBlanc, Steven A., and Katherine E. Register. *Constant Battles: Why We Fight*. New York: St. Martin's Griffin, 2004.

Lever, Christopher. *Naturalized Animals: The Ecology of Successfully Introduced Species*. Cambridge: T. & A. D. Poyser Natural History, 1994.

Lewis, Henry T. "Patterns of Indian Burning in California Ecology and Ethnohistory." In *Before the Wilderness*, edited by Thomas Blackburn and Kat Anderson, 35–116. Menlo Park, Calif.: Ballena Press, 1993.

Lightfoot, Kent G. *Indians, Missionaries, and Merchants: The Legacy of Colonial Encounters on the California Frontiers*. Berkeley: University of California Press, 2005.

Linebaugh, Peter, and Marcus Rediker. *The Many-Headed Hydra: Sailors, Slaves, Commoners and the Hidden History of the Revolutionary Atlantic*. Boston: Beacon Press, 2000.

Linnekin, Jocelyn. *Sacred Queens and Women of Consequence: Rank, Gender, and Colonialism in the Hawaiian Islands.* Ann Arbor: University of Michigan Press, 1990.

Lockhart, James. *The Nahuas after the Conquest: A Social and Cultural History of the Indians of Central Mexico, Sixteenth through Eighteenth Centuries.* Stanford, Calif.: Stanford University Press, 1992.

MacArthur, Robert H., and Edward O. Wilson. *The Theory of Island Biogeography.* Princeton, N.J.: Princeton University Press, 1967.

Mack, R. N. "Temperate Grasslands Vulnerable to Plant Invasion: Characteristics and Consequences." In *Biological Invasions: A Global Perspective,* edited by J. A. Drake, H. A. Mooney, F. di Castri, R. H. Groves, F. J. Kruger, M. Rejmánek, and M. Williamson, 155–79. New York, John Wiley & Sons, 1989.

Maly, Kepa, and Bruce A. Wilcox. "A Short History of Cattle and Range Management in Hawai'i." *Rangelands* (October 2000): 21–23.

Mapp, Paul W. *The Elusive West and the Contest for Empire, 1713–1763.* Chapel Hill: University of North Carolina Press, 2011.

Margolin, Phillip. *The Ohlone Way: Indian Life in the San Francisco-Monterey Bay Area.* Berkeley: Heyday Books, 1978.

Martin, Lynn J., ed. *Nā Paniolo o Hawai'i: A Traveling Exhibition Celebrating Paniolo Folk Arts and the History of Ranching in Hawai'i.* Honolulu: Honolulu Academy of Arts, 1987.

Marzagalli, Silvia. "Establishing Transatlantic Trade Networks in Times of War: Bordeaux and the United States, 1793–1815." *Business History Review* 79 (Winter 2005): 811–44.

Matson, Cathy. "The Ambiguities of Risk in the Early Republic." *Business History Review* 78 (Winter 2004): 595–606.

Matsuda, Matt K. *Pacific Worlds: A History of Seas, Peoples, and Cultures.* Cambridge: Cambridge University Press, 2012.

McCormick, E. H. *Cook & Omai: The Cult of the South Seas.* Canberra: National Library of Australia, 2001.

———. *Omai: Pacific Envoy.* Auckland: Auckland University Press, 1977.

McCoy, Drew R. *The Elusive Republic: Political Economy in Jeffersonian America.* Chapel Hill: University of North Carolina Press, 1980.

McEvoy, Arthur F. *The Fisherman's Problem: Ecology and Law in California Fisheries, 1850–1980.* Cambridge: Cambridge University Press, 1986.

McNeill, William H. *Plagues and Peoples.* New York: Anchor Press, 1977.

Meek, Ronald L. *Social Science and the Ignoble Savage.* Cambridge: Cambridge University Press, 1976.

Meeks, Eric V. *Border Citizens: The Making of Indians, Mexicans, and Anglos in Arizona.* Austin: University of Texas Press, 2007.

Melville, Elinor. *A Plague of Sheep: Environmental Consequences of the Conquest of Mexico.* Cambridge: Cambridge University Press, 1994.

Merrell, James H. *The Indians New World: Catawbas and Their Neighbors from European Contact through the Era of Removal.* New York: W. W. Norton and Co., 1989.

Merry, Sally Engle. *Colonizing Hawai'i: The Cultural Power of Law*. Princeton, N.J.: Princeton University Press, 2000.

Milliken, Randall. *A Time of Little Choice: The Disintegration of Tribal Culture in the San Francisco Bay Area 1769-1810*. Menlo Park, Calif.: Ballena Press, 1995.

Mills, Peter R. "Keanakolu: An Archaeological Perspective of Hawaiian Ranching and the Pacific Hide and Tallow Trade." TMK 3-8-01:9 (Draft Report Spring 2007).

——. "*Neo* in Oceania: Foreign Vessels Owned by Hawaiian Chiefs before 1830." *Journal of Pacific History* 38 (2003): 53-67.

Minnich, R. A. *California's Fading Wildflowers: Lost Legacy and Biological Invasions*. Berkeley: University of California Press, 2008.

Monroy, Douglas. *Thrown among Strangers: The Making of Mexican Culture in Frontier California*. Berkeley: University of California Press, 1990.

Morris, Melvin S. "Elk and Livestock Competition." *Journal of Range Management* 9 (January 1956): 11-14.

Najera-Ramirez, Olga. "Engendering Nationalism: Identity, Discourse and the Mexican Charro." *Anthropological Quarterly* 67 (January 1994): 1-14.

Najita, Susan Y. "History, Trauma, and the Discursive Construction of Race in John Dominis Holt's *Waimea Summer*." *Cultural Critique* 47 (Winter 2001): 167-214.

Newman, T. Stell. "Hawaii Island Agricultural Zones, circa A.D. 1823: An Ethnohistorical Study." *Ethnohistory* 18, no. 4 (Autumn 1971): 335-51.

Nunis, Doyce B. "Alta California's Trojan Horse: Foreign Immigration." In *Contested Eden: California before the Gold Rush*, edited by Ramón A. Gutiérrez and Richard J. Orsi, 299-330. Berkeley: University of California Press, 1998.

Obeyeskere, Gananath. *The Apotheosis of Captain Cook: European Mythmaking in the Pacific*. Princeton, N.J.: Princeton University Press, 1992.

Ogden, Adele. "Boston Hide Droughers along California Shores." *California Historical Society Quarterly* 8 (December 1929): 288-305.

——. *The California Sea Otter Trade 1784-1848*. Berkeley: University of California Press, 1941.

——. "Hides and Tallow: McCulloch, Hartnell and Company 1822-1828." *California Historical Society Quarterly* 6 (September 1927): 254-64.

Okihiro, Gary Y. *Island World: A History of Hawai'i and the United States*. Berkeley: University of California Press, 2008.

Palmer, Lyman L. *History of Napa and Lake Counties, California*. San Francisco: Slocum, Bowen & Co., 1881.

Peterson, Marcus Edmund. "The Career of Solano, Chief of the Suisuns." Master's thesis, University of California, 1944.

Phillips, George Harwood. *Indians and Indian Agents: The Origins of the Reservation System in California, 1849-1852*. Norman: University of Oklahoma Press, 1997.

——. *Indians and Intruders in Central California, 1769-1849*. Norman: University of Oklahoma Press, 1993.

——. "Indians and the Breakdown of the Spanish Mission System in California." *Ethnohistory* 21 (Autumn 1974): 291-302.

——. *Vineyards and Vaqueros: Indian Labor and the Expansion of Southern California, 1771–1877*. Norman: Arthur H. Clark Company, 2010.

Pitt, Leonard. *Decline of the Californios: A Social History of the Spanish-Speaking Californians, 1846–1890*. Berkeley: University of California Press, 1966.

Powers, Stephen. *Tribes of California*. Berkeley: University of California Press, 1976.

Pritchard, Diane Spencer. "Joint Tenants of the Frontier: Russian-Hispanic Relationships in Alta California." In *Russian America: The Forgotten Frontier*, edited by Barbara Sweetland Smith and Redmond J. Barnett, 81–93. Tacoma: Washington State Historical Society, 1990.

Prucha, Francis Paul. *The Great Father: The United States Government and the American Indian*. 2 vols. Lincoln: University of Nebraska Press, 1984.

Raab, L. Mark. "Political Ecology of Prehistoric Los Angeles." In *Land of Sunshine: An Environmental History of Los Angeles*, edited by William Deverell and Greg Hise, 23–37. Pittsburgh: University of Pittsburgh Press, 2005.

Rappaport, Roy A. *Pigs for the Ancestors: Ritual in the Ecology of a New Guinea People*. New Haven, Conn.: Yale University Press, 1967.

Ray, Arthur J. *Indians in the Fur Trade: Their Role as Trappers, Hunters, and Middlemen in the Lands Southwest of the Hudson Bay 1660–1870*. Toronto: University of Toronto Press, 1974.

Reséndez, Andrés. *Changing National Identities at the Frontier: Texas and New Mexico, 1800–1850*. Cambridge: Cambridge University Press, 2004.

Rich, E. A. *The History of the Hudson's Bay Company: 1670–1970*. 2 vols. London: Hudson's Bay Record Society, 1959.

Richman, Irving Berdine. *California under Spain and Mexico 1535–1847*. Boston: Houghton Mifflin Company, 1911.

Rigby, Nigel. "The Politics and Pragmatics of Seaborne Plant Transportation, 1769–1805." In *Science and Exploration in the Pacific: European Voyages to the Southern Oceans in the Eighteenth Century*, edited by Margarette Lincoln, 81–100. Woodbridge, UK: Boydell Press, 1998.

Ritchie, Robert C. *Captain Kidd and the War against the Pirates*. Cambridge, Mass.: Harvard University Press, 1986.

Ritvo, Harriet. *The Animal Estate: The English and Other Creatures in the Victorian Age*. Cambridge, Mass.: Harvard University Press, 1987.

Roots, Clive. *Animal Invaders*. New York: Universe Books, 1976.

Ryan, Lyndall. *The Aboriginal Tasmanians*. Vancouver: University of British Columbia Press, 1981.

Sackman, Douglas Cazaux. *Orange Empire: California and the Fruits of Eden*. Berkeley: University of California Press, 2005.

Sahlins, Marshall. *Historical Ethnography*. Vol. 1 of *Anahulu: The Anthropology of History in the Kingdom of Hawaii*. Chicago: University of Chicago Press, 1992.

——. *Historical Metaphors and Mythical Realities: Structure in the Early History of the Sandwich Islands Kingdom*. Ann Arbor: University of Michigan Press, 1981.

——. *How "Natives" Think: About Captain Cook, for Example*. Chicago: University of Chicago Press, 1995.

Salvatore, Ricardo D. "Modes of Labor Control in Cattle-Ranching Economies: California, Southern Brazil, and Argentina, 1820–1860." *Journal of Economic History* 51 (June 1991): 441–51.

Sánchez, Rosaura. *Telling Identities: The Californio Testimonios*. Minneapolis: University of Minnesota Press, 1995.

Schmitt, Robert C. *Historical Statistics of Hawaii*. Honolulu: University of Hawai'i Press, 1977.

Scott, James C. *The Moral Economy of the Peasant*. New Haven, Conn.: Yale University Press, 1976.

Scruggs, Marc. "Anthony D. Allen: A Prosperous American of African Descent in Early19th Century Hawai'i." *Hawaiian Journal of History* 26 (1992): 55–94.

Seed, Patricia. *Ceremonies of Possession in Europe's Conquest of the New World*. Cambridge: Cambridge University Press, 1995.

Sheehan, Bernard W. *Seeds of Extinction: Jeffersonian Philanthropy and the American Indian*. Chapel Hill: University of North Carolina Press, 1973.

Shineberg, Dorothy. *They Came for Sandalwood: A Study of the Sandalwood Trade in the South-West Pacific 1830–1865*. Carlton: Melbourne University Press, 1967.

Shinseki, Kyle Ko Francisco. "El Pueblo Mexicano de Hawai'i." Master's thesis, UCLA, 1997.

Shipek, Florence C. "California Indian Reactions to the Franciscans." *Americas* 41 (1985): 480–92.

Silva, Noenoe K. *Aloha Betrayed: Native Hawaiian Resistance to American Colonialism*. Durham: Duke University Press, 2004.

Silverman, David J. " 'We Chuse to Be Bounded': Native American Animal Husbandry in Colonial New England." *William and Mary Quarterly* 60 (July 2003): 511–48.

Simmons, William S. "Indian Peoples of California." In *Contested Eden: California before the Gold Rush*, edited by Ramón A. Gutiérrez and Richard J. Orsi, 48–77. Berkeley: University of California Press, 1998.

Slatta, Richard. *Comparing Cowboys and Frontiers*. Norman: Oklahoma University Press, 1997.

———. *Cowboys of the Americas*. New Haven, Conn.: Yale University Press, 1990.

Smith, Bernard. "Constructing 'Pacific' Peoples." In *Remembrance of Pacific Pasts: An Invitation to Remake History*, edited by Robert Borosky, 152–68. Honolulu: University of Hawai'i Press, 2000.

Smith, Gene A. *Thomas ap Catesby Jones: Commodore of Manifest Destiny*. Annapolis: Naval Institute Press, 2000.

Smith, Henry Nash. *Virgin Land: The American Myth as Symbol and Myth*. New York: Vintage Books, 1950.

Solberg, Carl. *The Prairies and the Pampas: Agrarian Policy in Canada and Argentina, 1880–1930*. Stanford, Calif.: Stanford University Press, 1987.

Spate, O. H. K. *Paradise Found and Lost*. Minneapolis: University of Minnesota Press, 1988.

Starr, Kevin. *Americans and the California Dream, 1850–1915*. New York: Oxford University Press, 1973.

Stauffer, Robert H. *Kahana: How the Land Was Lost.* Honolulu: University of Hawai'i Press, 2004.

Street, Richard Steven. *Beasts of the Field: A Narrative History of California Farmworkers, 1769–1913.* Stanford, Calif.: Stanford University Press, 2004.

Taylor, Alan. *The Divided Ground: Indians, Settlers, and the Northern Borderland of the American Revolution.* New York: Alfred A. Knopf, 2006.

Thompson, R. A. *The Russian Settlement at Fort Ross: Why the Russians Came and Why They Left.* Oakland, Calif.: Biobooks, 1951.

Tomich, P. Quentin. *Mammals in Hawaii: A Synopsis and National Bibliography.* Honolulu: Bishop Museum Press, 1969.

Truett, Sam. *Fugitive Landscapes: The Forgotten History of the U.S.-Mexico Borderlands.* New Haven, Conn.: Yale University Press, 2008.

Tucker, Richard P. *Insatiable Appetite: The United States and the Ecological Degradation of the Tropical World.* Berkeley: University of California Press, 2000.

Tuggle, H. David. "Hawaii." In *The Prehistory of Polynesia*, edited by Jesse D. Jennings, 167–99. Cambridge, Mass.: Harvard University Press, 1979.

Tutino, John. "Capitalist Foundations: Spanish North America, Mexico, and the United States." In *Mexico and Mexicans in the Making of the United States*, edited by John Tutino, 36–82. Austin: University of Texas Press, 2012.

Tyrell, Ian. *True Gardens of the Gods: California-Australian Environmental Reform, 1860–1930.* Berkeley: University of California Press, 1999.

Uhrowczik, Peter. *The Burning of Monterey: The 1818 Attack on California by the Privateer Bouchard.* Los Gatos, Calif.: Cyril Books, 2001.

Usner Jr., Daniel. *Indians, Settlers, and Slaves in a Frontier Exchange Economy: The Lower Mississippi Valley before 1783.* Chapel Hill: University of North Carolina Press, 1992.

Valeri, Valerio. *Kingship and Sacrifice: Ritual and Society in Ancient Hawaii.* Translated by Paula Wissing. Chicago: University of Chicago Press, 1985.

Valle, Rosemary. "Prevention of Smallpox in Alta California during the Franciscan Mission Period (1769–1833)." *California Medicine* 119 (July 1973): 73–77.

Van Kirk, Sylvia. *Many Tender Ties: Women in Fur-Trade Society, 1670–1870.* Norman: University of Oklahoma Press, 1983.

Wallace, Anthony F. C. *Jefferson and the Indians: The Tragic Fate of the First Americans.* Cambridge, Mass.: Belknap Press of Harvard University Press, 1999.

Warren, Louis S. *Buffalo Bill's America: William Cody and the Wild West Show.* New York: Alfred A. Knopf, 2005.

Weaver, John C. *The Great Land Rush and the Making of the Modern World, 1650–1900.* Montreal: McGill-Queen's University Press, 2003.

Weber, David J. *Bárbaros: Spaniards and Their Savage in the Age of Enlightenment.* New Haven, Conn.: Yale University Press, 2005.

——. *The Mexican Frontier, 1821–1846: The American Southwest under Mexico.* Albuquerque: University of New Mexico, 1982.

——. *The Spanish Frontier in North America.* New Haven, Conn.: Yale University Press, 1992.

Weber, Francis J. *Mission in the Sierras*. Los Angeles: Weber, 1982.

Weigle, Richard D. "Sugar and the Hawaiian Revolution." *Pacific Historical Review* 16 (February 1947): 41–58.

Weisiger, Marsha. *Dreaming of Sheep in Navajo Country*. Seattle: University of Washington Press, 2009.

Wellmon, Bernard Brian. "The Parker Ranch: A History." Ph.D. diss., Texas Christian University, 1969.

Wellmon, Bud. "Frontier Traders and Pioneer Cattlemen: A Hawaiian Perspective." *Hawaiian Journal of History* 7 (1973): 48–54.

West, G. James. "Early Historic Vegetation Change in Alta California: The Fossil Evidence." In *Columbia Consequences*, vol. 1, *Archaeological and Historical Perspectives on the Spanish Borderlands West*, edited by David Hurst Thomas, 333–48. Washington, D.C.: Smithsonian Institution Press, 1989.

Whaley, Gray H. *Oregon and the Collapse of* Illahee: *U.S. Empire and the Transformation of an Indigenous World, 1792–1859*. Chapel Hill: University of North Carolina Press, 2010.

White, Richard. "Animals and Enterprise." In *The Oxford History of the American West*, edited by Clyde A. Milner II, Carol A. O'Connor, and Martha A. Sandweiss, 237–74. New York: Oxford University Press, 1994.

———. *The Middle Ground: Indians, Empires, and Republics in the Great Lakes Region, 1650–1815*. Cambridge: Cambridge University Press, 1991.

———. *The Roots of Dependency: Subsistence, Environment, and Social Change among the Choctaws, Pawnees, and Navajos*. Omaha: University of Nebraska Press, 1983.

Whitehead, John. "Hawai'i: The First and Last Far West?" *Western Historical Quarterly* 23 (May 1992): 153–77.

Wyatt, David. *Five Fires: Race, Catastrophe, and the Shaping of California*. Reading, Mass.: Addison-Wesley, 1997.

Index

Brennan, Joseph, 143

British Empire. *See* English colonialism

Brown, William, 60, 88

Brucelosis, 49

Bryant & Sturgis, 105–6, 111, 112, 114, 132, 140

Bucareli y Ursúa, Antonio María de, 28

Buchanan, James, 86

Buffalo Bill's Wild West, 1, 4, 200

Bullock hunters, 120–22, 145, 147, 165, 184, 187

Bunchgrasses, 48, 211 (n. 43)

Byron, George Anson, 117

Cabestro, 119, 133, 148

Cabot, Juan, 52

Cabrillo, Juan, 16

Calico, 109

California, 16–17; as maritime settlement, 5, 31, 98, 106, 107–9, 175; political conflicts, 85; pre-Spanish environment, 39–40, 48; Spanish settlement, 9, 24–30, 36, 45, 67–68, 200; statehood, 196; trade, 103, 106, 109, 111–12, 123–25, 127, 138, 159, 176, 195

California Indians, 16, 27–29, 41, 83, 98, 130–31, 137–39, 142, 197; agency, 7, 69, 170, 189–92, 201–2; conflict, intertribal, 43, 51–54, 159; conflict with Spanish, 29, 53–54, 65, 67–68, 157–63; conversion to Christianity, 131–32; gender division of labor, 71, 113–14, 132, 161; horse riding, 75, 135, 138, 160–63; property, 172–76, 189–92, 197; subsistence, 41–43, 45–52, 54; trade networks, 50, 54, 159; views of animals, 42, 67, 69–70, 75–76, 113, 157–61

Callao, 84, 105, 115, 124

Campbell, Archibald, 61

Canton. *See* China trade

Cape Horn, 124

Caribbean, 14, 20

Carter, Alfred Wellington, 196, 199

Catalá, Magin, 74

Cattle, 5–11, 16, 18–21, 35–36, 83, 86, 200–203; in California, 24–30, 68–69, 75, 90–91, 99–100, 108, 130, 140, 160, 162, 171, 189, 190, 192; commodities, 100, 102, 105, 108, 112–13, 115–16, 119, 126, 133, 136, 141, 147, 155, 172–73, 176, 180, 200; competition with other ungulates, 48–50, 200; ecological change, 9–10, 37–38, 44–47, 50, 61–64, 200; feral, 60–61, 65, 79–81, 117–18, 120, 129, 142–43, 145, 148, 152, 155, 166, 184, 186–88; in Hawai'i, 30–32, 56, 77–78, 143, 153, 155–56, 178, 183, 185–86, 192, 198; natural increase, 26, 30, 44–46, 58, 69, 106, 208 (n. 58). *See also* Cabestro; Cattle culture; Domestic animals; Hide and tallow trade; Introduced species; Leather; Longhorns; Tallow

Cattle culture, 10, 82, 120, 127, 129, 200, 202; Californian, 130, 132; Hawaiian, 143, 146–51; Spanish, 26, 69

Cavenecia, José, 103

Charlton, Richard, 122, 125, 145, 166, 178–79, 187

Chia, 47–48

China trade, 5, 9–10, 16–17, 34, 58–60, 66, 84, 87–89, 92–95, 97–100, 118, 123–26, 157, 201

Chinese immigration to Hawai'i, 121

Chumash Indians, 41, 47, 53–54, 65, 73, 157

Civilization, European view, 15–16, 18–20, 22, 33–36, 156, 177–78, 180, 196, 208 (n. 52). *See also* Gente de razón; Pastoralism

Clear Lake, 141

Clerke, Charles, 23

Cleveland, Richard, 33–36

Climate, 63

Clyman, James, 137

Colonialism, 11, 44, 64, 136, 165, 194; role in conflict, 53–54, 59–60. *See*